RAVE NEW WORLD

Confessions of a Raving Reporter

Kirk Field

NINE
EIGHT
BOOKS

NEB 018

First published in the UK in 2023 by Nine Eight Books
An imprint of Bonnier Books UK
4th Floor, Victoria House, Bloomsbury Square, London, WC1B 4DA
Owned by Bonnier Books, Sveavägen 56, Stockholm, Sweden

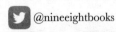 @nineeightbooks

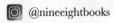 @nineeightbooks

Hardback ISBN: 978-1-7887-0770-1
Trade Paperback ISBN: 978-1-7887-0771-8
eBook ISBN: 978-1-7887-0772-5

A CIP catalogue record for this book is available from the British Library.

Publishing director: Pete Selby
Senior editor: Melissa Bond

Cover design by Paul Palmer-Edwards
Typeset by IDSUK (Data Connection) Ltd
Printed and bound in Great Britain by Clays Ltd, Elcograf S.p.A

1 3 5 7 9 10 8 6 4 2

Text copyright © Kirk Field, 2023

Every reasonable effort has been made to trace copyright-holders of material
reproduced in this book. If any have been inadvertently overlooked,
the publisher would be glad to hear from them.

Nine Eight Books is an imprint of Bonnier Books UK
www.bonnierbooks.co.uk

CONTENTS

INTRODUCTION

The rave scene helped make me who I am. It forged a generation's ideals and gave us a glimpse of utopia. We were one nation under a groove. We looked after each other regardless of class, colour, creed or sexual preference and expressed ourselves through dancing in places we weren't meant to dance – noble goals for any society, right?

It was a time of expression, experimentation and discovery. Yet many of us still feel we can't tell our kids about the fact we may have taken some mood modification once upon a time, before we moved on, matured, and took on the responsibility of raising children and becoming that person who tells them to tidy their room or limits their screentime. As a result, any parent who ever got lost in the lasers now has a problem: How can we tell our teenagers about our lives before they came along without lying?

By the mid-1990s, police estimated that over half a million UK clubbers took ecstasy every weekend.[1] That's

---

[1] According to ACPO (Association of Chief Police Officers). By 2002, 2.2 per cent of 16–59-year-olds had taken ecstasy, according to the British Crime Survey.

one in every hundred people. So do we we avoid the subject of recreational drugs altogether, cross our fingers and hope they emerge unscathed from the slings and arrows of outrageous partying – or do we jump on our moral high horse, waving a 'JUST SAY NO' banner, while hiding underneath a T-shirt that reads 'HYPOCRITE'?

I decided to write this book in the hope that (perhaps when I wasn't looking) my teenage sons could learn about the adventures I had before they came along; the ups and downs, the moments of revelation and despair – while learning something about the life I once led. If any of this resonates with you, please feel free to hand your teenagers this book when you have finished, with a knowing wink and those immortal words, 'When I was your age . . .'

There are no shortage of books covering the music, fashion, politics and seismic cultural significance of acid house. Some are written by those who claim to be instigators, others by established music journalists and considered 'definitive' discourses, and a few are 'written' by big name DJs (edited so they don't upset their corporate management or impact negatively on their careers, remember). While this book has elements of all three, it's written from a raver's perspective – a raver who decided to write about what he was watching explode.

I wasn't a protagonist or 'face'. I was just the guy who worked behind the bar flogging Ribena for a quid, keeping the rave hydrated and witnessing the wonder. But then I became the guy who decided to put pen to paper to set the record straight after reading tabloid lies about these amazing parties that I was witnessing first-hand.

What follows are personal recollections of that long, hot, crazy summer of 1989 and the decade of adventures

INTRODUCTION

it launched me into, which I hope will give you a flavour of that time: wide-eyed innocence, turbo-fuelled fun, and the freedom to party, lost in the moment, which doesn't exist now. It was a time of hope. Change was in the air. It felt like the old order was crumbling and a new era dawning – a 'rave new world', if you like.

This is what *really* happened on those overseas assignments. And when you read this, you'll understand why it couldn't appear in print at the time. Some anecdotes may seem far-fetched, but rest assured, they did all happen. I've only written about the raves I witnessed and talked to those whose accounts, like mine, have remained unheard.

Although it's my story, I've reached out to key people from that era who've never told their story before, having also been overlooked by other writers. People who risked their liberty to put on the best parties that a generation would witness. You'll be surprised and shocked by some of what lies in the pages ahead and, hopefully, transported back there, too.

As you'll discover, my experiences were enhanced in ways I'd never imagine. I was unable to write about them in *Mixmag* at the time, as dance music was under attack for its association with drugs. But with the interest in this era only increasing, and as a generation of ravers look back, I feel the time is right to spill the beans on the adventures I had, and the scrapes I got into as a result of living large and embracing ecstasy culture.

This book may not be the most definitive account of that era, but I hope it's among the most authentic and evocative. I hope you'll find it illuminating and entertaining – and a salutary lesson that like most things in life, choosing to alter your perception has many facets and is neither good nor evil, smart or dumb. It's all of these. At once. It's a choice. So choose carefully.

I had to laugh when I recently saw a DVD for sale on eBay which featured many of the raves I'll take you back to. It stated: 'Please remember there was no such thing as High Definition in 1989'. So it's bound to be a bit blurry around the edges.

Happy daze indeed!

1

A SUMMER OF LOVE

April 1989. The cell stank of piss.

My incarcerators – the Munich Airport Border Police – were just changing shifts and informing the new officer in charge that the pathetic creature in front of him, with ripped jeans and a body covered with black marker pen, was being held upon the discovery he was carrying a falsified passport.

With my passport in his hand, he strode arrogantly over to the cells to survey his prey, shaking his head at the obvious amendment before slipping effortlessly into aloof interrogation mode.

'You English think you're so clever.'

I wasn't feeling clever. I was feeling hungover, alone and vulnerable. Although my crime only involved changing the '2' to a '4' in the year of my birth in order to obtain half-price rail travel for another two years, they were running checks on me with Interpol. As each hour passed, my schnapps-addled, sleep-deprived mind was growing increasingly worried that they thought I was the Red Army Faction terrorist on the WANTED poster on the wall. He too wore a leather biker jacket and was unkempt and unshaven.

When they'd strip-searched me, they were bemused to discover the well wishes scrawled on my skin in thick black magic marker – 'LUV FROM ADAM + DOM' and 'THE CELLMATES ROCK!' – parting gifts from the previous night's final gig in the Scotland Yard Pub from the Mayrhofen ski bums.

As we'd been mid-song and wearing bedsheets (toga party) while the scrawling took place, myself and my fellow cellmates were powerless to stop them. And, having partied all night before we left at dawn, hadn't showered.

'Who did this?'

'My friends.'

'What kind of friends do this?'

How dare he! Those guys were the best bunch of people I'd met in years. We were one big family. But I was in no position to rebuke him. He was clearly trying to provoke me.

So I smiled at him and said truthfully, 'Those with marker pens.'

After eight hours in a cell and agreeing to donate all my cash (which I'd earned in the three-week stint in the snow) to charity, they released me while retaining my passport.

I bunked trains back into Austria and borrowed 40 quid to get 'The Snow Coach' back to the UK with the help of a friendly rep who 'forgot' to add me to the passenger manifest, covering me in coats on the back seat as we drove through each border.

A SUMMER OF LOVE

I disembarked into the rain of Trafalgar Square at 2 a.m., joining pissed office workers waiting for a night bus. No one noticed me. Was I that insignificant?

Until a few days ago I was singing and DJing in an Austrian ski resort and looking forward to a summer season playing on party boats in St Tropez. But at the last minute I was let down as my guitarist Colin had fallen in love with a German girl and had decided to stay in Frankfurt. As a result, I was alone and broke. I had nothing.

Looking back, at that stage the decks of my life were cleared, allowing me to have the best summer of my life.

As spring stubbornly gave way to summer, I crashed on ex-girlfriends' and holidaying mates' sofas around north London, lugging my suitcase from Swiss Cottage to Kentish Town and Harlesden. As I had no fixed abode I couldn't sign on, and so I signed up with an agency who had clearly cornered the market in mind-numbing, soul-destroying, poorly paid dead-end employment, which, looking back, was a great advert for automatisation. Or suicide.

I spent May earning a pittance doing grim, temporary work: folding bedsheets in a hospital laundry room to take silently around what was referred to as 'the AIDS ward' in hushed tones; scouring endless pans of grease and burnt food in the Unisys staff canteen; and monotonously cleansing 14-foot long rods of a coating of oil with a series of towels, prior to carrying each one 'tightrope-walker'-like to another clanging pile in a steel mill in Park Lane.

I was back in Britain and broke. I had no job and nowhere to live. My band had split up and my dream of pop stardom was dead. But as they say, as one door closes . . .

'The Rave' appeared in *Mixmag*, July '89: 'The latest trend among thrill-seeking youngsters is, of course, the much-publicised warehouse party. KIRK FIELD examines the appeal of spending a Saturday night in an aircraft hangar in rural Berkshire . . .'

This was the very earliest coverage of the rave scene to have appeared in *Mixmag.*

★

First off, I should point out that I had no intention of becoming a 'raving reporter' for a dance music magazine. As my long-suffering editors discovered, I had no experience or training as a writer, no ambition to commence a career in print journalism, and certainly no plans to break the law every weekend. But as John Lennon once said, 'Life is what happens when you're busy making other plans.' Although, truth be told, I had no plans either.

'Come and stay with me for a few weeks in Mill Hill. My girlfriend's moved out and I've got the flat to myself.' I was having a drink with another recently returned ski bum from Mayrhofen called Adam.

'But I haven't got any money for rent.'

'Just keep the place clean and answer the phone, that'll do.'

Adam and Tony (another former Mayrhofen seasonaire) had a new business venture: a mobile bar business aimed at bar mitzvahs, weddings and posh private birthday parties. So I moved in and the very next day I took a call, writing down the details on the message pad. The evening came and Adam came home from his job, which printed top-shelf porn mags.

'How was work?'

He grimaced. '*Fiesta*'s Naughty 40s today. Any messages?'

I handed him the pad.

'This Saturday: equestrian centre, private party 12–7, maybe later . . . around 2,000 people . . . no alcohol needed. Call Jeremy on 0836 . . .'

'Fucking hell, Kirk, all you had was one job to do . . .'

'What do you mean?'

'This is all over the shop; 12–7? You mean 7–12 right? Two thousand people? Who the fuck's it for, Macaulay Culkin? He probably told you 200. And it says here "no alcohol"? Okay, it's a kids' party, then? So it won't be kicking off at midnight, will it?'

He had a point. I was embarrassed and whimpered defensively, 'I'm sure that's what the guy said.'

Adam was right, it just didn't make sense and he wasn't alone in doubting my secretarial skills. However, I was relieved but no less confused when he called the number and confirmed my notes were in fact correct. The bloke on the phone had been cagey about the type of event it was. Just that it was a members-only party for adults. He had given Adam a huge list of drinks: 6,000 bottles of water ('still, not fizzy'), 1,000 cartons of Ribena, 1,000 bottles of Lucozade – and a crate of Champagne ('not for display, strictly for VIPs').

We figured it was probably a private launch party for the eagerly anticipated first 'Batman' movie, shot at Pinewood Studios and due to be released in a few weeks.

I couldn't go along as it was short notice. I'd already agreed to take a girlfriend out to my mate Marten's club, Paramount City in Soho, to meet Lemmy from Motörhead, who was a regular. Although intrigued at the prospect of going to an all-night movie party, I didn't want to let her down. Little did I know it was to be my last rock 'n' roll-orientated night out for over a decade.

I returned on Sunday evening to find Adam saucer-eyed, listening to a presenter on a pirate radio station who appeared to be talking with a mouth full of ski socks. Every advert appeared to have the same sultry sax riff (which I later got to know and love as 808 State's 'Pacific State') on a continuous loop, as someone who sounded like they were trapped down a deep well read what sounded like a shopping list for mobile DJs . . . '32K TURBOSOUND RIG . . . THREE COLOUR WATER-COOLED LASER . . .'

As I appeared, he rose to meet me, grasped my wrists and stared excitedly into my eyes.

'It was only one of them acid house parties! It was the absolute bollocks . . . everyone's on these pills called E, no fighting, and AMAZING music. I met so many people and we sold all the stock. AND we've been booked to do the bar at their next rave, called Energy!'

And then, while doing a funny octopus dance with his gangly limbs, he added, 'You gotta try it, Kirk, this thing's gonna change the world.'

I thought that was a bit far-fetched, but thirty-odd years later, it turned out he'd been absolutely right.

The unbearable lightness of E-ing

'I am astounded. Everyone must get to experience a profound state like this. I feel totally peaceful. I have lived all my life to get here, and I feel I have come home. I am complete.'

– The 'Godfather of Ecstasy' Alexander
Shulgin's journal

My own personal ecstatic epiphany took place one Saturday night in June later that year at the Dungeons, beneath Lea

Bridge Road in Walthamstow. It wasn't so much a night out as a rebirth.

The venue resembled a disused pub, with white bed sheets draping the windows, low ceilings that dripped condensation, Ribena sold off a table at a quid a carton and bouncers with Rottweilers patrolling the exterior. I was unsure whether they were there to keep people out or keep them in.

Adam insisted I try an E. Intrigued, I swallowed it and twenty minutes or so later began to feel dizzy. I was looking out of an upstairs window and the queasiness increased. A girl asked me if I was okay. 'I've just done my first E and I don't feel good,' I replied.

She gave me a hug and grabbed my hand, leading me downstairs. 'You've got to dance it off!'

I started dancing, but looser and more fluid than I'd done previously. I wasn't dancing to the music; I *was* the music. It flowed through my limbs, shaping my form like an LED graphic equaliser. My spine became a bassline, my legs the drumsticks and my feet were no longer just feet; they were my roots drawing up divine Earth energy. I couldn't feel where my legs ended and the ground began.

Then something elemental happened that ignited the future . . .

Evil Eddie Richards was playing on a flatbed truck in the courtyard when all of a sudden it started to rain. Have you ever seen summer rain through lasers? Billions of little blue sparks fizzed in the air like atmospheric static, triggered by the chemical kinesis of Lil Louis 'French Kiss'.

In that very moment, my life changed.

Like many who had seen the (strobe)light, I became evangelical in my belief that ecstasy and rave culture were not only the answer to my problems, but the solution to most – if not all – of society's ills.

We'd sing 'I'd like to buy the world an E' to the tune of the '70s Coke advert, and having witnessed the proliferation of ecstasy ending football hooliganism, quite reasonably believed that if Bush and Gorbachev dropped a pill together, the Cold War would melt in a maelstrom of MDMA-induced empathy and understanding.

I once met the guy who was instrumental in the initial mass importation of the drug MDMA. A convert himself and believer in its potential to change the world for the better, he told me of his unease that 'ecstasy' was known to be a drug used in the gay scene, therefore it might be necessary to subtly re-brand it for the *straight market*.

In fact, had it not been for a popular shampoo advertised on TV already using the name, the drug which changed the world for the louder would have been marketed under the name 'Empathy'.

June 1989: Sunrise, 'Midsummer Night's Dream' (White Waltham Airfield)

'It seems entirely reasonable to think that every now and then the energy of a whole generation comes to a head in a long fine flash.'

– Hunter S. Thompson, *Fear and Loathing in Las Vegas*

The next week we loaded up the 8-tonne truck with the plywood, pop-up bar and numerous pallets of soft drinks. Going forward, we would always use the same supplier, an astute wholesaler in Hammersmith who offered us stock on a 'sale or return' basis. This was essential as there was always a chance the police would get to the venue before we did and set up a roadblock. He was the only drinks merchant in London who offered this option, and as a result he supplied a lot of the orbital raves through that long hot summer.

If the Pay Party Unit had really been on the case they would have leant on him, cut off the only source of liquid available, and very few parties would've been able to go ahead. More on this later.

No promoter, however financially driven and morally challenged they might be, would've put on a party without the availability of water. Ecstasy can cause overheating and dehydration, so access to water is absolutely essential. Without it, people would die – something we pointed out one Saturday when we took the wrong turning on a country road in Suffolk and wound up in a farmyard. Dogs were barking, geese were honking and the smell of manure was overpowering. It was around midnight (which is late for mortals) and the middle of the night for early-rising farmers. Hearing the commotion, the farmer stomped out of his farmhouse brandishing a double-barrelled shotgun and screamed at us to 'Turn round and fuck off now!'

This was something we'd already realised we couldn't do, as the convoy of cars we'd led from South Mimms services had followed us – and were stuck. Bumper-to-bumper for half a mile back along the single-track lane we'd mistakenly led them down. By the time everyone had reversed, and we'd extricated ourselves, the boys in blue had turned up and were preventing anyone else from getting into the rave, which was being held in a disused airfield in Berkshire. The hangar, the largest in Britain at the time, was the main room, and an articulated lorry packed with speakers parked outside was 'the terrace'.

There were already a few hundred ravers who'd got in before the roadblock was set up and these numbers were swelling as many others parked their cars on verges and disappeared into adjacent fields, where they would scramble over hedges or holes in perimeter fencing. As the police reinforcements were still on their way, the dozen or so coppers were powerless to stop them.

We calmy pointed out that we were the only bar servicing the event, and if they didn't let us in there would be deaths and we'd go on record saying we were physically prevented from taking water into the event.

They conferred, and after making a radio call to HQ, reluctantly let us in. We arrived like the cavalry, to cheers like we were returning war heroes or victorious cup winners. Some kids were dangerously dry-mouthed and desperate, outstretched arms imploring us to stop. We pulled up, climbed into the back, dropped the tailgate and threw out bottles of water to those who needed them.

NRG

A lot was made at the time about the *extortionate* price of water in the orbital raves; in fact, the price was determined by practicality more than a desire to profiteer. Everything was a pound coin, because anything less was fiddly and involved change, which we'd invariably run out of (resulting in us having to temporarily close while one of us ran off in search of more loose change). Charging a quid also meant that spaced-out ravers didn't have to count out the exact money in small coins in a distracting environment. This also gave us a margin that would cover the amount of free stock we usually gave out. If anyone looked the worse for wear and didn't have any money left, we'd give them a bottle of water without hesitation. We must've given away thousands through that summer. They didn't mention that in the tabloids, did they?

At the time, Ribena and Lucozade were unfashionable. Ribena was for kids while Lucozade was something which was advertised as a convalescent drink or a 'health' tonic if you were under the weather. After seeing how perfect they were for raving, I wrote to Lucozade telling them they were missing a trick and asking if they'd be interested in developing a brand partnership with a party promoter like Energy. A few days later I received a snotty reply telling me that Lucozade was a health product and no association with acid house parties was *'sought, encouraged or something we are comfortable with'*.[2]

The party itself was mind-blowing in many ways. I witnessed no moodiness, no fighting, weapons or threats and no one was discriminated against. Cheesy quaver 'geezers', shirtless gay guys, lesbian couples, black, white, Asian, twenty-somethings, thirty-somethings, forty-somethings . . . this was one nation under a groove. And. It. Was. Out. Of. This. World.

Later on, the DJ played a version of 'French Kiss' which seemed to go on for ever, then spun Doug Lazy's 'Let It Roll' in there as an a cappella. The place went nuts. Who was he? No one played like this. I wandered over. There was no staging or elevated DJ booth in those days, just a

---

[2] In early 1990, after seeing a huge upswing in sales from an outlet in west London, 'Lucozade Sport' was launched with re-branded bottles, logo (NRG) and advertising to appeal to the new generation of drinkers. Coincidence?

few trestle tables behind the stacks. No passes were needed. Why would anyone want to go back there? Although respected, the DJs weren't stars and there was no such thing as VIP culture or backstage passes. There was a huge fella playing with three decks, totally concentrating, yet loving the music as much as anyone the other side of the speaker stacks. There was a girl dancing next to him who obviously knew him. I asked her what the DJ was called. She leant over and mouthed something, but I just couldn't hear. She reached in her pocket and handed me a business card.

DJ Carl Cox

Three-deck wizard. For bookings, call Maxine 0273 27857

At one point I recall the music stopping and a guy I recognised as Denzil, who was always on the door at Sunrise, announced that his bag full of cash had gone missing. And unless it was returned, the party was over. Whoever took it realised that they wouldn't be able to escape as security had been informed and everyone was to be searched on the way out, if necessary.

After what seemed like an eternity of silence (but was probably no more than five minutes), some fella with what looked like a bionic arm pushed through the crowds, holding the bag aloft. As he moved towards the front a cheer rose from those he passed; a rolling wave of euphoria which carried him to the DJ booth. Whether or not the bag was full no one knew, we all wanted to believe that honesty had won the day and there were no thieves in Paradise.

Eleven thousand people were at that party, and within hours, every household in the country would know about it.

After dropping the unsold stock off, we returned home late on Sunday evening, picking up pizzas and falling asleep utterly elated.

Front-page news

The next morning, I had a dental appointment, and after a few fillings I walked, numb-mouthed, back home. As I drew level with the newsagent's shop, I stopped dead in my tracks. Every newspaper's front page was about the best party I'd ever been to, except what they wrote bore no resemblance to what I'd witnessed:

The Sun's headline read 'Spaced Out!', followed by a double-page spread on 'Ecstasy Airport'. I bought every newspaper, ran back to the flat, burst into Adam's bedroom and threw the newspapers onto his bed. He sat bolt upright, like Bela Lugosi rising from his coffin.

'Fuck . . . nooooo!'

We headed to our usual greasy spoon café in Mill Hill, where every Monday morning we pored over the papers. What we saw was staggering in its hysterical inaccuracy: 'Youngsters so drugged-up they ripped the heads off pigeons!'

As any small child or dog will testify, it's really, really hard to catch a pigeon. (Indeed, the pursuit's complexity is such that it inspired a children's cartoon in the '70s starring Dick Dastardly and Muttley.) So the chances of some pilled-up raver being able to catch a pigeon, let alone bite the head off one after mistaking it for an ice pop, are infinitesimally small.

Another absurd claim was the observation 'at the end of the night, the floor was covered in empty ecstasy wrappers'. Recalling the now-deserted hangar floor when we'd packed up and were preparing to leave, it was littered with trampled plastic water bottles, flattened Ribena cartons and the colourful detritus of the confetti cannon slivers of silver foil. Headless pigeons were nowhere to be seen. And as for ecstasy wrappers ... They'll be with the unicorn horns, tooth fairy and rocking horse shit. The claim that really got my goat, however (not to mention triggering me to use a typewriter), was the headline: 'Children as young as twelve at acid house party.'

I saw virtually no one under the age of twenty at *any* party that summer. Tickets were £25, pills cost £15, *and* you needed a car in order to get there. This was the age of the yuppie, remember? There may have been lots of money about in London, but it wasn't in the piggy banks of twelve-year-olds.

The fashion at the time was baggy dungarees, accessorised with dummies and glow sticks. Very little make-up was worn as it would only be ruined by the dust and sweat, and with the absence of a well-lit girls' powder room to touch up, many girls wore no make-up at all to the raves. It wasn't about glamour or trying to look cool. In retrospect, the raves were an excuse to relive our childhoods: silly dancing, funny, colourful, comfortable clothes and an excuse to stay out *WAY* past your bedtime! Back in the day, bouncy castles and fairground rides were as big an attraction as the DJs. But just because people wear dungarees doesn't mean they're pre-pubescent (Super Mario, Dexys Midnight Runners and the Minions in *Despicable Me* are all proof of this).

Perhaps this explains the 'kids as young as twelve' claim.

As what we read sank in, the excitement was replaced by anger and a sense of injustice. All week the debate raged.

The media's narrative was that the 'spectre of acid house' hung over the nation's youth and not – as I saw it – like an angel of redemption. I was so incensed at the lies being peddled that I borrowed my ex-girlfriend's Olivetti type-writer and tapped out the aforementioned article defending the phenomena while explaining its attraction.

Two fingers and the truth

Country music and punk rock were once described as 'three chords and the truth'. I'd never driven a typewriter before; the keyboard was baffling, so I tapped out my features using a forefinger of each hand, using an entire bottle of Tipp-Ex to conceal my numerous typos. Adam read it and said it was 'the bollocks', so I sent it to *NME* (no reply), *The Face* (no reply), the *Daily Mail* (not a fucking hope, what on earth was I thinking?), the *Evening Standard* (likewise) and a title called *Mixmag* – a magazine for DJs, which a former girlfriend told me her old schoolmate, Dan, the son of Radio Luxembourg DJ Tony 'The Royal Ruler' Prince, was involved with.

The next day the editor of *Mixmag*, Dave Seaman, called me and informed me they loved my piece on raves and wanted to run it in their next issue . . . and, what's more, they'd give me £25 for doing so! I was to become a published writer AND be paid for it!

Upon hearing me repeat this, my flatmate Adam, who was listening to the conversation draped on the sofa with a spliff, muttered, 'Only £25? They're taking the piss.'

So I nervously told them this wasn't enough and that *The Face* were showing interest. Adam sagely nodded his approval.

Next thing I know, I hear a familiar voice I recognised as Tony Prince, the owner of DMC, who published *Mixmag*. As a kid growing up in the '70s listening to Radio Luxembourg, I'd listen to Tony with a one-piece earphone late at night under the covers so no one would hear and know I wasn't asleep.

'David tells me our offer isn't sufficient, Kirk. What figure have you got in mind?'

As he spoke, his mid-Atlantic accent transported me back to August 1977. I'm in a tent with my schoolmate, Tosh Winfield. We're fifteen years old and cycling to Yorkshire. Tosh is asleep, but I'm awake listening to a transistor radio. Tony Prince announces Elvis Presley is dead, as president of the Elvis Presley UK Fan Club, the all-night shift fell to him. He stayed on air for twelve hours, playing only Elvis songs. I drifted off just as the sun was rising. 'Are You Lonesome Tonight?' was never as poignant as it was that night.

'Hi Tony, nice to talk to you. I'm on the dole at the moment and get £32.75 a week. It would really mean something if my writing earned me a week's dole money.'

There was a pause. Had I blown it already?

'Okay, you've got a deal.'

This was the first coverage of the rave scene in *Mixmag*. Although it was only one small step onto that podium, it was one giant leap for me. I was caught up in the most thrilling, adrenaline-fuelled wave of excitement and rebellion ever to happen to my generation.

No sooner had we caught up on our sleep, we were loading that 8-tonner with soft drinks once again. This time bound for Energy II, which took place in a field next to a commuter trainline. The convoy that night was bonkers, stretching back miles behind our truck. The police sealed off an 18-mile run of the M25 to prevent more partygoers from attending, but they simply abandoned their cars on the hard shoulder and walked across the fields, following the lasers. The negative tabloid coverage seemed to act like an advert for acid house. This thing was spreading exponentially. Every weekend saw greater numbers of people searching for somewhere to dance.

The following week, Dave Seaman called me to commission another piece on the forthcoming Sunrise rave. My first feature had gone down well with the readers and this time the piece would run over three pages AND I'd get paid the princely sum of £65 ... equivalent to my fortnightly giro!

Every Saturday people would ask if we were going to '*the common*'. I was aware that on Sunday afternoons ravers were congregating on Clapham Common, opposite the Windmill pub, to come down from the night before with a few pints and spliffs – swapping stories of raves and roadblocks as the sun got lower in the sky and the weekend ended. As June progressed, these colourful gatherings grew; sound systems would arrive and impromptu raves began developing in the hazy evening sun.

As we had to return the unsold stock to west London, we'd usually be too late to catch the action. But one weekend in early July, Biology's 'DJ Convention' official after-party was to be held on the common. Come 11 a.m. on the Sunday morning, a convoy crept down the M1 into London from Watford beneath another cloudless sky. By the time we reached south London there must've been around 500 stay-awakes, raving on the road around parked cars and lounging about in groups on the grass. Some stood sipping pints of lager and girls skipped and danced barefoot in the grass like infants on a school trip. MC Chalkie White had found a car steering wheel and was pretending to park, shuffling back and forth along the road. Familiar faces recognised us from the bar and asked us where the truck was. That white DAF Drinks Wagon was the most recognised box truck in the UK that summer. These days it would have its own Insta account.

There was never any trouble on the common, yet the following week the police were waiting and refused to let the sound system in. But where there's a pill, there's a way and from nowhere a stereo deck and small generator appeared, carried aloft on shoulders through the crowd. It didn't matter that the generator easily drowned out the tinny stereo speakers: people still danced. On the roofs surrounding the common, the long lenses of police photographers glinted in the sun.

In 2004 I found myself back on Clapham Common surrounded by 10,000 ravers along with Sasha, Tall Paul, X-Press 2 and Erick Morillo. I was asked to manage and host the mainstage at my mates' SW4 event. It was my job to welcome the crowd, introduce the DJs, ask the postcode of SW4 how they were feeling, and – most important of all – ensure that the 10 p.m. curfew wasn't exceeded as it would cost the promoters a £1,000 fine for every minute they'd run over.

As I surveyed the vast crowd, excited faces were briefly illuminated, lit up by exploding pyrotechnics, and I thought about those innocent, impromptu gatherings on the common fifteen years earlier; the first expression of a new culture. A culture which despite state oppression, media lies and on occasion even having its sound system taken away, refused to stop dancing. Amen to that.

A SUMMER OF LOVE

August 1989: The big showdown

'Tony arrived, and after showing him my field, we sat in the kitchen. He opened his briefcase and I've never seen so many notes in my life. And to be honest, if you're in farming and see that many notes it does tend to sway you slightly.'

– Stuart McIntosh (farmer who rented the land)

One Friday in August, I called Tony Colston-Hayter to sort out entry arrangements so I could review his Sunrise organisation's forthcoming 'Back to the Future' event for *Mixmag*.

He told me he'd already sold 15,000 tickets and it was set to be Britain's biggest ever rave, but that the police were determined to stop it by putting pressure on the farmer and local council. This resulted in them serving an injunction, but as we spoke, Tony was on the other line to his legal team, who were onsite in Longwick, Buckinghamshire. I understood that if he could prove it was a private party, the injunction could be overturned as it wasn't a public event.

After closing the call with his lawyers, Tony relayed the conversation.

'If we can prove it's a private event, it's on. We have over 15,000 names and addresses of our members and as long as we don't take cash on the door, I understand we'll be fine ... though they'll probably set up roadblocks because we haven't told them the true number of attendees. You'd better get there early if you want to make sure of getting in, Kirk.'

I couldn't miss this party. *Mixmag* had reserved three pages for my write-up and what happened that night would define the summer. So we agreed that in return for getting in with the crew, I would marshal traffic for a few hours prior to commencing my raving reportage.

What I was aware of was that at the same time I was meeting Tony, the local council were threatening to take the farmer to court if he gave permission for the party to take place on his land – as were Sunrise, who had a signed contract with him.

'I was in the position that if it went ahead, the council would take me to court, and if it didn't, Tony Colston-Hayter would take me to court, so I was a bit stuffed,' farmer Stuart McIntosh later said.

After days of discussions between Sunrise's QC, the farmer, the council, local residents, the police and Environmental Health, the news broke that Sunrise's appeal was upheld. The injunction was lifted and the build continued with staging trucks and laser companies heading out of west London along the A40 on yet another scorching hot summer's day . . . with a car-parking steward wearing a DMC baseball cap.

As it turned 11 p.m., I was standing in a dusty field on the outskirts of Longwick with a torch and a whistle. It looked and felt like a scene from *Close Encounters* – surrounded by beams of light in all directions. Behind me, laser fingers waved through the sky, briefly exposing the silver pylons that crossed the site. To my left, a big wheel whirred, scattering excited screams into the warm night air. To my right, a bright halogen light illuminated the car parking area. In front of me, a convoy of headlights snaked from my torch beam to the horizon.

The sheer number of cars arriving was staggering. The police, still smarting from being beaten in court, refused to help, as did the local authorities, and despite us parking them as quickly as possible, the line of cars tailed back some 4 miles to the A40. Some ravers just abandoned their

cars and walked across the fields, following the lasers and
booming kick drum. No one walked from their cars; they
all ran or skipped and leapt like rodeo horses or jubilant
toddlers in a soft play car park.

I saw so many familiar faces arriving. George Michael,
Jonathan and Eko from London's top indie night 'Feet First'
at Camden Palace, French rockstar Axel Bauer, Philip Sallon
and Boy George (who was a regular that summer), *EastEnder*
Danniella Westbrook, a Pet Shop Boy, 'wild child' Amanda
de Cadenet, a British Olympic swimmer, at least two Page
3 girls, most of the cast of *Grange Hill*, Wee Papa Girl
Rappers, some bloke from TV's *The Bill* and a saucer-eyed
female ITN newsreader. More and more familiar faces I
recognised from various aircraft hangars, warehouses and
fields turned up. It felt like the whole world was at Sunrise.

After returning my torch and hi-vis vest to the
Portakabin, I entered the main arena and realised there
must have been around 20,000 people present. In addition
to the mainstage, there was a huge blue circus big top
overflowing with ravers who scurried around, illuminated
by glow-in-the-dark necklaces.

I picked up a bottle of water at the bar and was intrigued
to see a lone security man standing in front of a small
stretch of red rope which was strung between two traffic
bollards. Behind the rope, glumly drinking Champagne
from flutes – and being completely ignored – were the
immaculately attired and perfectly made-up popstars, Mel
and Kim. Overdressed and underwhelming, they were out
of sync with the 'Year Zero' aspect of 1989. Posing was
out, dancing was in. Popstars were passé, it was all about
the music. (Note: it still wasn't about the DJ in 1989. The
agents hadn't got their fingers in the pie at this stage.)

There were PAs too: Cry Sisco! performed their Balearic banger 'Afro Dizzi Act', E-Zee Possee vogued and rapped their quirky anthem, 'Everything Starts With An "E"', Razette grooved through 'Ready 4 Love', and Doug Lazy was received like an old friend, with 20,000 voices rapping along to 'Let It Roll'.

Although there was a performance on the stage, it felt somehow different to a concert, where a performer exudes energy that is absorbed by the crowd, who collectively give it back, empowering the performer to reach a higher level. This 'chemistry' was something I studied and worked with when I was a singer in the band for the previous five years. But here, something different and much more interesting was going on. The PAs and DJs weren't the focus of the energy, just the (largely anonymous) facilitators.

The crowd still responded as one entity but they fed off one another rather than the individual on stage. Instead of bouncing back and forth, the energy spiralled among and above us – a self-generating, unifying vortex unhindered by personality or a verbal manifesto.

At one point, I found myself in the middle of the crowd in front of the stage, where the traditional mosh pit would be. A tribal chant started up, urgent and affirmative and accompanied by collective fist pumps. 'Men-tal! Men-tal! Radio rental!'

Suddenly above our heads a police helicopter appeared and maintained its presence for the next hour, spoiling the music with its incessant, irritating staccato, but improving the light show with a huge searchlight, which when alighting on a group would prompt either a sea of 'V's or pleas of 'Beam me up, Scotty!'. A camera pointed out of the open side door, recording evidence until the chopper became low on fuel and finally wheeled away to cheers.

As I danced beneath the stars, it dawned on me that what I was doing wasn't at all new, but very old indeed.

It suddenly made sense. We were connecting with 'the great dance', something I'd quiz 'Psychedelic Saint' Timothy Leary about the following year.

At this moment, my merrymaking became a mission. A few years earlier, Margaret Thatcher had famously declared that there was no such thing as society. Yet the sense of unity I felt at these raves – ravers helping each other, accepting each other's differences, sharing not only their water with strangers but also their love of being alive and an unspoken sense of togetherness – showed me she was wrong. Society grows from community and a sense of belonging. In a rave, there is no individual, the crowd is one sentient being radiating energy. My ego dissolved into its mass, sacrificing individuality to become part of something bigger – something called society.

How could dancing through the night, to a drum, with thousands of other souls all celebrating life, ever be regarded as 'evil'? At this moment, my merrymaking became a mission. I've made my living from encouraging people to dance together to music ever since this night and would go on to explore paganism through the path of Druidry.

Just before dawn, Tony Colston-Hayter took the mic and made the announcement that over 20,000 cold people wanted to hear: 'I've just received the weather forecast and can tell you we're in for a glorious sunrise.'

This was most welcome, as like many, I was only wearing a T-shirt and was yearning for dawn. It didn't disappoint. Fifteen minutes later, a huge blood red orb appeared from over a hedge to the left of the stage, breathing life into tired bodies; rays of warmth that reinvigorated the rave and prompted countless reunions.

In the light, I found my mates and introduced them to those I'd just met – a pattern repeated across the site. The random nature of raving in unfamiliar venues coupled with the absence of mobile phones resulted in groups of friends inevitably being separated. I've lost count of the times a girlfriend would return from a trip to the toilets, hand in hand with some wide-eyed stranger: 'This is Alan, he's lost his mates.' Which led to a sympathetic, 'Aww, WE can be your mates, Alan.' At some point in the late afternoon, clouds started building, so we finally left and headed back to London. This was probably the best rave of the summer. All the elements came together – line-up, scale, production, weather – it was never matched.

As Tony's sister, Charlie Colston-Hayter, says about the farmer, 'Luckily he made the right decision, and the party went down in history.'

It wasn't the only thing which went down. Farmer Stuart McIntosh's popularity similarly sank. He was ignored when he dropped into his local, the Red Lion in Longwick, for a pint and stopped going.

More than thirty years later, does he have any regrets?

'Looking back, I'm quite proud of what we did. A lot of people had a lovely weekend and I'll bet a lot of them remember it to this day,' he told the BBC in 2006.

Stuart McIntosh passed away as this book was being written. His place in heaven is assured.

As the years rolled by, that Sunrise party became the rave equivalent of the Sex Pistols in Manchester in '76 – except with one difference. There was no way that the Manchester venue could possibly have accommodated everyone who claimed to be there that seminal night, but the thousands who claim they witnessed the biggest ever rave in the acid house era could feasibly all have been there indeed.

Tony Colston-Hayter gave the village of Longwick a cheque for £3,000 for all the inconvenience caused. This caused a hot debate in the parish council chamber with accusations that it was 'blood money'. After much discussion, it was accepted and spent on crocus bulbs and hanging baskets.

★

'For every action, there is an equal and opposite reaction.'
– Sir Isaac Newton

Tony, Sunrise and the rave scene may have won this particular battle, but with tabloid hysteria over the 'Sunrise' party and convoys of *'crazed teenagers'* tearing around the M25, the war took a different direction from this point on.

I recently discovered through a FOI request that former foreign secretary and Tory grandee Lord Carrington's estate was within earshot of the party and he received a guided tour of the site the following day. His report has never been published, so we'll never find out if Mel and Kim finished their Champagne.

The authorities needed someone who had the guts and guile to take on the promoters and bend the rules and exploit loopholes in a similar fashion. Enter divisional commander of north-west Kent, Chief Superintendent Ken Tappenden – a tough-talking, no-nonsense career copper who made his name during the miners' strikes when he blocked the Dartford Tunnel to prevent 'flying' pickets travelling from Kent to challenge strike-breaking miners at collieries in Nottinghamshire. When British bodies needed to be recovered from the Zeebrugge ferry disaster in 1987, they called on Ken. Fresh from a £21 million LSD bust, he was on a roll and, like the adversaries he faced, willing to bend the rules . . .

Tappenden set up the police's Pay Party Unit (or the 'Acid House Squad', as we called them). From the incident room in Gravesend, they started gathering information about everyone involved in the scene: from promoters and ticket sellers to staging companies, plant hire and mobile bar providers, which was entered onto the national HOLMES database, which had been set up after the Yorkshire Ripper case. As more resources were ploughed into this, they became more effective.

But there was still time to party. The next Energy rave was set to be the biggest yet, and what's more, I'd spotted a gap in the market. Everyone loved the artwork on the flyers: a mixture of the very old pagan imagery of suns or standing stones, juxtaposed with the very new computer-generated graphics, fractals and 3D effects. Surprised that no one had thought to put these on T-shirts, I outlined my idea to Adam. He was in. We'd go 50/50. We needed Energy's blessing and so a deal was struck with founders Jeremy Taylor and Quentin 'Tin Tin' Chambers, where we'd give them a fiver for each shirt we sold.

Soon came the final Saturday of August. Along with pallets of soft drinks and the crate of bubbly for 'VIPs', we also loaded 200 T-shirts with a choice of short- or long-sleeved options. I'd put what little money I had saved into this. Although I knew it was a risk, I was confident the shirts would fly out. We wore them as we worked behind the bar, prompting compliments and many asking where we got them from.

They say everything starts with an E, but in actual fact, for a few months, everything started with South Mimms services: ravers assembling and mingling, waiting for our bar truck to pull out of the car park. Having stripped the shelves of Ribena, water and chewing gum, they also cleared the services of those little packets of tissues. As everyone was starting to realise, ecstasy gets you moving in more ways than one.

One Saturday night I remember a small cheer drew us towards a van, around which a small group thronged. Someone in the passenger seat was reading out loud that day's *Guardian* newspaper, carrying the story that the Lost in Space promoters, whose rave had been busted the weekend after Sunrise, were suing the police for unlawful behaviour.

'The National Council for Civil Liberties who are supporting the action last night claimed the operation was "outrageous and unlawful and probably influenced by the sensational media coverage". Mr Keir Starmer, legal officer for the NCCL, then added that the operation was "an incredible abuse of police powers."'

'Fuck me, that guy should run for prime minister,' enthused Adam.

With regards to my merchandise venture, they all admired the quality and didn't baulk at the price but said they didn't want to carry it around as they'd invariably lose it, so would come back later 'at the end'. But this being an orbital rave, it had no specified end!

By dawn on Sunday 27 August, there were around 25,000 people at this party. As Biology and Raindance both got raided, people transferred to Energy . . . but did it help us sell any extra T-shirts? No. People would tell us they were saving their last 15 quid for another pill rather than spend it on a bloody T-shirt. I think we sold four ... it was a complete disaster.

On the same weekend, as the sun rose on a misty summer's morning, a well-connected and wealthy 82-year-old former merchant banker and magistrate gazed from the bedroom window of his eighteenth-century Grade II listed house. The incessant throbbing of a rave was clearly discernible from across his swimming pool and exquisitely designed gardens. Beyond the tennis court, down the Wey Valley and over-looking the hills of the Alice Holt Forest, intermittent pencils of light arched above the horizon, exciting an otherwise serene sky. With one hand on his hip and the other once again holding a telephone, he shook his head at the power-lessness he felt. Villagers were threatening to turn vigilante and if they did, he feared bloodshed. Urging them to park their anger, he reassured them he'd act.

A few hours later, utterly exhausted from not sleeping and fed-up of getting no response from the police, he picked up the phone to his nephew, an MP in Margaret Thatcher's government. It was to become acid house's 'Archduke Franz Ferdinand' moment, setting in motion a chain of events that would affect every promoter and raver in the land. The KLF may have been unsure of the time of love, but Gerald Coke would demonstrate this particular morning that the time of resentment is dawn.

TOP TUNE: 'Your Love', Frankie Knuckles

2

THE LADY'S NOT
FOR GURNING

Of all the summers I'd go on to mourn, that of 1989 remains the most fondly remembered: bathed in soft golden light, crazy and carefree . . . and, like the best summers, seemingly endless.

By late September of that year, my second feature had appeared in *Mixmag*: an attack on the hysterical tabloid coverage of the rave scene. It was enthusiastically received and every Saturday in South Mimms services, ravers would come up and shake my hand to thank me for being their voice. As much as I was a commentator, I was covering it from the inside.

'He's not just a roving reporter, he lives in the lasers and is *Mixmag*'s raving reporter!', quipped Tony Prince. He was introducing me onstage at the DMC DJ Convention at Hammersmith Palais, to chair a debate about acid house for a panel that included Tony Colston-Hayter from Sunrise, Radio 1's latest signing Dave Pearce and some politician or other.

The hottest summer in a generation was also one of the longest. Much to the delight of an ever-growing army of ravers (not to mention the police's disappointment), the autumn of '89 was largely dry and warm with the exception of Biology's 'Panorama' in the Kent countryside, near Meopham. The venue was located in a valley with the stage and production halfway up the slope. There were no under-cover areas whatsoever, and this was the first orbital rave at which it rained. There were around 7,000 people as Genesis's 'The Empire Strikes Back' venue was discovered and neutralised at the last minute. And so the ravers headed for Biology, swelling the numbers.

The slope soon turned into mud, with ravers sliding down in comical fashion. It was hilarious to watch, but a reminder of just how vulnerable our scene was to bad weather. I honestly believe that if the summers of '89 and '90 weren't as reliable weatherwise as they were, the orbital raves would not have attracted the numbers they did and acid house may not have made the front pages. On a summer's night when the air is balmy and sensual, and it's still light at 10 p.m., people are up for adventure. In the same way the long hot summer of '76 supplied sultry fermentation conditions for punk rock, the sunniest and driest summer in London since records began provided ideal growing conditions for a very vigorous seed.

There was a bigger problem than the rain at Meopham: it was on Ken Tappenden's turf. As national coordinator for the 'Acid House Squad', it caused embarrassment that one of these parties took place right under his nose (unlikely claims that he was still finding youngsters in hedges days later, high on drugs, only reinforce this). Meopham was just 10 miles from the Pay Party HQ. When Ken heard about another rave planned for the following Saturday, a few miles away in Wrotham, he personally served the landowner with an injunction – only to find he'd been bunged £3,000 to go on holiday to France. Outsmarted again, and unable to prevent people going in, police busted them coming out instead – filling six bin bags with clubbing contraband in the process.

Energy 'Dance '89' @ Raydon Airfield

A few weeks later, with the weather still holding, I found myself in an airfield in Suffolk chatting to the comedian, Griff Rhys Jones.

The party was supposed to be a fundraiser for the families of the victims of the *Marchioness* riverboat disaster, which claimed the lives of fifty-one people, many of them connected to the rave scene, and was to take place in Southwark Park in London, but the council folded under police pressure at the last minute. We sat in South Mimms from 9 p.m. to 2 a.m. waiting to hear if a venue had been secured. We understood there were three possibilities. One by one they were busted before the sound rig and security were in position. There were hundreds of ravers dancing around cars to the anthems of the summer, punctuated by muffled pirate radio presenters urging, 'Keep it locked' and 'Hold tight'.

Just as we were on the verge of giving up and driving home, Adam's pager started bleeping. 'It's on! . . . Junction 28, A12, more info to follow . . .'

It took the best part of two hours to drive there. No one overtook as we were the only ones who knew where we were going. I recall looking in the wing mirror and seeing a procession of dipped headlights dutifully following in a single file, slow lane convoy. No one else was on the motorway. It felt like we knew the biggest secret on the planet at that moment.

As we headed east, scything through golden wheat fields and parched verges in the still summer night, the first signs of dawn teased the horizon, its pale blue gape slowly swallowing the stars, leaving only the silver crescent moon. We'd finally reached our destination, and after being waved through security cordons, headed to a huge black building which reverberated to the THUD, THUD, THUD of a sound system. We drove into the hangar, turned off the engine and threw the rear door shutter up, revealing an MDF and chipboard pop-up bar and pallet upon pallet of our usual liquid refreshments. The clatter awoke the bar staff, who'd been asleep in the back of the truck.

'Where the fuck are we?'

'Just outside Ipswich,' replied Adam.

'Ipswich? What time is it?' yawned one dungareed corpse curled up in the corner.

'Wake up time, there's 15,000 thirsty ravers on their way.'

A few hours later, I was introduced to the genial Griff. His house was next door to the rave and, clearly intrigued, he had asked security for a guided tour.

He was a big star in those days, having appeared in *Not the Nine O'Clock News* and *Alas Smith and Jones*. This led to those present double taking when he passed. I presented him with an 'Energy' T-shirt. We had plenty left! I was in the process of chewing his ear off, explaining that the raves were friendly gatherings populated by adults responsibly enjoying a new recreational drug. A drug infinitely preferable to alcohol that didn't incapacitate people, wasn't addictive nor did it ruin their lives.

THE LADY'S NOT FOR GURNING

It was at this point a gurning raver who was passing by recognised Griff. The bloke was clearly E-ing off his tits and awestruck at seeing such a well-known face from '*off the telly*' at an acid house party. Griff saw him gawping, gently smiled, and politely held out his hand. The saucer-eyed creature grabbed it with his sweaty, squidgy palm and caressed it tenderly. Griff straightened and gently tried to withdraw his palm . . . which was now encased by the plucky pillhead's other hand, being caressed to smithereens.

'I can't believe it, man. It's really you, isn't it?'

Griff confirmed rather awkwardly that yes, it was definitely him. The bloke leant forward, gazing into the nervous comic's eyes with his pupils spinning in alternate directions. On their orbit around his eye sockets, they would occasionally disappear from view beneath his eyelids, leaving bloodshot snooker cue balls where his pupils should be. 'I'm a lumberjack, and I'm okay . . . right?'

A somewhat confused Griff tried to pull away, but the Python-loving pillhead did not relent, whispering something into the celebrity's left ear while dribbling a slow-motion silver thread of saliva onto his shoulder. Something which, although Griff could see happening, he was unable to prevent. I can still see his face staring aghast as the globule of gob dangled from the raver's chin, catching the light like a small disco mirror ball of spit.

'I cut down trees, I skip and jump, I like to . . . something . . . ah yeah, press flowers! I put on women's clothing and hang around in bars – mental, mate, fackin' mental! Wot a fackin' geezer!'

Griff then received a hearty slap on the back, making him stumble forward with its ferocity. The chemically challenged chap had waited all his life to meet Michael Palin and wasn't going to let this opportunity pass him by.

At this point Griff's security men extricated the saliva- and sweat-covered comic and succeeded in urging the raver to go on his merry way. Griff just stood there, looking disgustedly at his hand and the stringy globule of gob now running down his sleeve. Then, fixing me with *that* gaze said, 'Where were we? Ah yes, you were telling me about this *wonderful* new drug . . .'

As a result of the usual cat-and-mouse with the police, this party started late. The original venue had been spotted from the air and we'd had to divert to Suffolk. It had turned 3 a.m. by the time we'd got on site and set up. Consequently, it took place mostly in daylight hours . . . and ran for most of Sunday, as I recall. After a chilly autumn morning, the sun's warmth delivered a glorious afternoon. At one point early in the day, I recall dancing outside on the straw-like grass. By now there were around 15,000 at the party and a police helicopter overhead with a camera poking out, which people ritually gave the finger to. I remember thinking that this was probably the biggest party anywhere in the world at this moment in time. Nowhere were more people dancing and celebrating life together than they were here.

And then I saw him.

Dancing a few metres away without his shirt, in a pair of faded cut-off three-quarter-length denims, he had a small goatee beard, and a permanent grin ran across his earthy features. His hair was jet black and slicked back behind large ears. He appeared to derive energy from the ground itself; glancing with a conspiratorial glint at the two men either side of him. He was clearly the leader of the group. None of them spoke or interacted with any other raver.

Their frenetic movement caused the ground they pounded to release clouds of dust from the parched earth, reaching their knees and giving the impression they were dancing on air.

I looked down and could see no dust rising from my Reebok Ex-O-Fit Hi's, nor from anyone else dancing around me. Returning my gaze to the goatee guy, I peered into the disturbed dust cloud and found out why this was. Instead of two feet, I saw two cloven hooves pounding the ground.

This only served to reinforce my assertion that this was a premier planetary event. Here, before me, was *the* Satyr, the male nature spirit, the god of rustic music and impromptu gatherings. I was enthralled. You know it's some party when Pan turns up. Here I was, dancing with the devil – and on a Sunday, too!

The following Saturday night I found myself stuck in a traffic jam in a country lane just outside Reigate. We were on our way to Phantasy and had run into a police road-block. With cameraman Bela on board, I thought it a good opportunity to interview the officer in charge.

Phantasy promoter Dave Lambert was talking to a senior officer, insisting no licence was needed as the rave was on private land. With people already in the party and thousands more clogging up the surrounding lanes, the police realised they were outnumbered and made the decision to allow access. 'Go and have your party in the field,' the officer muttered.

'Did you catch that, Bela?' I asked my mate with the camera, but he was changing the battery and missed it. So

I asked the officer to repeat it, and a megaphone was passed to him.

'GO AND HAVE YOUR PARTY IN THE FIELD.'

This was greeted by cheers. I thanked the officer, who appeared very relaxed about the situation and even accepted the sweaty palms of a few appreciative ravers. The police withdrew and we walked back to our cars, spreading the word, and filed into the party.

Then something happened which would change the course of the war. A scuffle broke out when the police snatched a member of the security team for reasons unknown, which set up a 'them and us' situation between the police and the security, whose accessories included dogs and canisters of CS gas. Ravers tried to free the guard by trying to rock over the police van he was being held in, all in full view of BBC Newsroom South East cameras. In the following melee, fourteen police officers were injured, and the barrage of outrage prompted junior Environment minister Virginia Bottomley to swiftly announce that new measures would be brought in to stop the acid house craze.

This was the first time things had turned nasty. It was a watershed moment.

As September gave way to October, the days shortened, but no one complained because it just meant you could see the lasers earlier, assuming the police hadn't got there first, obviously.

Around this time Margaret Thatcher opened a letter from Michael Mates, one of her MPs and the nephew of the aforementioned uncle who lacked sleep.

With whispers of an imminent challenge to her leadership, this was another 'Falklands' opportunity which could play well in the Tory shires blighted by these parties, therefore demanding a robust trademark Iron Lady response. Ecstasy was the new Exocet threatening our way of life. The Gravesend Pay Party Unit were the new Task Force, equipped with the same zeal the Royal Navy had for the *Belgrano*.

Raves were getting busted more and more frequently as the Pay Party Unit upped their game. From an initial team of twelve, the detachment grew to 200 officers – many of them skilled and experienced detectives who expertly tapped phones and trailed staging companies, riggers, lighting and sound crews.

From Wednesday onwards, you'd hear police helicopters searching for steam rollers or fairground rides on the move around the M25. A mate of mine, who provided the sound rigs for many orbital raves, was visited by a supposed police sergeant, and told that he'd be prosecuted for conspiracy to commit an offence if they hired out the rig that weekend to Biology for the rave at Guildford (information he could only have known by tapping phone calls).[3]

Tarquin and his Biology business partner Jarvis were held without charge, their mobiles taken from them, and threatened with ten years inside for tax evasion if they persisted with that weekend's party. This was after the Inland Revenue and VAT bods were brought in to beef up the charge sheet.

Public Enemy were massive at the time, and the biggest name to appear on any flyer that summer. I was eagerly looking forward to meeting and interviewing them for *Mixmag*. The story which is told is that the only people to

---

[3] Years later, it was alleged that he wasn't actually a policeman at all, but an undercover MI5 operative . . . which would explain why the Pay Party Unit were so effective at intelligence gathering.

interview them were immigration officers at Heathrow, where they were held for four hours before being put on the plane back to New York.

What really happened was that Chuck D and Flavor Flav spent Saturday night drinking cocktails and snacking on peanuts in the bar at the InterContinental Hotel on Park Lane as the Biology party wasn't happening.

We were worried that our drinks wholesaler would be subject to the same bully boy tactics, so we did everything we could to conceal our supplier's identity. We started using public phone boxes to make calls, reading drinks orders from a piece of paper while holding our breath to avoid taking in the smell of piss. When we returned unsold stock, we'd ensure we weren't being followed, and if ever we were asked where we'd got the stock, we'd give them false information. I'd even made up a false invoice from a fictitious wholesaler, which I put in the glove compartment in case they asked for proof we hadn't stolen the drinks.

Looking back, our phone was definitely among the hundreds of numbers being monitored. Our truck was known by everyone that summer, so the police were well aware of us. But they didn't want dehydrated ecstasy cases on their hands, so if the party had started, we'd be allowed in. Just like they would never raid a party but contain it, as they knew it was the safest option. Many officers were bemused at what they witnessed and thought we were harmless. I witnessed no violence from either side and even Ken Tappenden, who was on the ground at times, could be grudgingly good-natured. 'I'm missing my bloody wedding anniversary for this and haven't had a Saturday night off in over a year,' he once told me at a roadblock in Kent. Before adding, 'Roll on, Christmas.'

THE LADY'S NOT FOR GURNING

Although poor Ken's Christmas also turned out to be rather hectic, as you'll discover . . .

★

We'd just dropped off the entire stock at the drinks' whole-saler, as the rave we were booked to provide for had been busted. This was the first time we'd been out-foxed and out-manoeuvred by the police and councils. We could feel the tide turning.

Normally we'd be listening to Centreforce FM, but it was 6.45 p.m. and chart day, so I switched to Radio 1. Straight away the gently undulating bassline was immedi-ately recognisable as Sydney Youngblood's utopian groover 'If Only I Could'. We turned it up; there are so many memories of the summer dancing to this. Trevor Fung would always play it upstairs early on at Land of Oz and we all identified with the lyrics, 'If only I could, I'd make this world a better place,' followed by a warm flamenco guitar flourish. Bloody hell, it was number three! Then a familiar hi-hat pattern filled the cab. It couldn't be, could it? IT WAS! A dry, assertive female voice confirmed it, 'Pomp up the jeam, pomp it op . . .'

In what was to become known as Carpool Karaoke thirty years later, two heads nodded and sang at the tops of their voices in a key far too high for either of them. '*Ow-Wa! A place to stay, git yer booty on the floor tonight, make my day.*' Three minutes later, Mark Goodier counted down and before that week's number one was announced, that pulse-racing, heart-quickening adrenaline-pumping staccato piano riff which we'd heard in fields, aircraft hangars, former police stations, underneath railway arches and on illegal pirate

stations A-L-L summer long . . . was being played on Radio
1. 'Ride on Time' by Black Box was number one! This was
the point at which rave went from being an illicit youth
craze to a mainstream cultural phenomenon. We may have
failed to sell one single bottle of water that weekend, but
this was the proof we had fuelled a revolution.

The rave scene was growing week on week, but by now
also attracting the attention of criminals. There were rumours
that promoters' houses were being raided and cash seized at
gunpoint. I became aware that 'shooters' would be secreted
in the box office, 'just in case'. One promoter of a well-known
rave (who shall remain nameless) approached myself and
Adam with an investment proposal. He told us he'd secured
Brixton Academy for a party but needed 'five grand sharpish'
for the deposit of artists. The return would be ten thousand.
As it was legal (Brixton had been granted a number of
6 a.m. licences by Lambeth Council and every rave there
had sold out), it was nailed on. Neither of us had that amount
of money lying around, but I knew someone who did: a
well-known advertising executive called Don. I asked him and
he agreed. His return would be seven, meaning Adam and
I would get a tidy three grand . . . and, more importantly, a
foothold in a legal party operation.

The next day we were called by the promoter's girlfriend.
She was hysterical, sobbing about guns and hoods.
Gradually I ascertained that they had opened the door,
thinking it was the pizza they'd ordered half an hour
earlier, only to find it was two masked men brandishing a
sawn-off shotgun and a knife. After roughing up her
boyfriend in an adjacent room, they obtained the combin-
ation to the safe, blindfolded them with pillowcases and
tied them up. They cleaned out the safe – including our

five grand – and left after threatening to set fire to the flat. Her promoter boyfriend was at the police station giving a statement and had asked her to break the bad news to us.

Months later, I bumped into her and she told me she was now his ex-girlfriend after receiving information that he'd staged the hold-up himself. He had paid a couple of heavies to steam in and knock him about a little and tie both he and his poor unsuspecting girlfriend up. Although she wasn't physically hurt, what she went through that night had clearly mentally scarred her.

It was early spring before we recovered all the money. We got it in dribs and drabs but eventually received it all and I returned Don's five thousand pounds. This incident marked the end of my innocence; there were snakes in Paradise and I was now aware that there was a power struggle going on for control of this burgeoning new cash-rich market.

There were stories of gangsters holding promoters ransom in their own houses and demanding a cut of profits. The pirate stations were fiercely competitive, and stories abounded of them nicking each other's transmitters and even grassing rivals up to the DTI. A DJ mate of mine who had a weekly show on one pirate station was told he could only play sanctioned events that advertised or were connected in some way to the station. He took no notice and was taken to a warehouse, hung upside down on a meat hook, doused in petrol and told to reconsider his future.

The Winter of Discoteque

It was the middle of October. The Tory Party Conference reverberated with chants of 'Ten more years! Ten more years!' as Thatcher's speech ended in adulation and the omnipotent triumphalism a decade in power brings. This was the moment Home Secretary Douglas Hurd chose to declare war on acid house, personally guaranteeing tough new powers to curb 'the evil menace to our children' and explained why the Pay Party Unit was able to draw on multi-agency support and with a limitless budget: 'If this is a new "fashion" we must be prepared for it and prefer-ably prevent such things from starting.' But prevent they could not.

The orbital raves, together with E, had given the clubs a new audience; every night in the autumn of '89 there was somewhere cool to go: Mondays was Spectrum/Land of Oz at Heaven. Tuesday was Rusty Egan's night at Crazy Larry's, Wednesday would be Café de Paris, Thursday back to Heaven for Rage, Friday Philip Sallon's Mud Club @ the Astoria, Saturday/Sunday a rave somewhere in the home counties before moving on to Clapham Common. Then, if you were still alive, Balou's in Whetstone . . . before starting it all over again!

Saturday, 28 October. BingoBangoBongo at Brixton Academy. The only rave or club I ever paid to get into! Although it was legal, the police had got wind that Sunrise were behind it, ensuring no door sales whatsoever, citing the flyer which stated, 'This is a private party, strictly invite only'. Normally this wouldn't have affected me as my name was always on the guest list, but with the Pet Shop Boys rumoured to be involved in the party, and them knowing everyone in the music business, *Mixmag* was bumped off the list by the likes of Duran Duran, Big Audio Dynamite, Janet Street-Porter and Normski. I was left with no option but to buy an unwanted ticket off a bloke across the road for £25. Looking back on it, it wasn't a bad price for a line-up featuring Frankie Knuckles, 808 State, Carl Cox, Paul 'Trouble' Anderson and Judge Jules.

It was interesting observing the Durans' toilet habits. Simon Le Bon and Nick Rhodes had synchronised bladders. They would disappear together and watch each other's backs as they took turns in using the urinals. But, as this was Year Zero, everybody ignored them except one gurner, who approached them for a light. After a brief exchange, it was left to Simon to tell the bloke they couldn't help him as they didn't smoke.

He shrugged and broke into the de rigueur raver greeting, shooting out a hand while hurriedly confirming his essential information.

'Davey, Barnet – a dove and half a trip . . .'

Simon looked down at him, somewhat confused. Davey repeated the information, staccato-like, and waited for a response, still fervently gripping Simon's hand. After an awkward silence he pulled Simon closer and bellowed in his ear, 'What's yer name, where you from, what you on?'

'Oh! Er . . . Simon, Richmond . . . Planet Earth!'

At this point the raver recognised him and started jumping around. 'Calling Planet Earth, Ba-Ba-Ba, Ba, Ba-Ba, Ba-Ba . . .', before disappearing down the sloping dancefloor into the crowd, arms whirling like windmill blades.

It felt at times like I was the only writer who was unequivocally on the side of the ravers. The *NME* had covered the crackdown, but generally the media were anti-rave. The orbital raves were despised by the Shoom brigade, who had lots of friends in the London print media, and the mainstream media's response is well documented.

As I was freelance and didn't have to toe the line to keep my job, I wrote as one of the oppressed, fully engaged in a fight for the right to party. I urged *Mixmag* to carry advice about minimising the risks of taking ecstasy (only take a half at first, drink lots of water, etc.), which they did, and read everything I could on this new drug (which wasn't much at the time), following the research and passing on useful information in my features.[4]

In one piece I mentioned that ecstasy can deplete magnesium and potassium and that bananas are a good source of both trace elements. My mate Beamish, who played a big rave at Brixton Academy one Friday night, called me to say that lots of people had taken note.

'I hope so, but how can you be so sure?'

'Because the road outside the Academy was strewn with hundreds of banana skins at 7 a.m., where the market stalls had set up. The traders were all complaining they'd been cleaned out of bananas and had none for their regular customers!'

Happy Mondays at Heaven

As everyone knows, Paul Oakenfold returned from Ibiza and wanted to replicate the same vibe he'd discovered at Amnesia. Sensing an opportunity to grow the seed he

---

[4] While the team behind *Mixmag* have always had a passion for dance music, it doesn't mean that they also indulged in any mood modification. I was keen to use the magazine to impart information about the dangers of recreational drug use, as well as its popularity, and present a balanced view, which led to the biggest drug survey in the world. Like this book, the Global Drug Survey doesn't condone or preach, just reflects reality.

planted at his Soundshaft night, the Future, he opened Spectrum every Monday at Heaven. The queue would extend right along to Embankment Tube station and was a great catch-up time as ravers swapped stories about their adventures during the weekend just gone. After *The Sun* ran a feature headlined 'Fiver for a drug trip to Heaven in Branson club', Spectrum closed its doors to allow the fuss to die down. A few weeks later it relaunched as Land of Oz.

The main floor would be Lisa Loud, Trevor Fung, Johnny Walker and Oakey, with a live PA from a big tune Balearic act like Raúl Orellana or Elektra, while Nancy Noise and Colin Hudd would host the upstairs long room. Then there was the Dakota Bar, a lounge with a circular bar which would reflect the promoter's imagination. On some nights it was 'The Leatherman's Bar', packed with clones in leather caps and chaps; other nights it was a VIP area, while on Mondays it was carpeted and draped in white to become 'The White Room'.

I wandered in and was struck by the sheer contrast to the intensity of the other areas. In front of a multi-screen video array, a scruffy duo I was introduced to as Alex and Jimmy would endlessly tweak and fiddle with three record decks, a cassette player, a CD and an Akai twelve-track mixer.

They would play bird song, which smoothly segued into what sounded like a large aircraft taking off, before morphing into ocean waves crashing onto the shore as a sweet, shrill female voice sang the words 'Loving you, is easy cos you're beautiful . . .' The DJs, Alex and Jimmy, were somewhat older than everyone else in the room. They were both friendly and as the weeks went by, I got to know them well. In return for carrying a mixer, I'd get in before the club opened and help them set up and chat. I reported back to *Mixmag* about this new sound and they agreed it was something they should cover.

So one Friday afternoon in early November 1989, I walked from Sloane Square Tube station to Alex's office at the bottom of King's Road at EG Records, to interview him for *Mixmag* about the emerging 'ambient house' sound.

Like many record companies, it was an open-plan set-up with a semi-transparent 'fishbowl' office in the middle of the room which served as the A&R Department. He spotted me and beckoned me in. I opened the door and entered what looked like a cloud. The unmistakable aroma of skunk enveloped me and Alex offered me a fat spliff with a mischievous grin. I declined. It was mid-afternoon, I had an interview to do, and felt uncomfortable as we were surrounded by typists and accountants who were all studiously working in silence – hardly the most relaxing of environments. But resistance was futile. The atmosphere in that glass bubble was so thick with potent smoke that it was like conducting an interview in a giant bong. Pretty soon the questions were forgotten and we just chatted while listening to the new sound of 'ambient house (for the e- generation)', as it was described on the sleeve of 'A Huge Ever Growing Pulsating Brain That Rules from the Centre of the Ultraworld' – Alex's 24-minute opus.

He played me some new tracks on his own label, WAU! Mr. Modo, and something he was working on with Jimmy, which was set for release in spring 1990. This turned out to be the seminal album *Space*, but without Alex's contributions, and as we sipped tea, chilling and chatting, things were going quite well. Then Alex stopped in mid-sentence, stared at me and declared guiltily, 'Don't let me stop you from what you came here to do.'

'Err . . . this IS what I came here to do, Alex.'

What did he think I was here for?

'Yeah, right. But best get on, eh?'

I looked straight at him and asked calmly, 'Alex, who do you think I am?'

He looked a little unsure, then offered, 'You're the bloke who services the photocopier, right?'

I was incredulous. We'd met half a dozen times at Land of Oz and I'd been there asking him about the Orb, KLF, Eno, Brain Machines and Smart Drugs.

'Alex, would you spend half an hour smoking a spliff, playing music and chatting about your new album with the bloke who fixes the flaming photocopier?'

He thought about it for a few seconds and replied, 'Probably.'

Then a brief frown appeared on his pale face like he was disappointed that I wasn't the photocopier bloke. There followed a long awkward silence which I broke by saying, 'I can take a look at it, if you want, how's the ink level?'

His eyes brightened. 'So you ARE the photocopier bloke!'

By the time I'd reassured him who I was by showing him my Land of Oz membership card, it was time to draw a line under the strangest, most confused interview I'd ever done. I pushed 'stop' on my mini-cassette recorder and Alex handed me a bunch of EG product (a fistful of seminal Brian Eno albums including *Music for Airports*, which was appropriate as Alex was going straight to Heathrow for a gig in Berlin that evening with the Teutonic Beats crew). We walked up the King's Road discussing our hopes for the new decade only weeks away, his interest in the Berlin sound, and at around 5 p.m., he bade me farewell as he went west on the District and Circle Line, and I east.

At that very moment, East and West were coming together in a seismic shift.

That night I watched the pictures on the *News at Ten* of thousands of people drinking and partying on top of the Berlin Wall – chipping away at it with chisels and hammers and forming a human chain along the top. Alex – the lucky bugger – would soon be there for the party.

There was always something childlike about Alex; never more so than when I called him after that weekend.

'How was your weekend, do anything interesting?'

He told me at the airport he was met by a driver who wanted to take him to the Wall. As a regular visitor to Berlin, he'd seen the Wall many times and just wanted to go to the hotel.

'You must see the Wall, it's unbelievable.'

'Mate, I just want a shit, shower and shave.'

But twenty minutes later he was witnessing history at Brandenburg Gate and spent the early hours walking around East Berlin, awestruck at what he was witnessing.

A few weeks later, the barbed-wire barricades were removed from the Czechoslovakia–Austria border as the Velvet Revolution replaced a joyless one-party regime with Václav Havel, a poet and playwright, as the president.

THE LADY'S NOT FOR GURNING

This was all confirmation that change *was* in the air. This wasn't a utopian Ecstasy mirage or hippy fantasy. We were witnessing a cultural shift. The old order was crumbling, giving us hope that barriers could be overcome and confirmed the belief that people did want to come together – the rave new world was happening!

TOP TUNE: 'Energy Flash', Joey Beltram

3

THE ACID HOUSE KING

When the promoter the media named 'Mr Acid House', Tony Colston-Hayter, handcuffed himself to Jonathan Ross live on television that autumn of 1989, it showed the chasm between the mainstream media and the new dance movement.

I caught up with him at the Sunrise shop opening in Islington on the Monday morning following the stunt, as he'd promised me the exclusive on the story behind the headlines. I arrived to be greeted by stress and panic as it transpired that, overnight, some raver had nicked the neon E from the SUNRISE sign above the shop. Tony fixed me a tequila sunrise.

So how did you become the most despised man in Britain, Tony?

'Ha! I used to play blackjack professionally at casinos and everything used to finish at 4 a.m., so I started going to after-hours parties like Shoom and what I saw there just amazed me. All these people from different walks of life, different races, ages and persuasions, all together just having a great time. I thought, Let's have more of this. Initially it wasn't a business thing. In fact, I can reveal we lost money throughout 1988, it was only after the NYE party that we saw any profits. From there it just got bigger and bigger.'

Tony maintained that they didn't fit in with the bohemian vibe and at the time he was as despised by as many in the dance scene as he was in the media and Scotland Yard, mainly for taking what was an exclusive secret scene of a few hundred white kids and turning it into an inclusive mass movement attended by 20,000 people of all colour, and attracting negative attention to their utopian drug. There was also resentment that Tony was deemed the spokesman for the scene. 'Mr Acid House', yet he wasn't one of the group of DJs who'd originally brought back the vibe from Ibiza . . . he wasn't even a DJ. Up until Sunrise, the nights were promoted by the DJs themselves: Rampling (Shoom), Oakenfold and Fung (Spectrum/Land of Oz), Holloway (The Trip), Eddie Richards (Clink St.). So this brash home counties posh kid was seen as an interloper, an outsider.

And I found him fascinating. His parties were out of this world and hugely important in that they were the catalyst for the dance music and clubbing explosion. To use a punk analogy, if Shoom was New York Dolls, Sunrise was the Sex Pistols on the *Today with Bill Grundy* show. He let the genie out, basically.

How did he do it? Well, firstly by fibbing to the venues he wanted to use. The equestrian centre in Buckingham were told it was a garden party and paid £500, another venue was told it was a private party for Michael Jackson (who was touring the UK at the time), farmers were frequently told their field would be used to film a music video for someone big like Queen, and if they started to feel the heat from the police, bunged a few grand and told to book a week's holiday away somewhere warm. At the time Sunrise had 15,000 *members*. This is vitally important as Tony discovered private *members* parties were not subject to the same licence requirements as public events, enabling the orbital raves to happen. Each *invite* (not ticket) had somewhere to write your name and address (as no one had phones, never mind email addresses).

This was all underpinned with canny utilisation of BT's Voicebank system to fox the police. Flyers would include no venue address, just a phone number, and at certain times on Saturday night the answering machine would be updated with a series of rendezvous locations. Finding a rave became an end in itself; a weekly treasure hunt around the M25. He had a cast-iron belief that his parties were legal. That if he possessed a legally binding contract with the owner of the venue, reinforced by the presence on the ground of a QC, the result was a loophole large enough for over 150,000 people across the summer to climb through.

Is all the media attention you receive a good thing? Isn't rave about the collective rather than any individual?

Another two tequila sunrises appear. It's 11 a.m. on a Monday morning.

'I didn't choose to be the voice of the acid house generation, but if I'm offered a platform to represent it, I'll take it.'

Even if there are traps? Was accepting the invitation to Jonathan Ross's show wise?

'I knew I was being set up. Paul Morley and Jonathan are good buddies and I heard them talking before the show. They spent half an hour trying to persuade me to take my Motorola on set, so I'd fit into that "yuppie prat" image.

When I finally saw the script was geared against me, I decided to go ahead with Plan B: handcuffing myself to Ross. I'd been practising it for two days in case.'

So how did they separate you?

'During the ad break the producer came up to me and said, "Okay, you've made your point, now where's the key?"'

'I said, "What fucking key?" So they searched me and realised I was telling the truth and called for some huge bolt croppers. All the time Jonathan's going, "Oh, my God, this is the worst thing that's ever happened to me on live TV – not only that, but I'm busting for a pee!"'

Any regrets?

'None. I'm glad I did it. Seven million people saw me raise the point that the authorities want to restrict people's movement – only they don't need handcuffs. They use last-minute injunctions and a draconian police force instead.'

At the outset of the show, Jonathan asked whether the spirit of rock 'n' roll rebellion was dead. The guests were Tony, goth-punk princess Siouxsie Sioux, and music writer Paul Morley. Tony had practised the move hundreds of times over the preceding week. He knew he only had a few seconds to execute the move, and after doing so smoothly, Ross asked him what was going on.

Tony replied that it was a protest on behalf of the Freedom to Party campaign at the restriction of movement felt by many who were unable to dance after 3 a.m. Ross's response was, 'Frankly, ladies and gentlemen, who gives a toss? Dancing in a field shouting, "I'm an Orange, I'm an Orange!"'

What should've been a debate on licensing and the funda-mental human right to party turned instead into an in-depth discussion on why Siouxsie's new band the Creatures couldn't get on TV, before degenerating into a slapstick tit-for-tat. Tony couldn't get a word in edgeways and was repeatedly told to 'shut it' before the conversation ended with the antagonistic Morley knocking Tony's Sunrise base-ball cap off, causing him to retaliate by throwing a glass of water over his fellow guest.

When Tony told them he'd lost the key to the handcuffs, Wossy was livid. I guess it was the wrong kind of rebellion for the former punk rocker. Once again it showed that the movement was an irritant to be ridiculed, one that if ignored long enough, might go away.

It's a grin up north

At Christmas I returned to my hometown of Ulverston in Cumbria and couldn't wait to tell my old schoolmate, Rob, all about my new life . . . and neither could he wait to tell me about his! I was thrilled to hear that he was a regular at the Blackburn warehouse raves every weekend, and my Christmas present was a place in the van for the next one on Boxing Day. I was so engrossed in the orbital scene, that I was completely unaware that acid house was now a national phenomenon – and it appeared Blackburn was the epicentre. One roadside chevron sign we passed read BOOMTOWN, as hundreds of cars in convoy slowly snaked around the streets before arriving at the venue.

'It'll be all over by Christmas.' Ken Tappenden's megaphoned prophesy was realised before my eyes. And it was – 'all over' the country. But this was only the start: within a few years it would be all over Europe and by the end of the decade the world.

Upon reaching the door I automatically went into blagging mode, introducing myself and telling them I wasn't on the guest list as I'd only found out about the party a few hours ago.

'What's a guest list, mate?'

'Err . . . well, it's a list of people who get in for free.'

The orbital raves I'd been working weren't cheap to get into, sometimes £25 a ticket. I simply didn't have that amount of cash on me, so I went into a long self-important spiel about how I'd write about their party to justify letting me in for free. Still somewhat confused, they let me in. However, my sense of achievement soon turned to embarrassment when Rob joined me inside a few minutes later.

'You do know it was only three quid to get in, right?'

I was mortified. 'Three quid? No wonder they were baffled by my blag, they must've thought I was a right tight bastard.'

Rob leant over and whispered in my ear: 'The unemployment around here is twice the national average. It's usually a quid to get in.'

The production budget reflected the door charge: no lasers, smoke or lighting rig. Just one incessant strobe, a sound rig and thousands of ravers from across the north dancing with the same expressions to the same tunes, offering the same hugs, and sharing the same sense of illicit togetherness. Except in empty red-brick warehouses in a Lancashire mill town as opposed to an aircraft hangar in the Home Counties. The north's unlicensed party scene inspired the KLF's (as the JAMs), 'It's Grim Up North'. Essentially a roll call of hitherto unglamorous towns whose drizzle failed to dampen the spirit of staying up for ever. They briefly regained their former glory by becoming reborn as countercultural hubs of hedonism, giving rise to a new civic pride through the reclamation of warehouses and mills laying empty in Thatcher's Britain. The revolution wasn't limited to urbanites: a slate quarry in the Lake District played host to a series of ever-larger free unlicensed 'cave raves'. There are accounts of a huge smiley being cut into the bracken above the village of Coniston. At first glance, this small former Lakeland mining village appears an unlikely location for people to speed their tits off, but this is where Donald Campbell lost his life in 1967 at 328 mph trying to break the world water speed record. Twenty-five years on, people were once again rushing big time in Coniston.

The track finished with a prophesy: 'The north will rise again.'

The north had already come up.

Little was I to know that battle between the police and the second Summer of Love orbital rave scene would be fought in another warehouse, a few days later, 220 miles away . . .

★

NYE 1989 was momentous. The end of a tumultuous year which had seen the rise of the biggest youth movement since punk rock. This was the night when everyone was going out, to dance the decade away and welcome in the new one. A new decade for a new music, a new fashion and a new drug. For the major promoters the gloves were off for NYE '89.

Three rival parties announced events and, for the Pay Party Unit, it was getting personal. Extra resources were given to Ken Tappenden. More manpower, a bigger budget, all leave cancelled. The police were determined that the year would end with roadblocks rather than Robo Scans and with disappointment instead of dancing. From a conflict that had been a good-natured, non-violent confrontation, things were beginning to turn ugly after a rave in east London saw heavy-handed security take baseball bats to the police who were raiding the party.

It felt like the net was closing in. There were rumours of a new law being prepared which would make it very hard to pull off a party in future, so this New Year's Eve was regarded as the last big opportunity. Naturally, everyone wanted a slice of the action and had begun hyping it for all they were worth.

Tony had talked about his Sunrise event being the biggest party to date, with a production budget in excess of £100k, multi-coloured lasers, a 100,000k sound rig with 3D computer graphics on huge screens, Carl Cox playing on three decks . . . and FIFTEEN bouncy castles!

This was in response to Jarvis from Biology, who'd set the bar in the *Evening Standard* a few months earlier when he announced that he was planning a NYE party for 100,000 people. All autumn, there were rumours that Wembley Stadium was being lined up.

As the sun rose on New Year's Eve, the final score for 1989 was that out of 223 raves, ninety-six of them had been closed down or prevented. As usual, we were waiting for the call in South Mimms. We'd go to whichever venue was secured first.

The police (thanks to the input of the security services) were getting better at picking up intel, and there were rumours that they were incentivising landowners who may have seen neighbours' land being utilised by rave promoters to inform them. In addition, they were monitoring info-lines and posing as ravers to get the location of the venue before the convoys had a chance to get there. Having confidence in the venue's secureness, Sunrise broke tradition and printed the venue on the flyer. This led to the farmer being pressurised by the Pay Party Unit, who threatened him with all manner of charges.

On the day of the party, with perimeter fencing erected and production vehicles carrying sound and lighting rigs en route, the landowner caved in and cancelled the show. We were told to fill up with petrol and prepare for Plan B, which was a two-hour drive away in Norfolk. But the local council got wind and at an emergency licensing committee meeting served an injunction forbidding any event on that land. They'd won. There would be no Sunrise on New Year's Eve, or Energy for that matter.

We drove back to Mill Hill with heavy hearts and full pallets. This was meant to have been the biggest party night of the year.

A pirate station was playing on the stereo and just before 11 p.m., the DJ made some muffled reference to Sunrise joining up with Biology and Genesis before concluding with 'Hold tight, Heston!'

We exchanged glances.

Although no tickets had been sold for Genesis and Biology's 'Future Power People' and the venue not known until 10 p.m., over 15,000 people attended. Biology promoter Tarquin de Meza: 'For the previous ten weeks, we had been flying clubs all over the South-East and beyond with laminated cards which contained a telephone number on which people could validate their membership or register for information about future parties. What the public didn't know was that they were putting their details into the first fibre optic digital voice bank in the UK. We'd hooked up with a crazy ex-Mossad agent who had access to a secret digital exchange under Marylebone High Street.

'Usually, we'd advertise on the pirate stations, but on this occasion, rather than advertise a venue, we simply told people to stay tuned in on New Year's Eve and all would be revealed.

'When we were ready, the digital voice bank called over 40,000 people either at home or on their mobiles in the space of three and half minutes. This was unprecedented at the time.

'The voice message simply stated, "Welcome to Biology",' de Meza went on. 'And gave out a series of different meeting points, depending on where the person was travelling from. Each meeting point was manned by someone who knew where the venue was. Wayne Anthony was responsible for one. When the time was right, we'd call the one's furthest away, before mobilising the groups nearer to the venue, meaning everyone would arrive at the same time . . . making it impossible for the police to control and prevent them accessing the party.

'Course, the police were listening to the pirate stations and had probably infiltrated the membership, so they arrived at the same time . . . except with dogs.'

Had Sunrise's Tony and Dave done a deal with Jarvis, Tarquin and Wayne from Biology? If so, this would be an epic unification of the scene. Ten minutes later, we pulled into Heston Services and were immediately recognised by the Sunrise ticket holders, who confirmed that the message line told them to wait at Heston for more information.

Most people never knew who was playing at the orbital raves. And what's more, most people didn't care. Each DJ played for an hour and wanted to play the bangers, and as there weren't that many tunes out at the time, this meant they all played the same ones in any case!

You'd hear 'Come Get My Lovin'', 'Ride on Time', 'Strings of Life', 'Pump Up the Jam', 'Monkey Say, Monkey Do', 'French Kiss', 'Your Love', 'Afro Dizzi Act', 'Let Me Love You for Tonight', 'Break 4 Love', 'Promised Land', 'Real Life', 'Salsa House', 'Lost in Paradise' and, a particular favourite, Raul Orellana's 'Real Wild House' . . . four or five times through the party. Remember that often the party had no scheduled finish time, and those scheduled to play later were regularly stopped from reaching the venue by the police roadblock. Meaning those already there would have to step in and cover for them and play the same records! No one complained at the lack of variation though.

One sneeze from disaster

Something that's never been reported is how close this legendary epoch-defining party came just a stifled sneeze away from not happening at all.

The police were going above and beyond the call of duty that day. Not content with searching for potential rave sites in the Home Counties with helicopters, following promoters in unmarked cars and tapping mobile phones, they were also methodically searching trading estates in the Greater London area and checking *every* empty warehouse for signs of activity.

Paul Marston, who did the sound that night, was parked up in Slough with a 10k rig waiting for a phone call.

He was unaware of the location as his phone was bugged ('every two weeks a "GPO worker" would be climbing up the wooden telegraph pole outside our house to reset the tapping device, as the Home Office needed to reissue them every fourteen days,' he recalls).

When it became clear the other raves had fallen, he received the address on his pager and sprang into action. It had turned 11 p.m. and time was tight, thousands of ravers would soon be descending on a trading estate in Slough. He arrived to find the warehouse door opened, though completely unlit. He drove in and parked his van alongside some others that had been left by the construction company who were taking out some offices.

Hearing cars screeching to a halt outside, he quickly locked his van and together with his assistant, Stuart, scaled a nearby scaffolding tower up and over the partly demolished plasterboard wall, where they hid in a recess in one of the offices.

Perhaps acting on a tip-off, twenty uniformed officers ran into the pitch-black warehouse and began searching for signs of life. Their torches flashed around like killjoy lasers, briefly illuminating the piles of rubble, parked vans and skips.

'It was like a film,' Paul told me later. 'One copper strode into the office we were hiding in, and he was literally inches away. I could've reached out and touched his shiny boots. Then Stuart pointed to his nose, like he was going to sneeze. If he did there would be no party, rioting from around 10,000 pissed-off partygoers and, what's more, I'd be arrested and not paid . . . and it was a double-bubble payday, remember!

'I slapped my palm over Stuart's mouth and held his nose with my forefinger and thumb. I could feel his body spasming as the sneeze built. The more he twitched, the tighter I gripped. Eventually the copper, satisfied no one was in there, left. As I heard his footsteps get quieter I released Stuart, who collapsed on the floor panting, "You bastard! I nearly died!" – poor bugger! There then followed a commotion outside, so the coppers all piled out. We could hear shouting and the barking of dogs. We removed a window from the office, climbed out into the cold night air and could see hundreds of ravers had arrived, with more cars arriving.'

A stand-off soon developed, with the police throwing a cordon around the warehouse. Tarquin ran forward and addressed the crowd: 'We've come this far, are we going to party or not?' The crowd's response was a definitive 'YES!' Tarquin darted through the police lines, with dogs snapping at his heels and reached the shuttered door, which appeared closed. Mindful of the huge numbers, and understanding he was trapped against a closed door, a few police officers approached slowly, giving Tarquin time to roll through under the shutter into the warehouse and press the button that electrically released the main door. The crowd rushed forward through the police lines. Tarquin didn't see them though, because as he stepped back he fell down a manhole cover, breaking three ribs.

There were far too many ravers for the police to stop – and as the warehouse was currently soundless, they figured there was no harm in letting them wander around. It would avoid any immediate confrontation and allow them to set up a roadblock to stop the sound van from coming in.

What they didn't realise was that the sound system was already in there!

Seeing this, Paul and Stuart pulled their baseball caps down and coolly walked into the dark silent warehouse with the ravers.

Five minutes later, a small amp, monitor speaker and one deck was set up, allowing the Face to put on his first record ('Meltdown' by Quartz). Although it sounded like a transistor radio in the huge space, the crowd didn't care, erupting into a cheer as they heard the quirky, plinky-plonk intro. As the system was built around him and more lights added, the crowd grew exponentially, greeting every tune he played like a football crowd celebrating a goal.

'There's no time for a warm-up set when the New Year's Eve party starts at around midnight!' he told me afterwards.

When it became clear the party had started, the police had to let the bar truck in for public safety reasons. And then when an ice cream van chugged in behind it, it got a guard of honour!

This was a celebration of the culture we'd created – and for all we knew, the end of an era. So we partied like it was the last night on Planet Earth . . . and the crowd kept on growing.

At some point near the end of the rave, a car miraculously appeared from nowhere in the middle of the room. I later found out that it was being used as a makeshift dance podium and obscured by ravers. This would explain why I wasn't aware of it from my own podium – a 10-foot-high tower of breezeblocks.

It was a black BMW 5 series, that night's raffle prize. Now I'd been to a few raves at this point and had never witnessed a raffle before. The MC announced that tickets were a fiver each and ticket sellers would be moving among us. Sure enough, fellas carrying red buckets appeared amid the shoulder-to-shoulder mass, which stretched from wall to wall across the warehouse. People were throwing notes into the bucket in return for raffle tickets. This went on for around twenty minutes, the buckets filling so quickly that those carrying them had to leave the arena to empty them. Upon returning, they would be mobbed, and the buckets would be full again within minutes. It was a frenzy of *Loadsamoney-esque* excess which summed up the late '80s.

The raffle was drawn in the slow section of 'French Kiss' (or 'the lady cyclist reaching the summit of a steep hill song,' as we referred to it), an orgasmic release as one shimmering shape raced to the stage, cloakroom ticket aloft. His ticket was checked. It wasn't right. This happened another few times before eventually the number on the ticket matched the one that was read out (the confusion may have resulted from the different coloured tickets being used. There were four 926s: a yellow, green, pink and blue).

Eventually, after another ten minutes, a wildly grinning skeletal bloke was presented with a set of keys, to weary cheers from a crowd who just wanted to get on with the party.

When the music ended, the security formed a guard of honour and the crowds parted Red Sea-like to create a clear path to the exit. On a cue, the doors were opened and the cheesy quaver who'd won the Beamer roared out of the warehouse to cheers.

The police, realising the rave was over, allowed everyone to file out – leaving the floor littered with the usual bottles of water and ice-pop wrappers, but also an inordinate number of banknotes. The decade of greed and Thatcher's policy of materialism, which she justified by citing 'trickle-down economics', was in full effect: the cleaners went home rich in cash, discarded drugs and jewellery.

As we left the site in the morning gloom, we passed a black BMW which had been pulled over by a police motor-cyclist, who was taking down the particulars of the somewhat chemically challenged driver.

Afterglow

As regards to the government clampdown triggered by that letter to Maggie, in March 1990, MP Graham Bright introduced the Entertainments (Increased Penalties) Bill. This raised the fine for organising an unlicensed party tenfold – from £2,000 to £20,000 – in addition to a custodial sentence of up to six months' imprisonment. Nicknamed 'The Acid House Party Bill', it was a clear attempt to push the free-party scene into the licensed leisure industry, so it could be regulated. And it worked. Throughout the following decade, the combined capacity of West End late-night music and dance venues steadily grew from 33,000 in 1990 to 128,000 people by the millennium – an increase of more than 300 per cent.

The influence of acid house continues to permeate through mainstream culture. The National Marriage Guidance Council changed its name to the orbital rave-esque 'Relate', and how many of us smiled when the Post Office adopted the slogan 'Sorted!' It's surely only a matter of time before the words 'double-drop' appear on paracetamol instructions.

As this book was being finished, BBC Two's *Mastermind* featured a contestant whose chosen specialist subject was '90s drum 'n' bass. A Sunrise flyer from 1989 on eBay recently sold for £320. There are websites dedicated to walking routes taking in the orbital rave sites. And I was

recently approached by a student writing his degree disser-
tation on the 'cultural impact of the summer of '89'!

There's a sad irony that an underground movement so
reliant on young people's desire to have a good time by
using a drug which promotes feelings of euphoria, love and
empathy attracted moodiness, violence and greed. However,
after retiring from police service in 1993, with an MBE to
his name, scourge of the orbital rave promoters Ken
Tappenden appeared to have mixed feelings about events
of the previous decade.

'Even the army couldn't move people like those promoters
did. Some of the parties were amazing, attended by really
nice people. I sometimes wonder why we bothered. We
never had any trouble from the ravers. Great lights, lovely
people. I wish them well.'

TOP TUNE: 'Chime', Orbital

4

INTO THE '90S!

'How much longer will the masses tolerate muddy fields, sound systems so muffled they sound like they're on loan from British Rail and £25 tickets to parties that don't exist?

The sheer scale and spectacle of the '89 raves earmarks them for a place in the nightlife history books, but all the signs are they're on the way out.

The powers that be are now grimly determined to put the boot into "acid house" – and it's a bloody great steel toe-capped size 13 that kicks to hell . . .'

– Mixmag, January '90

The onset of winter, the increasing effectiveness of the Pay Party Unit in closing down parties and the impending legislation to deter their very existence formed a formidable triple threat to the new culture in which I was now immersed.

Led by Paul Staines, the short-lived Association of Dance Party Promoters (ADPP) launched the Freedom to Party campaign at a press conference in mid-January 1990, which I attended both as a journalist (for *Mixmag*) and a promoter (I'd started working for Raindance, handling press and PR). After impassioned speeches claiming that the promoters were not enemies of the state or dark underworld criminals, a photo-call took place (but only after one member moved out of shot as he was 'a person of interest' in an ongoing police investigation and therefore a little camera-shy).

I was familiar with everyone behind the desk, including the bloke who dodged the cameras – and held them all in respect. Between them, they'd given my life a new impetus and direction, introduced me to a new set of friends and inspired me to start writing – and earning money. But I also suspected that for the mischief they'd made and the nuisance they'd collectively caused, the likelihood of any of them ever getting a large, licensed event again was minimal. But with the wind in their sails there was still time for one last hurrah . . .

Saturday, 27 January 1990: Freedom to Party rally, Trafalgar Square

Misery doesn't fall in raindrops. It drizzles like a damp shroud, slowly bringing you down with a million tiny blows.

From my position seated on the shoulders of a bronze lion, I gazed across Trafalgar Square, south through Admiralty Arch down Whitehall, and north to the National Gallery. No ground was visible, only a sea of kaftans, kagoules, curtain haircuts, beanies and the occasional umbrella. Around me, 8,000 people had assembled to demonstrate their support for the Freedom to Party campaign.

INTO THE '90S!

I understood Tony and Paul (Sunrise) were responsible for the campaign and rally, with Jarvis and Tarquin (Biology) assuming responsibility for the party afterwards. From the granite base of Nelson's column, everyone associated with the organisation of the major parties stood surveying their audience. Anton Le Pirate gee'd up the crowd through a megaphone, followed by a succession of speeches demanding the right to dance all night. Cheers greeted the first beats of a kick drum as builders on the roof of the National Gallery in hi-vis jackets downed their tools and started raving. But this was Central London, not an airfield in Suffolk, and police swiftly moved to confiscate the sound system as amplified music wasn't allowed.

I remember watching an animated Tarquin talking into a huge mobile phone. This was encouraging. I was pretty confident he wasn't ordering a pizza. It may well have been the moment he heard about a newly built warehouse in London Colney from an electrician mate who was in the process of wiring it up. He told Tarquin he'd run out of time to finish the job by Friday afternoon and assured him the alarm on the side of the building wasn't live but a dummy and would be replaced with the real thing on Monday morning.

Within minutes he'd spoken to Tony Colston-Hayter and meeting points had been drawn up.

Word spread through the crowd that something was stirring. The soggy ravers disbanded, knowing there was something planned for later that night . . . as did the police helicopter overhead. Peacefully protesting in Central London was one thing. Raving through the night in an unlicensed venue was something else and must be stopped at all costs. The pressure was huge and felt by everyone who had something to lose if it all went tits up.

Hours later, the generator supplier and the vans carrying the sound equipment were parked up a few miles away from the venue in Radlett, Hertfordshire, waiting for the call to proceed to the site. Once again, the helicopter stuttered overhead, this time lower, its searchlight briefly illuminating them as it scoured the area for signs of activity. The generator and burger van owner (let's call him Frank) felt exposed and demanded Tarquin give him the location. But Tarquin, also under severe pressure while dealing with DJs, meeting point staff and security and trying to coordinate the party, ignored Frank's repeated calls and hung up on him.

Eventually, fearing his mobile might be tapped, he drove over to speak to him face-to-face and, in his own words, 'lost his shit'. Next thing he knew, he was staring at a loaded 12-bore shotgun and the threat of a shallow grave. Frank didn't take kindly to being told he wasn't important. As the supplier of the generator and various other elements, he felt he was key personnel and deserved to know where the venue was. Immediately.

Paul Marston, who supplied the sound that night, stood by, frozen to the spot. The risks they were both under were clearly taking their strain, but thankfully they sorted it out. Tarquin apologised, Frank accepted and agreed they were in an extraordinary situation: 20,000 people would be descending on what was an empty warehouse which was under intense police surveillance. It wasn't only their reputations that were on the line, but their liberty.

Fifteen minutes later, the sound, generator, bar and burger trucks drove into the huge warehouse. The next challenge was getting the ravers to the venue before the police. As luck would have it, another party took place that night, just down the road and completely unconnected to the Freedom to Party event. The police latched onto this smaller affair and set up roadblocks. Without knowing it, the organisers had created a classic act of misdirection.

Gavin (DJ Face) Mills and Genesis promoter Wayne Anthony were managing the South Mimms meeting point. Wayne's mobile rang; it was the green light they'd been waiting for, allowing them to mobilise the hundreds of cars of gum-chewing, Ribena-slurping ravers who'd filled the car park.

Other meeting points were similarly actioned; some formed convoys, others scrawled the address down on the back of a fag packet. The pirate stations got behind it and for one night only, Colney became the epicentre of UK youth culture.

Although basic in terms of sound and lighting, the atmosphere was electric inside. Tarquin's girlfriend Geri – six years before the world would know her as 'Ginger Spice' – was dancing on a PA stack in a skin-tight white catsuit.

'Seen who's outside, Kirk?' Simon Sutton beckoned me over to the main door, which was being buffeted from the other side and bulging like something out of a Poltergeist movie. At eye level there was a row of small, thick, reinforced windows no more than one square foot large. Through the windows I could see a cordon of angry policemen who were attempting to barge the doors while one pointed his video camera up against the toughened glass. On the inside of the warehouse stood a line of security. It was like a medieval siege except with Maglite torches rather than pikes, and

CS gas rather than boiling oil. The coppers were goading the security, challenging them to open the doors and try their luck.

The insults continued as the smell of generator smoke mixed with adrenaline. If the police were to break the door down, it would've been carnage. What happened next will stay with me to my dying day. Someone, I think it may have been Dave Roberts (Tony's partner in Sunrise and not a man to be messed with), had clearly had enough of being filmed and insulted. Through the glass, he beckoned his opposite number.

'Closer,' he mouthed, so his ear was up against the small window. He then punched the glass, loudly shattering it, showering the goading officer and causing him to recoil in horror. This was enough to get them to withdraw, realising that although they had the place surrounded, confrontation was best avoided.

The case of the disappearing PA

The last set that night, as was usually the case, was played by Frankie Valentine. Frankie was a wise owl and had patience. Unlike other DJs who'd get 'on it', Frankie would sit patiently on a flight-case cradling a bottle of water and was often the last man standing capable of playing. He used to love playing the last set as he could play some really interesting and out there stuff, as the hardcore ravers who remained were up for anything.

As the law had the venue surrounded and were looking for arrests, soundman Paul Marston knew he would be the biggest prize, having hoodwinked them earlier in the evening. He was a marked man and already in their sights.

Once when arrested, he was taken to the Pay Party Unit's HQ incident room at Gravesend, where he was shown a white board titled 'Persons of Interest'. It read like a *Who's Who?* of the rave scene at the time. At the top was his name. Paul clocked it and smiled.

'You're still number one. Been there all summer,' said the arresting officer.

He couldn't afford to get nicked and have his gear impounded as he had to return the reggae scoops to a Jamaican guy the next day. More importantly, he'd promised his family he'd be back for their Sunday roast beef lunch. But how on earth would he get two transit vans of kit past the police cordon?

Paul looked out across the crowd, which was starting to thin as people drifted into the grey new decade. Less people soak up less sound, which enabled him to turn down the volume a little, reducing the demand on the amps. It was at this moment he came up with a cunning plan . . .

During Frankie Valentine's last set, he began surreptitiously loading the sound system into the two Luton transits parked inside. One by one the speakers slowly disappeared during Frankie's mix, a speaker removed after every other song, prompting double takes from a disbelieving DJ. The crowd were largely oblivious, although I did notice the top end disappearing but put it down to my hearing loss and a tablet called Phantasy that was doing the rounds that night.

By the end of the last record, there were only a few bass bins left. As soon as the track finished, they were loaded into the Lutons and driven out among the exiting crowd, who provided a human shield, thus preventing the boys in blue from nabbing him and impounding the sound.

The reggae sound system got their speakers back and Paul got his Yorkshire pudding.

As much as the night felt like a victory to many, for the promoters who cared hugely about their production, it felt their brand had been compromised.

Only months earlier Biology were hiring U2's stage and the Encore Sound System used by Live Aid at Wembley. They had just been reduced to putting basic 20k rigs with minimal lighting in a dusty old warehouse.

'We were always pushing,' Tarquin told me thirty years later. 'Always pushing the envelope in terms of how we could be doing things bigger and better. Always trying to outdo our rivals because competition was good, it ensured the bar was always being raised higher.'

The orbital raves demanded innovation. Instead of unloading the flatbed, the speakers were strapped down with a generator in tow, meaning they didn't have to be unloaded and could be moved at a minute's notice, if required.

Rivals they may have been, but the main players were wise enough to choreograph their events so as not to clash. Ironically, as more events got busted, there was a safety net in having two raves planned for the same night, as it provided a Plan B. A brief telephone call was made. A deal struck and tickets accepted to the party still standing, with its face value split between the two promoters 50/50, as happened on NYE.

'Ecstasy! The party's over'

Freedom to Party was the last battle in the war with the authorities; the equivalent of giving a bully a bloody nose just before he breaks your jaw and knocks you unconscious – a spirited but ultimately futile act of defiance.

The second Summer of Love, or whatever the media called it, was well and truly over. The government were actually doing what they said they were going to do and Graham Bright MP was crossing the t's and dotting the i's of his 'Acid House Bill', or the Entertainments (Increased Penalties) Bill, to give it its proper name, for the reading in March.

But the bill's creation in itself ironically confirmed the claims being made by the Freedom to Party movement: that there was undeniably a demand for these types of events.

Initially the Brixton Academy and the Eclipse club in Coventry managed to obtain all-night licences. As the year went on, Turnmills in Clerkenwell received the UK's first 24-hour licence, resulting in Trade becoming the first 'after-hours' party, starting at 3 a.m. But this wasn't until October. One club which was firing all year was Nicky Holloway's Sin at the Astoria. Upstairs was the place to be, people dancing on the tables and in the aisles. I remember a religious nut job used to walk up and down the (1,000-person, four-deep) queue outside holding a placard above his head that read: 'Repent, and turn back, so that your sins may be wiped away' (Acts 3:19).

Far from discouraging anyone, this only added to the allure. The most sinful thing about the night was that it sometimes closed at 3 a.m. . . . then it was next door to Busby's for 'The Breakfast Club'. Mind you, their all-dayers on a Bank Holiday Monday were pretty memorable, if I could only remember them . . .

The significance and influence of the UK orbital raves is huge. Tomorrowland is Sunrise without the sense of naughtiness. The EDM festivals in the States, Ushuaia in

Ibiza, and Creamfields all owe a huge debt to the orbital parties. No one had seen anything like them. It felt, and looked, like a spaceship had landed.

After the poorly attended Freedom to Party rally in March and when the 'Graham Bright Bill' was receiving its first readings, everyone knew the game was up. I next met Tony Colston-Hayter at his weekly Saturday nighter at the Park on Kensington High Street a couple of months later. I was putting together a feature entitled 'What Tony Did Next' for *Mixmag*. We sat in the VIP area sipping cocktails as he spanked his willowy blonde girlfriend, who was wearing tight black diamante shorts as she bent over his lap.

'You're such a naughty boy, Tony!'

And, as time has proved, she wasn't wrong . . .

Tony's sister Charlie appeared, somewhat flustered. She told him that the Crystal Palace football team, fresh from their post FA Cup final dinner, were at the door with their WAGs, asking if they could come in. 'They're staying at the hotel opposite and look pretty straight. Naff C&A suits, but we're not that busy and they're only staying for one.'

Tony agreed and Geoff Thomas and co. assembled at the bar, ordering cocktails. Charlie was right: the suits *were* naff.

I moved into the smaller room where Frankie Valentine was playing and started losing myself in his set, eyes closed, completely focusing on the music. After a while I realised there was only myself and another guy dancing. He wore a suit with a white shirt hanging out unbuttoned and, like me, had his eyes closed, 'locked in'. For around an hour we lapped up Frankie's set, passing a bottle of water between us like you did in those days and exchanging knowing looks when a mix hit the spot. Occasionally a footballer would encourage him to join them at the bar, but he'd just shake his head, sometimes not even opening his eyes. Ian Wright – who had come off the subs bench and scored twice at Wembley earlier that day – was in the zone.

The orbital raves lit a fire in me and countless others, showing us what was possible when you demanded the impossible. The parties may have been over, but the new decade was just beginning.

Afterglow

Tony Colston-Hayter hit the headlines again in January 2014 when he pleaded guilty to the theft of £1.3 million from Barclays bank and sentenced to five and half years' imprisonment. In December 2018, he pleaded guilty at Southwark Crown Court to his involvement in another scheme that involved using an 'ingenious' card-reading machine he had built at his home. He was sentenced to twenty months' imprisonment. In February 2023, he was sentenced to ten months for stealing mail from letterboxes.

His Twitter profile reads: 'Lucid dreamer, hypnotist, rave pioneer, inventor, entrepreneur, raconteur. Ex-professional blackjack player, ex-husband, ex-fraudster, ex-convict'. I always liked Tony, he was a catalyst in the evolution of club culture and for anyone who was at Longwick, he will always be remembered warmly for throwing the best party of that summer – which is saying something.

TOP TUNE: 'Hypnosis', Psychotropic

5

BERLIN WALLPAPER

What would resurface a few months later and almost 3,000 kilometres away behind the Iron Curtain and cause all manner of madness in Ibiza, began its journey in a humble house party at what turned out to be a major LSD factory – where the A1 intersects the North Circular at Henlys Corner in north London.

In 1991, I was clubbing editor for *Evolution*, the ravey rebirth of the notorious independent London magazine, *Encyclopaedia Psychedelica*, whose tripped-out contributors included Zen terrorists Dr Timothy Leary and Ken Kesey, and the Grid's Richard Norris. I spent the first month of the New Year in their commune in Formentera, Ibiza's sister island, in a secluded finca hideout belonging to a fugitive German bank robber, where we spent our time writing, editing and exploring New Age fads. Smart drugs, brain machines, fractals and hallucinogens all featured during the week-long moratorium.

This appeared in *Mixmag* as a double-page spread entitled 'Children of the Evolution'. The resulting article talked about psychoactive soft drinks . . . .because I couldn't really write about what really happened that day at the *Evolution* launch party.

It was held one Bank Holiday Sunday in early May 1990 and was attended by a few media types, DJs and promoters, along with every major acid dealer and 'head' in north London at the time. At one point the host (we'll call him Gerald) approached me with a glint in his eye and suggested I pay a visit to the kitchen. A few minutes later I was stood looking at a large table draped in a coarse cardboard roll of wallpaper backing, on which stood a bottle of advocaat, a few tins of Heineken, an empty box of Milk Tray and the remnants of a plate of Twiglets.

'Help yourself, there's some scissors on the sink.'

A woman was stood at the table, carefully scything her way through a stained section of the makeshift wallpaper tablecloth. Having extracted a small inch square, she held it between her finger and thumb and raised it to my chin while sticking her own tongue out, beckoning me to do the same. I opened my mouth and presented my tongue in readiness for receipt of Holy Communion. Looking into my eyes throughout, she gently placed the paper onto my tongue. What on earth was she doing? What on earth was I letting her do? I stood there with my mouth open with a piece of wallpaper on my tongue.

'Now close your mouth and chew it slowly for five minutes.'

She then took my hand and led me out into the large garden. A quarter of an hour later I was buzzing with a frazzled, sparkly energy and everything felt a touch more intense. If life was a fuck, I'd just removed the condom. I felt alert and sensual. But I also felt lucid; it was the hallucinogenic equivalent of feeling a little tipsy after a glass of Champagne. I always thought the trouble with taking acid was that there was no escape; eight to ten hours of a trip which twisted and turned from fun to terrifying in the blink of an eye, and from which there was no escape. This was somehow different.

'What IS this stuff?'

'It's wallpaper stained with acid. When the sheets of acid are drying, it's preferable to do it on a flat surface, as the last time Gerald hung them on the clothesline, the liquid acid slowly drained to the bottom tabs, making them super strong, which caused all manner of problems.'

What was that accent? Was she Australian? She was gorgeous. It turned out she had just appeared in a racy TV mini-series which everyone had watched the previous year. She was a regular on the rave scene for a few months and went on to a *very* successful career in stage and screen work on both sides of the Atlantic.

I was in. Everyone should try this; it was Acid Lite, KitKat acid – the psychedelic you could eat between meals without ruining your sanity. What's more, it never had a name, so I could name my very own unique mood modifier. And so was born 'Berlin Wallpaper' in recognition of the fall of the Wall the previous autumn: a seismic event which only proved to us that 1989 really was Year Zero and peace, love, unity and revolution were the order of the day.

I left the party with a roll of wallpaper under my arm, ran across the road and jumped on the running board of a departing red 143 double-decker London bus, buzzing at my discovery, and the fact no one around me had a clue I was carrying it. The beauty of Berlin Wallpaper was that it didn't look suspicious. It wasn't a capsule, joint, phial or powder. It was invisible, just an odourless stain on a piece of paper.

Naming a new drug was the pinnacle of every creative involved in the acid house movement. It was the street equivalent of coming up with an advertising slogan everyone used; 'For Mash get Smash', or 'Coke Adds Life' – except it was better as you were naming the product itself. Naturally, pills were named after their appearance, the colour and any stamp used to give them an identity and reputation.

While I remember thinking California Sunshine was a great name for pills during the utopian Summer of Love of 1989, no one really cared what was on the pills. It was their strength and purity which forged their reputation. 'Mitzis' (pills with the Mitsubishi logo) were huge at one time, but not because ravers appreciated the solid reliability and economic urban fuel consumption of the Mitsubishi Sigma; it was because they were considered 'clean' and a mark of quality in an unregulated sphere. Such was their appeal. Some (Gate)Crasher kids even got the logo tattooed or cut into their hair. The year 2020 saw Donald Trump pills, which were then usurped by Bern-E Sanders tablets. If someone had tried to sell an E shaped like Margaret Thatcher's head back in the day, they would've been laughed out of town.

At the time of writing, Bitcoin, Tesla, Mastercard and Rolex are all trending on the tongues of the aspirational, designer-desiring generation of ravers. Late summer 2020 even saw a smiley in a facemask pill doing the rounds.

Like the politicians we elect, the pills we swallow reflect the sign of the times, I guess. Bet none will have the impact of the humble dove, though . . .

Despite its name, ecstasy is not an aphrodisiac. In actual fact, there was very little lurve going on in the Summer of Love, but the Summer of Hugs hasn't got the same ring to it, has it?

> **TOP TUNE: 'Made in Two Minutes',
> Reel to Reel**

6

HOLA, IBIZA!

'Kirk, are you available to cover a party in the biggest club in the world for us and interview Sylvester Stallone's girlfriend?'

I loved it when Dave Seaman called me. One minute I'm jogging around Ally Pally hill working out how to make what's left of my giro last until Thursday, the next I'm on the guest list for a huge party and getting paid to write it up for *Mixmag*.

'I'm in, where is it?'

'Ibiza. It's a concert to celebrate the Barcelona Olympics in a few years' time, featuring Adamski, Beats International, the Beloved and Aztec Camera – with Cesar and Alfredo in the DJ booth.'

'Right. Where does Stallone's girlfriend come in?'

'Brigitte Nielsen is launching her dance-pop career. Try to grab a word with her as well as Adamski and Beats International.'

This was what's known in the trade as a 'press junket', a promotional event that media are invited to and expected to give a glowing write-up in return for a few days in the sun and free booze.

On the flight out I met my fellow journos: the dry-humoured Chris Heath from *Details* magazine, Tom Doyle from *Smash Hits*, lovely Louise Gray from *The Face*, an aloof media wanker from *Number One* magazine, Peter Willis from *The Sun*, Rick Sky from the *Daily Star*, and self-publicist and motormouth Robert Elms, who was covering the story for the *Sunday Times* (who in the end chose not to run his copy, which, after his superior posturing throughout the three-night trip, provoked considerable mirth from all of those previously mentioned).

On the flight out, I read a newspaper interview with the director of a new film called *Hardware*. Richard Stanley was in Afghanistan, filming and fighting in the Soviet-Afghan War. He and his wounded cameraman had to escape the minefield-strewn area of the war-torn country at short notice. Believing he was going to die, he took a huge amount of LSD, as he'd 'rather die tripping'. Miraculously, he survived, claiming his heightened state of consciousness saved his life, allowing him to see in the dark and smell the landmines beneath the ground. This fascinated me.

We waited for the press bus for over an hour in the bar, swapping music biz gossip. Tom Doyle, a fellow Clash fan, shared my excitement at the prospect of meeting Mick Jones and I was thrilled to discover he knew Roddy Frame as one of the exiled Scots living in London. *Hard Land, High Rain* remains one of my favourite albums, and to finally meet its composer along with someone from the Clash was a dream come true.

The bus eventually arrived and we were driven along a dusty single-track road for a mile or more. It was largely scrubland, very few buildings, the odd car park and occasional souvenir shop. The road ran parallel to the sea some 50 metres away on the left, providing tantalising, twinkling turquoise glimpses. Eventually, at the end of the peninsula, we reached a huge nine-storey modern hotel which stood alone and exuded the type of bashful air of someone who'd turned up overdressed to a casual party. Either it was ahead of the game or a white elephant in the middle of nowhere.

Fifteen minutes later and I was in the pool drinking cocktails with Norman Cook's Beats International, who'd had a number one with 'Dub Be Good to Me' a few months earlier. After establishing I wasn't from *The Sun*, Norman relaxed: 'I'm not talking to those fuckers after what they wrote about the rave scene last summer, please don't repeat anything I tell you.'

Sure enough, after Norman left to play tennis (you read that correctly), I went to the poolside bar. 'Bizarre' column's Peter Willis was waiting and primed me for info.

'Mate, he won't talk to you. He hates *The Sun*. And seeing the rate at which Beats International are downing those cocktails, I'd leave the pool area now if I were you.'

He shuddered uneasily, muttered something about the Showbiz desk not being responsible for the lurid headlines and crucifixion of acid house, and explained that his new editor, Piers Morgan, was keen to 'build bridges'.

'We'll build it as long as he agrees to jump off it,' was Norman's response when I fed this back.

Peter was a nice chap though for a tabloid hack, although he was pretty naive. In fact, as the trip progressed, we wound him up countless times. We would feed him absurd nonsense about Beats that was actually printed. According to *The Sun* that week, Norman Cook was buying a submarine, recording a single with Paul Gascoigne and, my personal favourite, retiring to open a tennis academy called Baseline Inc.

Also on the junket were a group of freelance photographers, or 'paps': snappers who sell photos to agencies for syndication. Unlike the journos, these were an approachable and fun-loving bunch who were dive-bombing and knocking back big blue jugs of cocktails. I got on immediately with two of them, a gooner called Graham and his skinny perma-grinning mate, Justin.

Insisting I share their Blue Lagoon, they regaled me with some of their daring tabloid tales until a voice from the balcony sliced through their story and alerted the paparazzi into action. 'They're here!' They leapt out of the pool and, grabbing their cameras, sprinted into the hotel.

Seeing my bewilderment, the snotty bloke from *Number One* flounced by and patronisingly pouted, 'Paul and Stacey' like it was the most obvious thing in the world.

I wasn't even aware Paul Young was playing. He'd married Stacey Smith, a lingerie model, in the summer of 1990. Funny to think it now, but after Charles and Diana, they were the UK's golden showbiz couple. Pictures of them arriving on the holiday isle of Ibiza would be wanted by every showbiz editor on Fleet Street.

When the sound of smashing glass is followed by a blood-curdling scream, you instantly freeze. In his hurry to get the shot, one of the paps ran straight through the glass door, shattering both the wall-to-ceiling panel and himself. Writhing around in blood and broken glass, the poor bloke was in agony in the reception. Just then Paul and Stacey walked through the door, their faces turning white with horror. The paps ignored them – one of their men was down and they were more concerned with him.

He was rushed to hospital with severe lacerations to the head, face, arms and chest and missed the entire event, but his agency never found out, as the other snappers donated images on his behalf, covering his end and ensuring he never lost any money. Honour among thieves, you might say!

Later that afternoon we were taken to Ku for the sound-check and artist press conference. The superclub had been ordered to put a roof on only months earlier and this was the first time anyone had seen the new structure. On a lush Mediterranean hillside stood a skeletal aircraft hangar complete with retractable roof and huge space age dome: there were so many palm trees in the building that a permanent ceiling wouldn't allow them to survive. The roof was over 80 feet high and the glass walls let in so much light that the club managed to retain an al fresco feel. The décor could best be described as 'bonkers botanical'. Within its cobbled confines were fourteen bars, four terraced gardens, outdoor balconies with views across the island, palm trees on dance podiums and an Olympic-size swimming pool with water slide.

At the time I visited, Ku was the new Studio 54, a playground where the polysexual jet set played out their hedonism. Grand, theatrical and completely over the top, Ku was the natural choice for the launch of Freddie Mercury and Montserrat Caballé's 'Barcelona'. And now Brigitte Nielsen's dance music debut.

When we arrived at the club, it was in chaos; the playback machines weren't working, the minibus carrying the photographers hadn't arrived, and to top it all, the star of the show, Ms Nielsen, was nowhere to be seen. And at 6 foot 1, that's quite an achievement!

With no sign of Brigitte and with the other artists tied up with my more illustrious press colleagues, I was presented to a well-dressed, middle-aged man in a silk shirt with rather large ears: 'The owner of Ku, José Antonio Santamaría.' He smelled of money, influence and designer fragrance. I introduced myself. He smiled. I smiled. While I had a list of questions for Adamski, Jon Marsh from the Beloved, and Norman, I had nothing prepared for the club owner. He handed me a flute of Champagne, we clinked glasses and resumed vacantly grinning at each other in silence like a couple of mute Stan Laurels. It was unbearable. I had to think of something sharpish.

My eyes darted around for inspiration. Up above the dancefloor a narrow strip of azure sky was visible through the opening. I pointed up and gave him the type of knowing look a retractable roofing expert might deliver upon spotting the nuances of a state-of-the-art traction and support system.

'Great roof!'

'Gracias. Very expensive.'

'Let's hope it works.'

He winced. 'If it does not . . .' and he made a gun shape with his free hand, which he slowly raised to his temple and pretended to shoot.

I laughed loudly. But I laughed alone: he was deadly serious.

I made a lame joke about Spanish builders and spotted Adamski was on his own, so I thanked José for the drink, wished him luck with the roof and awkwardly backed away, grinning graciously like an idiot.

Adamski recognised me from a Turnmills' Sunday-afternoon rave which we'd both attended a few weeks earlier and was relaxed and open. He confided that the Ku show was just a mimed TV slot which he'd only accepted as it gave him the opportunity to play a show at Pacha the following night.

This was great news. I'd visited Pacha back in January when I met the resident DJ Pippi and loved the place.

We shared a cab back to the hotel and reminisced about the previous summer and how his name accompanied by the words 'keyboard wizard' was on every flyer.

Back at the hotel, they were still repairing the glass door to the pool but this time I noticed the door had a sticker at eye level. The words 'lock, stable door, horse' and 'bolted' sprang to mind.

Something strange afoot

I showered, found some clean socks in my case and put them on. After dinner we were all taken back up to Ku to watch the actual show. TV cameras occupied most balconies and were currently trained on the DJ booth, which was suspended high above the swimming pool. The record ended and one by one the acts came on, did their thing and left. Nick Kamen, the Pasadenas, that year's Spanish Eurovision flops, Azúcar Moreno, followed, somewhat incongruously, by Ryuichi Sakamoto, whose haunting theme to *Merry Christmas, Mr Lawrence* appeared to trigger everyone around me to start moving in slow motion. Having never heard the tune in a club before, I just assumed it was the ambient equivalent to sitting on the floor to 'Oops Upside Your Head'.

Graham and Justin appeared and grabbed a beer from the complimentary press and artists bar, located in what I came to know intimately throughout the next decade as the Coco Loco Room. Even they were moving in slow motion, 'Bloody Brigitte is nowhere to be seen . . . again. We have to get back to the pit, do us a favour and if you spot her, Kirk, let us know, will ya?'

I wandered off to explore the vast tropical surroundings, following staircases, balconies, past red ropes and outside into the balmy night air, where I discovered intimate tiered terraces populated by beautiful people and a chorus of invisible cicadas, whose collective cracking ribs conjured a sultry and bewitching cacophony. I was aware my feet were tingling to the degree that it felt I was walking on air. I could feel nothing below my ankle. THIS must be the Earth spirit of the island I'd heard so much about.

As I stood on that small outdoor terrace, caressed by gentle conversations and laughter, my body and the island became adjoined.

Then I saw her.

Stood alone, smoking a cigarette in the doorway. Statuesque and more beautiful than I'd envisaged, if a little shorter and slighter than I expected. I looked around and to my surprise no one else had noticed that the elusive Brigitte Nielsen was in their midst. Nervously I approached and, gesturing to my pathetic plastic camera, asked if I could take her photograph. She smiled benignly and nodded, stubbing her cigarette out, twisting it to death with a high-heeled shoe.

I was fully expecting to be bustled out of the way by the other paps or autograph hunters, so kept clicking until I had no film left. Which, seeing as I only had twenty-four exposures, didn't take very long.

'A few words for *Mixmag*?'

She shrugged, which I took to mean, 'Why not?'

After rummaging around in my bum bag, I produced my Walkman and started to interview her. I lost the cassette years ago, but recall asking her (predictably) if she'd brought her boyfriend ('No, I'm working'), what was her favourite club ('Ku!'), who was her favourite DJ? ('Cesar'), and had she ever been to a rave in the UK? (an embarrassed shake of the head). One-word answers at most, but answers nonetheless! No one else had got anything from her, including the tabloids.

I thanked her and, elated at my exclusive, threaded my way through the crowds to below the stage, where the photographers gathered in the pit area. Aztec Camera had just taken to the stage and had struck up the opening twangy guitar introduction of their new single, 'Good Morning Britain'. The track featured Mick Jones from the Clash on guitar and this was the first time it would be played to an audience of more than 500 million people in 24 countries. As a huge Clash fan, I was excited at the prospect of meeting both Roddy Frame and the former Clash man, and Tom from *Smash Hits* had offered to introduce me after the show.

I found Graham. 'Brigitte's over here. She's on her own, I just spoke to her.'

Upon hearing this, the paps, who had been unable to get any shots of her since they arrived (and under increasing pressure from their editors and agencies), lowered cameras and to a man followed me out of the pit. Like a Pied Piper in a DMC baseball cap, I led around a dozen photographers through the heaving throng to Rambo's gal, leaving the pit empty to Roddy Frame's understandable dismay.

A few minutes later we burst through the door to the terrace and to my relief she was still there, exquisitely smoking another cigarette. She looked more gorgeous than before and radiated a shimmering white aura.

She recognised me and smiled, before spotting the pack of sweating, salivating dogs accompanying me. Her smile turned instead to a frown as the pack approached.

'My friends want to photograph you, is that okay?'

But when I turned around, they were walking away, shaking their heads. Only Graham remained, camera around his neck on a strap and hands on his hips.

'Wotcha playin' at?'

'Sorry?'

'We've just missed Aztec Camera for this?'

I ran after him: 'What do you mean? You told me if I found Brigitte to let you know.'

He looked at me, examining my eyes, peering closely at my face. Instinctively, I backed away. Where was his gratitude? And why wasn't he taking photos of Brigitte Nielsen, who by now had drifted away back inside the club?

'Are you on acid, Kirk?'

'No, why?'

'Because only someone on acid could think that a 5-foot-4 brunette could be Brigitte bloody Nielsen.'

I went straight to the toilet. My pupils were indeed dilated. Although I felt psychedelically 'tipsy', I was lucid and able to focus on thoughts.

Another wave flowed up my lower leg, a sensual ripple which pulsed in time with the music on the mainstage above the toilets.

Leaning against the wash basin, I eased my feet from my Reeboks and removed my right sock, turning it inside out on my hand as if I was making a glove puppet. Nothing. Then I reached down and felt the bottom of my foot.

Stuck to the sole was a moist piece of card no more than a few centimetres square. I'd completely forgotten that I'd unknowingly brought some Berlin Wallpaper out in my socks to optimise the observance of the sunset and attempt to align with generations of those who'd explored consciousness in Ibiza.

Tom emerged from one of the cubicles and paused to wash his hands.

'Alright, pal?'

I told him I was tripping by accident. He shook his head and laughed: 'The *Mixmag* journo's on one? A normal day at the office, I guess.'

This was the hallucinogenic equivalent of accidentally pulling the trigger of a loaded gun while cleaning it. What I was doing was unplanned and irresponsible, not to mention illegal. But, that said, it felt good. I was in control, in Ku and in Ibiza, so I decided to make the most of it.

I replaced my socks and went back to the VIP bar to apologise to Graham and the paps, but they were nowhere to be found as the real Brigitte Nielsen had taken to the stage and was launching the raunch in leather boots, fishnet tights, a black leotard and shades as a troupe of dancers writhed and flirted with each other like they were all on heat. Brigitte towered above them all and lolloped around the stage like a peroxide prop-forward in drag. None of them could leave their crotches alone. I think it was meant to be sexy. It wasn't.

In one corner of the bar I spotted Tom talking with Mick Jones and Roddy Frame. I grabbed a piña colada from the tray of complimentary drinks which were being offered to guests by the 5-foot-4 brunette I'd interviewed earlier. She smiled benignly – or was it pitifully? Roddy had also spotted me across the bar and appeared to be frowning. Undeterred, I walked over and waited for a gap in the conversation for Tom to introduce me to my heroes. I brandished my disposable camera, completely forgetting that I had no film left, having used it all on the bar girl. Roddy kept glancing at my cap and glaring at me. Did he recognise me as the person responsible for clearing the pit for their one song? I was sure he did. But I could explain it was a mistake and I was a huge fan of both him and Mick. They'd probably laugh about it and we'd party together long into the night. The longer I waited, the more I convinced myself it was an opportunity to apologise and explain.

As I waited, I felt my nose starting to itch. The perfume of a small group of drag artists who were stood nearby was overpowering and I was struggling to control the urge to sneeze. With one hand on my camera and the other holding a bowl-glass of creamy piña colada, I had no means of covering my mouth. It was building . . . I started to do that light stuttered panting in the hope I could avert it. The group moved closer. The perfume got stronger. They were passing a mini fragrance stick around, applying it to each other and comparing notes. I was jammed in and aware that I was in danger of covering two of my heroes in spit and phlegm. Tom looked to me and, turning to Roddy, said, 'Kirk from *Mixmag* has asked me to introduce you . . .'

And just at that moment, my nose exploded.

As it did, I involuntarily raised the glass of cocktail in my left hand to catch some of the blast on my wrist, but the recoil caused by the supressed explosion caused my head to rise slightly, meaning a short sharp gust of air whipped across the top of the glass, lifting a wave of froth into the air and onto Roddy Frame's neck. I'll never forget the first words one of my favourite songwriters said next: 'Who's this cunt?'

Tom, bless him, replied, 'Nah, don't worry. Kirk's okay, he's just been spiked with acid.'

Mick Jones leant forward.

'Somebody spiked yer drink, mate?'

This was Mick Jones, who together with Joe Strummer had written the soundtrack to my teenage years. Mick Jones, the tousle-haired guitarist in the only band that mattered. Mick Jones, the musical genius who introduced me not only to chainsaw punk but also to reggae, rap, samples and drum machines in his next band, Big Audio Dynamite. How I'd longed for a chance to chat with him and here it was. But, having unknowingly spiked myself, I simply mumbled, 'My sock.'

Mick was incredulous: 'Somebody spiked yer SOCK?'

Roddy was similarly shocked. 'While you weren't looking? Jesus, that's a new one!'

A photographer arrived and asked them for a photo. I saw my chance, shrunk away utterly devastated and found a place on the dancefloor where I could dance until dawn on my own, trying to shake off the embarrassment.

I decided I needed to find the source of the beat. The place where the pulse starts. Inspired by the tripped-out film director in Afghanistan, I felt sure that I could locate the beating heart of the 'World's Biggest Club'. To little surprise, I found myself drawn to the area behind the DJ stand. The vibrations, of course, were more powerful here. I didn't move from that point for hours, feeling the energy flow as it charged my mind, body and soul.

As I danced, my body began to move instinctively, requiring no thought whatsoever, leaving my mind free to explore things. The *rave*lations included the theory that a strobe represents our lives on fast forward, day/night/day/night/day/night, and that the universe must be a ball, as the only thing which is truly infinite is a circle (boy, did I bore my mates *that* night). But as I danced alone in the biggest club on the planet after embarrassing myself in front of my heroes, I took it as confirmation that my life had moved on from bands, guitars and looking up to heroes. The culture I had embraced (and was being embraced by) was egalitarian and there were no stars. In those days we often didn't know which DJ was playing, and as long as it sounded good, we didn't care.

The piña colada I 'shared' with Roddy Frame and Mick Jones represented a severing of ties with rock 'n' roll, and the act of leading the photographers away from the stage a symbolic gesture in support of the belief that in a nightclub, everyone's a star. At least that's what I told myself as the sun rose through the 75-foot-high rear window, ably assisted by my lysergic-ally enhanced socks

Seven years later I was interviewing Andy and Dawn, promoters of Manumission, for the *Time Out* Ibiza guide. I asked Dawn to tell me something about Manumission no one else knew. After hesitating, she swore me to secrecy on the condition I wouldn't divulge it in my magazine feature. I agreed. She then led me off through an underground passage which rattled with bass and shook with the thousands of feet dancing above us. We stopped upon reaching a pale green tarpaulin. She looked at me mischievously and gestured for me to help her lift it. A low circular stone wall appeared. I looked down into the blackness. It was a well. This meant that Ku was built over a freshwater spring! There are no rivers on Ibiza and fresh water is precious. The significance of this was considerable . . . and controversial. As anyone who's gone clubbing in Ibiza knows, the tap water is unpalatable; acidic and prone to giving you bad guts. Given the importance of water when dancing in a hot climate – *especially after taking ecstasy* – water sales account for around 75 per cent of a club's bar revenue. Imagine if it *was* possible to drink the tap water . . . the club's profits would nosedive. No wonder this was a closely guarded secret.

It was only when we replaced the tarpaulin that I realised the location of the spring was directly under the spot where I'd danced seven years earlier.

Although I never included this fact in any Ibiza guides I was asked to write as I'd promised Dawn, I did tell anyone I took to Ibiza subsequently and made use of it myself when requiring hydration. When challenged by other clubbers, I'd insist it was safe. Word eventually got out and from 2008, so many clubbers were doing this that the club blocked off the cold-water taps, meaning only warm water flowed.

The morning after

My press pass gave me access to a free cab back to the hotel and I could navigate the rest of the evening without having to worry about communicating, sneezing or interviewing anyone. I watched the sunrise on the beach behind the hotel and after a few hours' kip, a shower and change of clothes, I hired a scooter. I had a special delivery to make.

Dave Ball and Richard Norris had given me some copies of their first release as the Grid, which they'd asked me to help distribute on the island by taking some vinyl to a record shop in Ibiza Town. So in I breezed with half a dozen 12-inch singles and interrupted two Italians sipping their coffees. Gianfranco and Pippi became friends, the former running M15 Records (the premier vinyl outlet in the premier DJ town anywhere on the planet), while his diminutive friend was a resident DJ at the best club in the town (and on some Wednesdays, the planet), Pacha.

We chatted for an hour or more. They told me about the myths surrounding Ibiza: that nothing harmful to man could prosper after the island was blessed by a Phoenician prince who decreed that whichever land he reached would be sacred ground.

They told me I had to experience the sunset from a place called Café Del Mar in San Antonio on the other side of the island, so I pointed my Vespa towards the descending sun. There were no signposts to the sunset in those days, and no 'strip' where superstar DJs played as the sun went down. Just an isolated solitary concrete residential tower block decorated with washing lines, served only by a bumpy dusty track.

I bought a bottle of beer from a supermarket and spent the next hour sipping San Miguel on razor-sharp volcanic rocks in front of the tower block. The shelf I perched on was gently buffeted by small waves as the DJ played a serene soundtrack of undulating laidback music. I was surprised how popular the place was, located beneath a scruffy block of flats and on the outskirts of town, but there must have been around fifty people there.

Two northerners sat behind me; from their conversation I gleamed they were holiday reps. One was explaining the science of selling a sunset boat cruise.

'Now then, lad, make sure to mention dolphins, folk luv 'em. But don't promise 'owt – just tell 'em we saw them last week and the fishermen say they're still around. Next, sunset. The sun's not as unreliable as the soddin' dolphins, but there's still no guarantee they'll see it. Quite often, it'll get cloudy just by the soddin' horizon and the bugger disappears. But don't give up 'cos sometimes just when you think it's gone, it'll come back. We call those herpes sunsets. Last of all, if any guest says there weren't a sunset and asks fir a refund, tell 'em to call NASA and if they verify it, say you'll pay out. Never fails! C'mon, sup up, wet T-shirt contest starts in half an hour.'

This conversation led to me doing my utmost to avoid San Antonio for a whole decade. I would always stay in Ibiza Town or Figueretas and only visit 'San An' for the sunset – which is simply sublime. Once the reps had departed, the serenity returned. Although alone, I felt connected to everyone who was there witnessing the marriage of Fire, Air, Earth, Water and the fifth element, Music.

I'd never been anywhere like this before in my life and at the moment the sun disappeared beneath the horizon and the sliver of gold dissolved into the sea, a ripple of gentle applause moved through the crowd. I was unsure whether they were clapping the sunset, the DJ or both. This appreciation and awareness of nature and music was a powerful affirmation that I had found a special place. A place I felt I belonged.

I was smitten. I thanked the DJ, a small fella called José, bought a cassette from him and with the air growing immediately colder, jumped on my scooter and headed back to Playa d'en Bossa. As I reached the summit of the hill at San Rafael, a new moon rose over the large spaceship on the lush green hillside where I'd spent the previous night.

After dinner with Gianfranco, I met Pippi at a bar he was playing in the new Marina Botafoch area called Keeper. As I stood at the side of the booth, I could see he was 'within' the music. It consumed him, fluidly riding each mix and breakdown. He was on fire as three or four souls whirled around the small dancefloor. Without speaking, he offered me what looked like the remnants of half a lager. I hesitated.

'Drink,' he urged. 'It's very special.'

So I did as he said and finished the contents in two swallows. He nodded his agreement, reached over the booth and grasped my hand.

Around 2 a.m., the bar fell silent and we drove the short distance along the portside to Pacha. The headlights of the oncoming cars appeared like diamonds, sharp shafts of light like stars on a cold winter's night, twinkling hope through millions of miles of darkness.

We walked straight through the front door and I found myself immersed in a traditional Spanish farmhouse, except with a canvas roof and the best sound system I'd ever heard. The bass vibrated my chest and each thump of the kick drum sent a bolt of lightning into my hips. The middle frequencies swirled around my head; a benign and beautiful murmuration of nightingales. Yet I could hear conversations and these included my own. Always the sign of a great sound system.

'What *was* in that drink?'

Pippi looked at me like someone who'd cracked the safe code or realised he was holding the winning lottery ticket.

HOLA, IBIZA!

'Liquid MDMA. Just arrived from New York!'

The next hours were spent on the dancefloor listening to Pippi. It was a wondrous induction to Pacha, blissfully dancing alone and losing myself in the moment. After moment. After moment . . .

At 5 a.m., Adamski appeared and, despite blowing the system, still managed to deliver a storming set. This time playing live rather than miming and turning everyone inside out with his relentless jangle. Every journalist on the trip was being mercilessly wrung out. Jenni Rampling appeared from nowhere and joined in. Looking back, this was the moment the British took over Pacha; it was an invasion which saw UK parties dominate the club across the next two decades – Renaissance, Miss Moneypenny's, Sundissential, Ministry, Underwater and Pete Tong's Pure Pacha.

At 8 a.m. we all staggered outside, squinting as God's spotlight heralded another cloudless day in paradise. We had an hour to get to the airport.

But a few hours later the press posse were sleeping on the tarmac at the airport after the plane wouldn't start. Rather than escort us back to the terminal building, we were made to spend the next seventy-five minutes dozing our way through what was left of the morning. Our rucksacks served as pillows and Robert Elms as our cuckoo clock: 'We've been here thirty minutes, we've been here forty-five minutes . . . we've been here for an hour now.'

The way I felt, I could've stayed there the rest of my life. I didn't want to get on the plane home. Sound familiar?

As we took off and banked to the right, I caught a glimpse of a spectacular, jagged-edged mountain island. Although it was the first time I'd set eyes on it, it felt powerfully familiar. I craned my neck as we left it behind.

What was this place I was drawn to? All the way home it haunted me. This was the moment I first felt a connection with Ibiza.

Afterglow

José Antonio Santamaría's fears turned out to be well founded, as was my hunch about the Spanish builders. The 'great' roof fell in a few months later and had to be completely rebuilt from scratch, financially ruining him. The year after I met him he was implicated in a cigarette smuggling operation, then the following year he was arrested as part of a huge drug-smuggling sting and faced allegations of bribing policemen. The net was closing in and his close friendship with a leading Basque politician may have been the reason why, just a few years after I met him, a known assassin posing as one of the kitchen staff in a restaurant in San Sebastián shot him at point-blank range in the back of the neck. He was killed instantly.

Despite our wind-ups, Peter Willis went on to become editor of the *Daily Mirror*, *Sunday Mirror* and *Sunday People*. One of his biggest achievements was conceiving and launching the Pride of Britain Awards. I met him again at the 1997 Dancestar Awards at Ally Pally and he remembered my face from somewhere. I somewhat guiltily confessed my part in feeding him false stories in Ibiza years earlier, reassuring him that it wasn't personal but down to the fact he worked for the '*Scum*'. He laughed about it, before adding, 'I'm at the *Mirror* now, so if you hear anything juicy . . .' and handing me his business card. Peter died suddenly as this book neared completion. He was that rarest of things, a charming and decent tabloid journalist.

The Grid achieved deserved success and are best known for 'Floatation', 'Swamp Thing' and their collaborations with Andrew Weatherall, Billie Ray Martin, Robert Fripp and Dr Timothy Leary. The DJ I met at Café del Mar was José Padilla, who became the 'Godfather of Chillout' and curator of the *Café del Mar* series, which sold millions of CDs. The reps on the rocks inspired fellow rep Colin Butts to write a book about the 'Lads in Ebeefa' culture, which became the basis for the popular Sky series, *Is Harry on the Boat?*

And, to my knowledge, Robert Elms still hasn't shut up.

> **TOP TUNE: 'Dub Be Good to Me',**
> **Beats International**

7

ANIMAL PHARM

My brief was simple: 'Capture the festival-rave crossover. Witness the moment dance music hits Glastonbury. Share a pint of scrumpy with Adamski, grab a chat with the Happy Mondays and try to get into the booth when Oakey plays the Pyramid. He knows *Mixmag* will be there and is looking forward to seeing you. This is an important moment in rave culture. Oh, one more thing – this will be a front-cover strapline and four-page centrespread, so don't get too messy!'

Sounded simple enough. What could possibly go wrong?

When it did hit the shelves though, my (two-and-a-bit-page) feature contained no live reviews of the Mondays, no booth banter with Oakey or cider-fuelled craic with Adamski. My report was no era-defining exclusive or epoch-defining despatch for the clubbers' bible. If anything, it almost destroyed *Mixmag*'s reputation and my burgeoning career as a writer.

Let me explain. I initially met Glastonbury co-creator Michael Eavis in late 1989, when I sat in his farmhouse

108

kitchen enjoying his wife Jean's delicious homemade vege-
table broth. I was interviewing him for *Encyclopaedia Psychedelica*
magazine's *Evolution* ('The psychic surfer's New Age bible for
the '90s') for a dual feature on the bearded Somerset farmer
and the wide boy of Acid House, Tony Colston-Hayter. Two
characters who shared a love of bringing people together
but who could not have been more different.

Having failed my driving test some years earlier, I needed
a lift to Michael's farm at Pilton, as Glastonbury station
was closed due to the Beeching cuts and the nearest station,
Castle Cary, was 16 miles away by road.

I put the word out and within hours I was called by
Jethro, a character who I suspected supplied half of north
London with mood modification. The deal was simple: I
would cover his fuel and square it with Michael that they
could wander over the festival site and do a spot of metal
detecting while I was conducting the interviews.

It was one of those grey days in December which never
really gets light. The sky couldn't even be arsed to rain
properly. The landscape looked drained of colour. Salisbury
Plain was shrouded in mist, ghost smoke from 3,000 years
of campfires. The stones huddled together on the bleak
landscape, lop-sided yet magnificent. Garish dayglo orange
barriers blocked the road leading to the visitor centre and
car park.

'What's going on?' I asked.

'Winter Solstice is approaching. They don't want to
encourage any gatherings,' Jethro deduced.

'Fackers,' added Slug, his Aussie sidekick who had joined
us on the excursion.

Slug had spent the whole journey rolling joint after joint,
with Jethro sharing the spoils of his friend's endeavours.

As the effects of the devils lettuce resulted in uproarious laughter and increasingly confusing non sequiturs from the front seats, I sat in the back engulfed by the fog, the broken rear window arm frustratingly rendering fresh air beyond my grasp.

The duo began to regale me with the myths and legends they'd heard about the Pyramid Stage. How it was built to the same dimensions as the Great Pyramid of Giza in Egypt, its location determined by the Glastonbury Abbey and Stonehenge ley line and possessed Earth energy in abundance. Jethro explained to his avidly listening Aussie mate some geo-mysticism:

'A pyramid is a very powerful shape, man. The apex projects energy upwards, while energy from the stars and sun are drawn down.'

Slug nodded in agreement, took another drag and surmised as only an Aussie stoner could: 'Too right: a big black, fuck-off prism transmitting pure vibrations into the night.'

Jethro told how he'd heard that lighting jocks suspended in the rigging beneath its point would leave old razor blades overnight and claim to return the next morning to find them miraculously sharpened. Another tale told of how water was observed dripping UPWARDS from a pool of condensed water that had collected in a parabolic dish which was a part of a band's stage set in the '80s, and of a half-eaten ham sandwich which had been left forgotten in the lighting truss for the duration of the festival and didn't go stale.

We arrived at Worthy Farm and I explained to Michael that my mates wanted to spend some time metal detecting around the Pyramid Stage. Michael agreed but pointed out that each year, after the site was cleared, a local bloke got 'first dibs' and they'd be lucky to find anything at all other than an occasional Red Stripe ring pull which had been trampled into the mud.

From my seat at the large kitchen table, through the window I observed my hippy companions walking away from the farmhouse, Jethro carrying a bulky rucksack and metal detector and Slug with what looked like a spade slung over his shoulder. Jean delivered a bowl of steaming broth and crusty bread onto the table in front of me and we started to talk.

Michael explained his involvement in the festival was probably a result of his non-conformist upbringing by Quakers and preachers, who would constantly question the established way of doing things and society's values. Despite his evident affection and sympathy for the '60s counterculture, he was clearly concerned at the latest expression of rebellion, namely acid house.

'Those pirates have ruined it for responsible festival promoters. I refuse to be tarred with the same brush as some of the dodgy cowboys out there who appear to be only in it for a fast buck.'

He also spoke about the history and future development of the festival, which he felt would be about more than merely music and increasingly 'visually immersive'. I asked him if the public's growing awareness of environmental issues and alternative lifestyles could perhaps cause the festival to become a victim of its own success.

'I hope not. From 500 festival-goers in 1970, we now have over 60,000 and I honestly don't know how many more we can accommodate safely and comfortably.'[5]

---

[5] Glastonbury 1990 was attended by 70,000 people. In 2020, the event had a licence for 210,000.

I tried to reassure him that the rave scene was here to stay, and my belief that the festival needed to embrace the movement and music if it was to continue to reflect what was going on beyond his lush green pastures. I urged him to remember his roots and consider that the demonisation of the rave scene had parallels with the way the establishment saw the hippy movement in the late '60s as a threat.

He saw the irony. 'What they said about freedom being eroded and the environment is now everyday language and mainstream political cause.'

I told him that there was a lot of love in the lasers and that the raves had a positive aspect, bringing together black, white, gay and straight people who were unified into one nation under a groove. It sounded like this was the first time he'd heard anyone speak up for the phenomenon and I got the impression he had a downer on the scene through the negative media coverage, coupled with the impact the scene would have on his festival in terms of increased penalties. The furore caused by the orbital raves the previous summer had resulted in tighter licence conditions for music events, prompting him to change its name to Glastonbury Festival for the Contemporary Performing Arts.

Michael figured that describing it as a 'theatre festival' to the local council would help him obtain the licence. (My advice to 'factor in any expected legal costs like the rave promoters did and put a fiver on each ticket' was perhaps heeded, except a tenner was put on each ticket!)

After speaking to him about the chill-out movement (which I described as acid house's quieter little sister), he agreed to look favourably on an arena for the 1990 edition – Glastonbury's twentieth anniversary, which sounded promising and would serve as a bridgehead for the dance scene to infiltrate and ultimately dominate what I've always thought is the greatest music festival in the world.

After we finished, Michael said he needed to take some feed to the cows at the Pyramid Stage, which doubled as a cowshed throughout the winter months, and offered me a lift in his tractor. As we drew near, I could make out two figures on the stage. I jumped out of the tractor, waded through the cow pats, and climbed up the steps at the back to join them. The three of us stood on the most famous festival stage on the planet in the midwinter gloom. My nostrils were filled with the smell of cow shit. In six months' time, there would be 70,000 pairs of eyes on us, but our audience on that grey Wednesday afternoon consisted of a herd of disinterested cows, a farmer and a lone buzzard which hovered above.

'So tell me about the buried treasure on my land. Am I a rich man?'

Slug went white and looked sideways at Jethro, who uneasily shifted his weight to his other leg, 'Erm, nothing, I'm afraid. Think me detector needs a service, but thanks for letting us have a go.' Slug coughed and smiled nervously.

We bade our farewells after Michael gave us a ride back to the farm. On the way back, after miles and miles of trying, and the offer of a full tank of fuel and some munchies at Heston Services, the duo eventually divulged their secret. There *was* buried treasure involved. However, it wasn't discovered by the dopey duo . . . but hidden by them.

Jethro explained how each year, his stash would part company from his vehicle at the same police roadblock on the A303 . . . by the same officer.

'Every fucking year he does me, and so this year I've come up with a cunning plan.'

That plan involved taking his drugs down prior to the festival, thus avoiding police, their dogs and security. Using my interview and metal detecting as an excuse, they found the perfect opportunity to bury copious amounts of weed, pills and tabs of acid on the festival site. Between them, they'd spunked all their savings *and more* on building up a hoard with a street value of around £10,000 for distribution to the expected influx of ravers.

After climbing over a five-bar gate, they found they were looking down on the famous black Pyramid, which was being routinely ignored by a herd of grazing Friesian cows. They walked down to it and scaled the side stairway onto the mainstage. As they looked out, Jethro's eyes were drawn to a magnificent oak tree a few fields away. He recalled that the field was not a popular one for camping, as it sloped down, and any rain would turn the lower part into a quagmire of Glasto mud. So as long as he avoided the lower field, it was the perfect hiding place.

Arriving at the tree, Jethro removed his compass and set it to north. He then carefully walked twenty paces and stopped. Looking at his compass, he turned 90 degrees and walked another steady twenty paces west. He then turned back north and counted out a final twenty precise steps, stopped, made a quick check that no one was watching, and began digging.

After filling his hole and taking care to replace the grass sods by stamping them down firmly, the two returned to the Pyramid Stage, where they pretended to metal detect and wait for me.

A few weeks later I found myself helping to put together a who's who of the emerging chill-out scene: the Grid, KLF, the Orb, Mixmaster Morris, Neutron 9000 and the

Shamen – who had all agreed to play for petrol money and a few free tickets at what was set to be the Dance Village in the expanded Green Fields – a space devoted to the expression of movement through a variety of media. DJ workshops, mixing demonstrations, 'bring-a-bongo' percussive jam sessions and live performances by the nascent scene's main players, which was being coordinated by a fellow 'evolutionary', Neil Oram.

Then, a few weeks beforehand, the plug was pulled after someone got cold feet after spotting the demonic word 'house'.

'Ambient house' was a name used by the Orb and KLF to describe their sound, although there was no similarity to house music in terms of rhythm, arrangement and tempo. The use of samples and the cut-and-paste approach meant the phrase immediately identified it to the generation (indeed the sleeve for the Orb's debut single was adorned with the phrase 'Ambient House for the E Generation').

But some in the Glastonbury hierarchy were spooked when, in March 1990, Graham Bright's 'Acid House Bill' became law, and the Dance Village was pulled within weeks of the festival.

There may have been no official chill-out tent, but this was the first post-Summer of Rave edition of the festival and so it was that dance music did feature – in the form of Adamski, Happy Mondays and De La Soul on the Pyramid Stage, with Paul Oakenfold becoming the first DJ to play the NME Stage.

The opening act on the Pyramid Stage on Friday was Adamski – dressed in a *Clockwork Orange* chic of orange hair, black bowler hat and a flame-red kaftan with jogging trousers. He was rapturously received. It felt like a moment.

RAVE NEW WORLD

Dance music on the Pyramid Stage (only six songs, mind). Welcome to the future!

As he played, *NME* staffers wandered through the crowd handing out '24 Hour Party People' badges and Paul Oakenfold took over Pyramid plastic-playing duties from Andy Kershaw. It was official: rave had come to Glastonbury, whether Michael Eavis liked it or not!

Happy Mondays, Friday's headliners, had appeared to spend their £50,000 fee on a photocopier, a laminator and enough pills for a Roman legion. They had a reputation for putting all their mates on the guest list when they played, and when it was made clear that not everyone on their list of over 200 would be accommodated, Shaun's dad Derek reportedly printed up their own *AAA* passes in his hotel room – hundreds of them. As a result, the backstage area was more Ancoats than Avalon . . . Madchester had taken the M5 to Somerset. 'Putting the pills in Pilton, man!' as Bez described it to me before I was ejected from the backstage area for having a suspected forged pass.

This was supremely ironic as my pass was probably one of the few genuine ones in there! But they were ejecting everyone from that area with jogging bottoms, a fringe or a bum bag . . . and I was found guilty on all counts. Oakey had started playing and waved me over, but the stage manager just wasn't having it. To make matters worse, Jonathan flamin' King stood gurning in a baseball hat and blazer next to his Rolls-Royce (registration plate: JK 9000), which he'd driven into the backstage area. He was nervously guarding the car from the encircling Baldricks, who saw the bonnet sculpture as prized booty . . . after JK had informed Bez the silver figurine was called 'The Spirit of Ecstasy'! There were rumours of a reward of a bag of pills

ANIMAL PHARM

for any scally who could nab the bonnet ornament and
present it to Shaun.

After the set finished, everyone headed to the 'rave tent'
in the traveller's field, which pumped out an all-night-long
relentless soundtrack of 303-driven 130-BPM acid techno
(this was fast for 1990) courtesy of Spiral Tribe, DIY and
Tonka, and a strobe which appeared to be stuck on 11.

On surrounding hills, in tents and sleeping bags, World
Party fans and Cure-loving goths cursed the snotty ravers
for keeping them awake. But these weren't raves as I knew
them. There was no love, unity or a shared sense of awe
and headline-making. Some dreadlocked revellers made the
ravers feel distinctly unwelcome, and there were reports of
theft and intimidation. Lawlessness is great – as long as
everyone behaves. The security presence at the orbital raves
I attended in the summer of '89 possessed very little in the
way of actual security. It wasn't needed. No one carried
weapons, there were no fights, and everyone respected
everyone else. In fact, everyone loved everyone else.

But here, people were on different buzzes; some were on
Red Stripe, scrumpy and/or acid, others were stoned, and
the ravers were all on E, being touchy-feely and all 'Hello,
matey, where ya from?', along with wild-eyed New Age
travellers who were more interested in tearing around the
site on motorbikes with no helmets and even less common
sense and consideration.

It was while walking back to the Green Fields, leaving
the throbbing sound systems behind, that I spotted two
familiar faces sat around some bloke playing a didgeridoo.
They each wore a blanket and smelled, I'm sorry to say,
like they'd shat themselves.

'Fellas! Everything okay?'

They briefly looked up, acknowledged me with a tiny wave and the slightest of smiles, before continuing to stare, statesmanlike, into the distance. I couldn't work out whether it was in awe or sheer disbelief. I sat down next to them, and over the course of the next twenty minutes heard, first-hand, what had happened.

Yesterday, on the third Thursday of June 1990, they set off in Jethro's spluttering van, which had undergone a rare vacuuming and valet to remove any traces of forgotten spliffs or incriminating little plastic bags. As he approached Somerset, the traffic started slowing. Up ahead blue flashing lights indicated that Avon and Somerset Police were pulling some vehicles into the lay-by. Sure enough, upon one look at the LOVE + PEACE sun strip, they gestured for him to pull over.

The officer in charge even recognised him. 'A familiar face! Off to the festival again, are we, sir?'

The boys in blue proceeded to turn the van over, even removing the door panels and back seats, but found nothing. As Jethro looked on, he took great delight in telling them he'd turned over a new leaf and had found honest employment at the festival as a toilet attendant and litter picker.

The coppers, clearly disappointed to have wasted twenty minutes and not upped their statistics, scratched their heads but wished him well. He pulled out of the lay-by and headed towards the festival, grinning from ear to ear. They'd made it!

After setting his tent up, he waited for darkness to fall, and by 2 a.m, when the central site area lights were extinguished and things got quiet, Jethro set off, alone, to unearth his buried treasure. There was but a sliver of a new moon, but despite the darkness he soon located the oak tree. As he had calculated a few months earlier, there were only a few tents scattered at the top of the meadow, but other than that, the field appeared uninhabited as he had imagined it would be.

Looking at his compass, he set it to north and carefully measured twenty paces. He then turned and walked twenty paces west. Turning back north, he was aware he was racing, which may lead to shorter or longer steps, so very deliberately, looking at his compass all the time, he counted the final steps to his loot. Thirteen, fourteen, fifteen, sixteen . . . but as he got to seventeen, he could go no further. Inches in front of his nose was a plywood wall, 7 feet high and stretching 50 feet in length. He looked up and saw the sign: LONG DROP TOILET.

His precious treasure had been buried where a shit pit had been dug.

Now, anyone else would've given up at this stage, but not Jethro. After returning to his tent, he tossed and turned until dawn's first light a few hours later. At which time he made enquiries and ascertained that each day, the endless stream of human excrement was sucked into trucks and decanted into a huge cesspit elsewhere on the site, known as 'The Lagoon'. From where it was filtered, prior to being taken to the sewage works . . . which would explain why two figures were wading, knee-deep in shit, at 7 a.m. on Friday morning, sifting through the poo, in a vain search for their tightly wrapped black plastic stash of drugs.

It was not in vain. I'm pleased to report that they didn't emerge empty-handed. Slug stumbled upon something solid, reached down and recovered the item, holding it aloft in disbelief, as the brown goo dripped to reveal . . . a false prosthetic leg.

Higher than the sun

By Saturday afternoon the clouds had cleared. The thick, gloopy mud which turned Somerset into the Somme very slowly dried. Optimism spread across the site.

I was sat with some of the Tonka and *Evolution* crews in the Green Fields, discussing life extension through nutrition, the use of 'smart drugs' while hearing Patrick from Wow! Foundation's idea for a rave culture-inspired boardgame,[6] which we called Monopoly with MDMA, as they passed around a huge spliff containing Tibetan Temple Balls hashish – the 'Dom Perignon of dope' apparently. Everyone was relaxed, yet I felt somewhat excluded as I didn't smoke and hated the idea of filling my lungs with anything other than air.

It was mid-summer, it was sunny, it was Glastonbury, and I was supposed to be experiencing the festival for the *Mixmag* readers. Being honest, I felt like a bit of a fraud by standing on the sidelines and observing. I was, after all, a 'raving' reporter, not just a bystander with a Biro. So I decided to fully immerse myself in the spirit of the occasion just as a crazy-looking guy with no shirt stumbled into view, carrying one of those trays that cinema ice-cream sellers wear, shouting, 'Space cake, fiver a piece!'

The tray was almost empty, but for two pieces of what looked like flapjack in one corner. They weren't very big, so I offered to take two pieces for £8, which he accepted.

---

[6] Rave the boardgame came out the following year with artwork by Tank Girl co-creator, Gorillaz founder and suspected Banksy Jamie Hewlett. It was years ahead of its time and didn't take off. Occasionally one crops up on eBay. I'm mentioned in the credits as 'Kurk'.

I wolfed the first down in a couple of bites, waited for twenty minutes and felt nothing. This was the first time I'd ever bought drugs at a festival and I'd been ripped off! So I foolishly ate the second piece of flapjack and within a few minutes I began to find everything really quite funny. Hilariously funny.

A nearby stall of homemade Aeolian harps – string instruments powered by the wind and which emanate a low-frequency hum – advertised its presence with a sign that read 'Pleasure Through Wind'. This triggered uncontrollable mirth. Every turn of phrase spoken, every expression, everyone was hilarious beyond explanation. I was literally crying with laughter to the extent that my mouth became dry and I was saved by one of the *Evolution* team (a beautiful Californian girl who has since returned to the States and set up a multi-million-pound cruelty-free cosmetics brand and nutrition line), who handed me a lush slice of melon.

'Cantaloupe?'

I bent forward and sank my teeth into the fruit. It was the sweetest thing I'd ever tasted. Its juice ran from my mouth, sweet rivulets of goodness which I intercepted with my fingers and rubbed across my lips.

A few minutes later I'm lying in her lap, feeling her fingers massage my scalp. As I looked up at the endless pale blue sky, a bongo workshop started up nearby, adding to the primitive mood. Everyone seemed to have a nose ring. I checked to see if I did and became fascinated by how my nostrils felt like a marshmallow between my forefinger and thumb.

It looked, felt and tasted like I was in the Garden of Eden. I was at the Dawn of Man. After twenty minutes, my mates Adam (Adam – of course!) and Fraser, clearly bored of watching me giggle and guffaw, suggested we go for a wander.

★

As they walked, the journalist became aware of this trio from a viewpoint around six feet above their heads. Then it dawned on him that the grey figure on the left in the crimson robes with his arm around his shoulder was God the Father and the classically Italian-looking bloke to his right was St Peter. They paused at a stonemason's stall. Industrious workers in sack cloth chipped at blocks of stone with hammers and chisels. They walked to the next stall, which featured a bloke with bellows working a fire, as another hammered a piece of red-hot metal into a sword. The Stone Age followed by the Bronze Age! He was being walked through the history of mankind! More craft stalls demonstrated leather tailoring, willow craft, carpentry and pottery making. Mankind was amazing! They walked through jugglers, accordion players, some bloke dressed as an orange. When a person in Victorian dress rode by on a unicycle eating fire, he stood open-jawed and utterly dumbfounded at what he was witnessing.

His consciousness would flit back and forth between his head and an aerial viewpoint within 10 feet of his body, like an out-of-body drone. His senses were ultra-receptive, receiving on all channels: the gentle brush of a stranger's clothes as they passed by, the cacophony of performers, market stall holders hawking their wares; a distant band on a faraway stage wafted in on the wind before fading out once more. Millions of multi-coloured made-up faces and fluttering flags and an ever-changing stream of contrasting aromas: damp ham bales, Japanese noodles, the whiff of piss from a Portaloo and the earthy, sickly sweet scent of marijuana. He was inhaling and exhaling existence itself, filling his lungs with festival flavours, breathing in the beauty of life.

The wavering whine of a mosquito distracted him. He waved it away and walked on, but it grew louder. His field of vision was filled by a brown-skinned man in a scarlet turban with a white feather playing a flute. Hundreds of pearls hung around his neck and wrists. The realisation that he was a snake charmer was proof that this *was* the Garden of Eden. This was the serpent which tempted Eve to taste the fruit, who in turn tempted Adam. His afternoon stroll had led to the Fall of Man. His head swam and his vision blurred the colours into a spinning, collapsing kaleidoscope of chaos and confusion. His senses had reached overload and he felt and heard a sizzling in his head as his synapses frazzled and short-circuited.

His friends could see he was struggling and slowly walked him back to Fraser's tent, like an injured Tommy retreating from the trenches. He was relieved to find himself in a quiet orchard campsite.

When it came to altered states, Fraser Clark knew a thing or two. But as much as the young journalist felt in safe hands, he knew he was in trouble and requested to be taken to a medical station. Fraser gently dissuaded him from the idea, suggesting to him that after hearing him describe his feelings, it appeared that the space cake contained LSD and would be in his blood by now, and any vomit-inducing treatment or stomach pump would not only be ineffective, but it would also be traumatic beyond words. He promised to keep an eye on him and gave him his tent to use for as long as he wanted.

One by one, the other *Evolution*aries dropped by after hearing their dance music editor was experiencing the ultimate trip, with many expressing envy or reverence.

'I know it's tricky for you at times, but believe me when I say I've known smokers, seekers and sadhus spend years – and huge amounts of money – to be in the state you're in right now. Make the most of it!' whispered Fraser, handing him a canteen of water.

'But I'm missing all the action, I haven't seen one band play today . . .'

The old zippy drew closer to the young raver. 'I've always said that one of the best things about Glastonbury is all the big-name bands who you can MISS. And, Kirk, the action is in here.' He touched my head.

He considered this, and after accepting he was in no physical, mental or spiritual state to do anything which required muscular coordination, crawled clumsily into the tent, where feeling safe and secure, he remained for over twelve hours. As he lay motionless, he heard Jasper the orange-robed sadhu tell the tale of a pilgrimage he and other hippies in the late '60s made to Shiva's home, a sacred cave high in the mountains of Kashmir.

'We trekked for weeks through treacherous passes, through revolt-ravaged valleys, along icy streams, frozen glacier ice sheets, dodging guerrillas and government troops. We were heading for the very cave where Shiva revealed the secrets of life and immortality to his consort. It's a revered shrine because each year a stalagmite grows and forms an ice phallus that stretches from the floor to the roof of the cave, 15 feet high. No Westerners had witnessed it. We were the first. As we climbed higher, it grew colder and colder. When we finally reached the cave, which is nearly 13,000 feet above sea level, it was just after sunset the day before the full moon – when thousands would be arriving for the annual festival. We were exhausted and on the verge of hypothermia. So we lit a fire, dropped some acid, smoked some potent Kashmiri and spent hours transfixed by the flames. We were finally warm and oh, did it feel good. Eventually at dawn we crashed out and the next thing I knew, we're being awoken by cries and shouts. I opened my eyes and the ice penis was nothing but a stump. We'd fallen asleep and the fire melted the bloody thing! They were livid and chased us out, saying it was a bad omen.'

He heard laughter from the others, which grew distant. Then . . . silence.

Some hours later, consciousness slowly returned. He was fully clothed, in an unfamiliar dark-green, two-man tent. It was darker than previously and, although motionless, he was aware of breathing. He wasn't alone. He opened his eyes and saw he was sharing the tent with a mongrel dog in a snug-fitting black designer leather jacket.

The bald, black hound looked around at him and yawned. 'Awl roight, yeah . . . yeah . . .' The yobby Cockney drawl was familiar. It wasn't the dog speaking. 'Dogs can't speak,' he told himself, before pondering the fact that dogs didn't wear designer leather jackets either.

'Let's 'ear ya!'

It wasn't coming from the dog; it was a band! But who? It didn't sound like Robert Smith, but the Cure were playing at some point on Saturday night. He was spending hours in a moment, splitting time like it was the atom, going ever inwards and finding more space . . . the first secret was unveiled. Infinity applies to inner space as well as outer space. He imagined cutting a round cake in half, then in half again and repeating the motion until he needed a series of ever-smaller, sharper knives. But no matter how infinitesimal the piece he'd just cut, something of substance still remained. There was no end until you'd split the atom – nuclear fission . . . and then it was the end for everyone. Wow!

The music from the mainstage invaded his ears. 'One flight, two flight, three flight, four . . . Five, six, seven flights, eight flights more . . .' He recognised the lyric from Eddie Cochran's song 'Twenty Flight Rock'. Fuck me, was Eddie Cochran the surprise act? Was Eddie Cochran still alive . . . was *he* still alive? Lying there motionless with a bald dog watching over him, he vaguely remembered that according to Greek mythology, a dog stood guard at the gates of the underworld to prevent the dead from leaving.

Missing the headline band when he was reviewing a concert is one thing, but to die of a drugs overdose wasn't a good look either. He needed to claw his way up and out from the sub-molecular level he was exploring. That voice again, brimming with positivity and optimism, 'Ty-i-i--ime is on my side . . . yes it is!'

Suddenly he was aware that not only was he alive but he was missing the Rolling Stones finally play at Glastonbury! Lying on his back, still paralysed, he wanted so much to leave his green nylon cocoon but accepted the best he could do was make mental notes about the setlist, and which songs were received the best, so he could still review the show.

In an act of perfect synchronicity, Mick confirmed this was the best course of action: 'You caint always get what you want, but you get what you neeeed!' Then the entire crowd joined in, chanting this over and over. It was like everyone was rootin' for him, aware that his lust for life had prevented him from joining them.

'WHHHHHOOOOOSSSSHHHH!!!!'

The tent was suddenly alight with red light. An intense circle of scarlet shrank in size as it streaked high into the sky. The smell of cordite drifted into the open doors of the tent, causing the bald dog to splutter and the stricken journalist to gasp in awe. As he focused on the descending scarlet orb, he began to expand, filling the tent, then outwards over the camping area. Although uneasy, the novel experience was something he couldn't control even if he wanted to. Imagine inhaling and feeling your chest expand, but not stopping until you have absorbed everything. Literally, everything in the universe. He felt immense, but comfortable.

Then a second secret unveiled itself. *If there's no separation*, he thought, *we can't engender conflict or war, because it doesn't make sense to go to war with ourselves.*

He was aware that this was a time and place (out of time and in no particular place) when he could ask anything. All would be revealed. All he had to do was ask. And he took the opportunity and received all the answers he needed. But as this was a non-verbal exchange, the wisdom arrived without words.

(He's thought about it many times since and the closest he can come to it is, '*We have everything we need.*' This can apply to renewable energy, resources, possessions or love. It's something which, as the years go by, reappears ever more frequently.)

Another red flare illuminated the tent and faded to reveal the sound of a helicopter. He was now in the Mekong Delta in *Apocalypse Now*, battling fever, flashbacks and the horrors of a one-way ride up the river into the heart of darkness. He was so sensitive that he was acutely aware of every single skin cell which was being crushed as he lay down. Moving was no escape. It just meant other cells got squashed instead. Just like life, he thought, there's pain and suffering no matter what course you take. So he decided to lie absolutely still to minimise the cellular destruction, and he wearily resigned himself to his fate of certain death – if he wasn't dead already.

He closed his eyes and rued the fact that for the first time ever he was finally going to miss a print deadline, something he prided himself on never doing. He would die with the wisdom gained during his incredible experience, but would be unable to share it with others. How very unsatisfying. He drifted off after Jagger thanked the audience and the last bars of 'I Can't Get No Satisfaction' dissolved into rapturous applause and the roar of an appreciative audience suddenly faded into silence. Outside he could hear the voices of his friends as they sat around laughing, talking, drinking and smoking.

Off he drifted once more, to a place which is everywhere. He'd already been in the tent since mid-afternoon, and it now felt like the middle of the night.

It's hard work being the universe. He slipped into the void.

Sunday

'Shorty, are you alive, or what?'

I recognised the deep deadpan voice immediately. I opened my eyes to see Adam peering into the tent. I could feel my arms and my legs and was relieved to find I'd returned to my body.

'Hello, mate. Yes, I'm alive! More alive than I've ever been.'

'Good, let's get out of here. It's gonna rain and I'm fed up with eating lentils.'

We'd had more than enough.

In order to get proofs to the printers and go to print at midday, I had to file the *Mixmag* copy by 10 a.m. the next morning and so began typing as soon as I got home.

I sat in front of a blank page with my arms folded. How on earth was I going to write 3,000 words after what had just happened?

I began calling round, but as the festival was still on Sunday night, I couldn't verify anything about Oakey, Jesus Jones, Gary Clail, De La Soul or the Stones. These were the days before 24-hour rolling news and Glastonbury was considered New Age subculture, not mainstream newsworthy coverage. So I had no way of corroborating anything. I was flying solo, trying to piece together what happened while I was, erm, somewhere else. *Everywhere* else.

Here's a section of the original copy I filed. A few faded typewritten pages of A4 I found recently in a dusty time capsule of rave paraphernalia in my loft, filled with thirty-year-old magazines, flyers and a board game called Rave!

After all these years, it will finally be read:

Satisfaction!

After twenty years of rumours, false start (me up)'s and disap-pointment, the Rolling Stones have finally played Glastonbury Festival. All weekend long (and boy, was it a long weekend . . .)

the mystery band's identity was, along with the forged backstage passes distributed/sold by the Happy Mondays and the Scrumpy Bus, the hot topic of conversation. Rumours that it was Sting in the helicopter which sporadically buzzed overhead mercifully turned out to be untrue.

The Stones show was such a closely guarded secret that many present missed the show entirely; busy elsewhere becoming one with a bongo, a bong or a piece of space cake.

Opening with the 'Under My Thumb' and the staccato 'Start Me Up', the hits flowed and flowed, delighting the ever-growing crowd, whose cheering and whooping eclipsed anything any other performer had received all weekend. They say time waits for no man, but Mick Jagger just three years from his FIFTIETH birthday appears to have found the PAUSE button; more gobby imp than middle-aged man. He strutted and pouted like a 'Little Red Rooster' on heat, a Pan-like presence, pumping out hit after hit: 'All Over Now', 'Honky Tonk Woman', 'Jumpin' Jack Flash' . . . the sound at Glasto can reflect the fields it soars over and be muddy, unbalanced and confused − but after thirty years on the road, I guess it's no surprise that the Rolling Stones are more than capable of getting the live mix right when it matters most.

I know it's only rock 'n' roll, but no matter whether the crowd preferred Adamski, Aswad or Archaos − they liked it.

The next morning at 10 a.m., I walked to Raj's Newsagent's and faxed my copy.

I returned home and the phone started ringing. Every Monday morning a few DJs would call me for a catch-up. We'd swap notes on which events went off, which tunes were the biggest, and ascertain where the scene was heading. John Digweed usually called just after eleven, Mixmaster

Morris was around midday and Tony de Vit was usually later in the afternoon.

Tony was lovely, humble and clearly passionate about playing, but his was such a hard sound that I always worried he'd struggle to get gigs in London, which was ruled by the relatively more laidback Balearica Boy's Own at the time as well as the breakbeat jungle going off in Essex. I knew that neither scene would be interested in Tony's sound, so I was so pleased it happened for him a few years later at Trade. His untimely death at just forty years of age was a massive loss to clubland.

Anyway, that Monday morning I spoke with none of the above, as I had unplugged the phone and was frantically rewriting my copy in a state of utter panic. As I returned from the newsagent's, my answerphone was receiving a voicemail, which ended just before I reached the phone. I pressed the red flashing message button.

It was James Hamilton, one of Fraser's closest cohorts and former editor of *Encyclopaedia Psychedelica:* 'Kirk, it's James. Hope you got home safely and have recovered from your trip. You lucky sod! Listen, man, I'm aware you left the festival early yesterday morning, as you needed to write your review, and I'm wondering if either yourself or your pal Adam packed my cassette player by mistake? It was outside Fraser's tent. I can't remember the make, but if it's got a Stones tape in it, it's mine! Give me a call, I'm at home, cheers.'

I played it again. And once more. My head spun. I called him straight away to tell him I hadn't got the cassette player but would ask around for him, before asking him in a random, just-making-conversation manner,

'Which Stones' album is it?'

'Their live one, *Let's Spend the Night Together* – it was the last tape we played on Saturday night.'

This wasn't happening. I'm still in a tent with a bald dog, imagining the whole thing, aren't I? Any minute now I'm going to snap back into reality and when I tell the guys at *Mixmag* about it, they'll find it utterly hilarious.

But it *was* happening, and I was consumed by guilt. Mixmag *will be the laughingstock of the publishing world if they run this*, I thought. I was aware that they'd just secured a distribution deal which placed the mag in every newsagent's shop in the country. This demanded credible journalism and radical reportage of the most dynamic thing to happen to music for a generation. And what did I send them? A fucking review of a ten-year-old Rolling Stones live album. I had to stop it! But what if it had gone to press already? I recalled the words 'increased print run' and '70,000 copies' from my last face-to-face at the DMC DJ Convention a few months earlier. If this was published, I'd never write again, and any respect I had in the club scene would turn to ridicule.

My next call was to *Mixmag*'s deputy editor, Nick Gordon Brown, who had the herculean task of proofing my copy each month. He confirmed my faxed copy had been received.

'But you haven't read it yet?'

'No, just going through the Mica Paris piece, then I'll take a look.'

'Don't!'

'Sorry?'

'I sent the wrong draft. It was a heavy weekend, you know, and my flatmate faxed it for me, but sent the wrong pages. I'll get it to you in a bit, just got to wait in for a washing machine delivery. You'll have it by midday, I promise.'

'Okay, look forward to reading it. How did the Mondays go down?'

'Great, I gotta go, Nick, speak soon.'

An hour later, my vintage blue Olivetti typewriter sat smoking in the kitchen, exhausted and spent from the merciless abuse my jabbing forefingers had subjected it to.

Emerging from Raj's with a carton of Ribena and a fax receipt which showed that at 11.57 a fax had been sent to Slough 01628 668552, I had maintained my record of never missing a deadline.

Loose ends

- The helicopter I heard was real – making an emergency landing behind the Pyramid Stage during the Cure's set after a member of the crowd had a heart attack.
- The infamous 'Battle of Yeoman's Bridge', as the clash became known, resulted in 235 arrests, £50,000 of damage to vehicles and ties being severed with the travelling fraternity. The festival then took a year off to allow everyone to calm the hell down, not least the local council.
- The Rave boardgame was released in time for Christmas of that year. I was honoured to get a credit on the instructions (even though they spelt my name 'Kurk'). They now sell for over £100 on eBay.
- Fraser's dog wasn't wearing a designer leather jacket . . . but he was wearing a leather jacket! He was a Xolo, a hairless breed. Just typical to come across one when I was in the state I was in.

- Glastonbury returned in 1992 with a 10-foot perimeter fence and swapped its 'edge' for a slow mission creep to mainstream respectability: Hell's Angels, travellers, and space cake vendors were replaced by the BBC and vegan sushi – from Mad Max to Pepsi Max, you might say.
- Dance music had to wait until 1994 when Orbital's performance was beamed into living rooms across the country on Channel 4. Effectively a respectable rave showcase, it paved the way for the Chemical Brothers, Leftfield and Underworld to play, leading to Dance Village becoming an annual fixture from 1995.
- The Rolling Stones eventually played the festival in 2013 . . . twenty-three years after I reviewed them.

> **TOP TUNE: 'WFL' (Paul Oakenfold Mix), Happy Mondays**

8

TRANSCENTRAL TALES . . .

. . . or how I helped the KLF burn £1 million

The first time KLF appeared in the national press was in an interview *Mixmag* carried on the cover in January 1990 entitled, 'The Ambient Age'.

The address I had to find was typically cryptic. On a note scribbled in a biro I'd borrowed from the bar at Heaven a few days before were the words, *Transcentral, Jeffreys Rd, SW4.* It was only when I emerged from Stockwell Tube in darkening skies and pulled the note from my pocket that I realised Jimmy had forgotten to add the house number. This is what happens when you ask DJs for their addresses mid-set at 2 a.m. In those pre-mobile/email days I had no way of reaching him, so I set off with a *London A-Z* under my arm, as I have no sense of direction.

I reached a long road of period Georgian houses with grand white bay windows and pillars framing the front doors. They all looked alike, as Georgian terraces tend to do. I'd promised my editor Dave Seaman 600 words and an exclusive of the artwork for their much-anticipated album, *Space*. The print deadline was 6 p.m. the next day, so I had no choice other than to locate the mythical Transcentral studios that day or lose the scoop.

This was a very respectable road, the badges on the cars told me so. Mercedes, BMWs and Range Rovers lined both sides of the street, bumper to bumper in middle-class comfort ... but then I came upon a vehicle covered in green tarpaulin, which although completely obscured, looked strangely familiar. I moved on to the road to take a look from the front. The sleek coupé shape, the unmistakable width and the bulges on the roof of the siren and loudspeakers ... it was the infamous Ford Timelord: The '68 Ford Galaxie which starred in Jimmy Cauty and Bill Drummond's number-one hit, 'Doctoring the Tardis'. A former Detroit police squad car that Jimmy had bought for £300 in Dagenham a few years earlier, after it appeared in the *Superman III* movie, it remains the only saloon car to have reached number one.

I couldn't resist lifting up the tarpaulin like a naughty schoolboy, and sure enough, there was the Timelord logo on the driver's door. It felt like discovering the Tomb of Tutankhamun or the Lost Ark of the Covenant on a quiet, south London street.

I knocked on the door of the house nearest to the obscured vehicular pop icon and was relieved when Jimmy Cauty opened it. We descended down a green metal spiral staircase into a basement which cradled a huge mixing desk and several strategically placed buckets to catch the incessant drips from the leaking ceiling. The walls were bare plaster and were adorned with a wall-mounted wooden cabinet marked 'Roll of Honour' – below which was a wooden cross. The floor was filled with boxes of vinyl, wires ran like spaghetti between stacks of effects units, a turntable, a keyboard and a Roland TR 909 which occupied central position on a large wooden workbench, at which Jimmy beckoned me to sit as he relit a roll-up. After ensuring it was lit, he smiled and said softly, 'Welcome to Transcentral!'

After catching up on the raves we'd been to, we commenced the interview. As this was the band's first national press, the name seemed like a good place to begin. Jimmy was adamant that KLF was not an anacronym for 'Kopyright Liberation Front', before adding, 'We don't know what it stands for – yet. When we find out, we can stop what we're doing now.'

Jimmy's partner Cressida appeared with two mugs of tea. Jimmy placed a slab of vinyl on the turntable. It read SPACE Test Pressing 003 and as it played, he showed me some artwork. It was stunning: an astronaut floating within a floating blue Planet Earth and in the bottom left corner, Théodore Géricault's *Raft of the Medusa* shipwrecked characters implore and reach out. Closer inspection revealed some were wearing KLF T-shirts.

I was surprised to see this, as they'd told me *Space* would be an Orb release; it was to be the vinyl expression of the duo's White Room sessions. But confusingly, Jimmy told me the artist name was Space, but would appear on KLF Communications. (I later found that all of Alex's contributions were replaced/re-recorded by Jimmy.)

To run this as an exclusive before *DJ MAG* would have been great. However, as it was the original artwork and pre-internet, there was no way of scanning and sending and it was way too intricate and colourful to be sent by fax. Jimmy offered to colour photocopy it for me but had no money. So I gave him a fiver (my food and drink money for that evening) to pop to the nearest Prontaprint, while I was left to drink tea with the beautiful Cressida and listen to the album in its entirety, in the very room in which it was conceived.

It was now raining quite heavily outside and the buckets and containers that were strategically placed to catch the leaks from the roof plopped and dripped as accompaniment to the lush minimalist soundscape which unfolded over the course of the next hour and a half. Jimmy returned with the colour copy and I bade farewell in the pouring rain, pausing only to stroke the green tarpaulin of the Timelord on my way out. Jimmy stood in the doorway and shouted, 'I'll give you the fiver next time I see you.'

Of course, every time I saw him after that was in a club or rave, usually with one or both of us working, so as a result, communication was both brief or non-verbal.

I invited him to Raindance on New Year's Eve 1991 and we had a thing where everyone on the guest list would pay a fiver as they entered (which we donated to a children's charity like Great Ormond Street Hospital). It was all cash and the scope for immoral types pocketing a bunch of fivers when the bucket was emptied every half an hour was too obvious. So I decided not to carry any cash in my pockets when I worked the guest list, so that any searches showed me not to be the one with light fingers.

Naturally, this was the night Jimmy offered to pay the fiver back. I declined, saying I'd see him inside later, which I never did. Hardly surprising given there was no VIP area, just one huge marquee packed with 4,000 ravers and a funfair. The 'FREE FUNFAIR' was an integral part of the furniture at most London/orbital raves back in the day, symbol of the happy-go-lucky, back-to-childhood fun the early rave scene espoused. Along with dummies, dungarees and lollipops.

On the way home an hour or so after the party had finished, we spotted someone who looked a lot like Jimmy on the North Circular. He was sat in a small beat-up yellow car, stationary on the inside lane. It was only as we got a few hundred yards up the road that my mate said, 'Was that Jimmy in that car we just passed?'

I did call him a few days later and he explained that he'd run out of petrol on the North Circular while driving home from the party. No garages were open and he was so adjusted that he didn't realise he had stopped. It was only when the police dawn patrol car stopped to enquire why he was parked on the flyover did he realise why all the cars that overtook him were going so fast! Apparently, he was concentrating so hard on driving carefully and not speeding that he didn't realise his tank was empty and that he was stationary. 'That would explain why I kept going slower and slower,' he laughed, before adding, 'And I still owe you that fiver!'

The next few years brought huge success for Jimmy and the KLF. They had a string of hit singles, topping the charts across Europe, and would go on to become the biggest-selling pop artists of 1991 in the UK.

★

It was 25 September 1994 and I was in bed reading the *Observer* magazine, which carried a feature by Jim Reid describing how he witnessed the K Foundation (Jimmy and

Bill's post-KLF retirement project) burn £1 million in a deserted boathouse on the Isle of Jura in the Hebrides.

Some stories grab the public's attention immediately, while others slowly seep into their consciousness. Strangely, this crazy cremation of cash didn't really register. It was just those misfit popstars turned art terrorists up to their old tricks again. They didn't really do it, did they? I mean, who would burn a million quid?

Jimmy would, especially if Bill Drummond was involved. I was aware that their infamous 1992 BRIT Awards performance, which saw them fire machine-gun blanks over the heads of the audience and dump a dead sheep on the red carpet of an after-party, was actually a compromise gesture brought about by Jimmy. I'd heard from someone connected to them that Bill's original plan was to cut his hand off and toss it into the crowd. I knew Bill was capable of contemplating self-harm and his distaste for the music biz was public knowledge.

I've always believed they did burn the money, and that was confirmed the next summer. I was working as guest list manager at the Forum, north London. The Orb were playing, and I was pleased to see Jimmy and Cressida's names on the list.

Cressida arrived slightly in front of Jimmy, who was engaged in conversation with someone a few steps behind. As she approached the box office window, she recognised me. I hadn't seen her for a few years but had to ask, 'Did Jimmy really burn a million pounds?'

She looked me in the eye with a look of regret and nodded. 'Yes, he did.'

'And was the fiver he owes me among it?'

'He still owes you that fiver?' She shouted him over. 'Jimmy, it's Kirk, you still owe him a fiver, remember?'

Jimmy shook my hand and fumbled in his pocket, then offered me a screwed-up, grubby blue note. This was the moment I'd been waiting for.

'Thanks – but keep it, Jimmy. Just see it as my contribution to the big burn.'

When regaling this tale, I'm often asked for my thoughts on why they burnt the million pounds (and they *did* burn a million pounds, of that I have no doubt). While there may have been numerous reasons behind it, I've always thought the main driver was guilt. Bill despised the music business and felt uncomfortable with the huge financial rewards they received for using other artists' work. ('What Time Is Love?' bears an uncanny resemblance to Anne Clark's 'Our Darkness', which in turn is very similar to 'Judas' Death' in *Jesus Christ Superstar*.) 'Doctorin' the Tardis' wasn't meant to be a novelty pop record. Try as they did, they just couldn't make it hip and so went for the chart jugular, but were embarrassed about it – hence the car fronting the video. They did exactly the same with the 'Stadium House Trilogy', which started as credible album tracks but were re-worked into chart fodder with snappy raps, featured vocals and accompanied by epic videos which were perfect for MTV.

Maybe they felt the same way about the vast financial rewards their pop canon gave them? According to Bill, Jimmy came up with the best reason they burned the money while watching Michael Jackson on *Top of the Pops* in 1995 with his kids and remarked, 'We'll never be as talented as him.' My personal view is that they just felt unworthy of the riches they had accumulated. Jimmy appeared to confirm this in 1996: 'I was a bit worried about it at first, but I think it's probably the best thing we've done. It was all the profit we'd made from selling records, after we'd paid off tax and stuff.'

While looking back over my features, I found a prescient quote from Jimmy in a *Mixmag* interview from March '91, which may provide a clue: 'Everyone has crazy ideas. The difference with us is that we can sometimes make these things happen. It's frightening, really. The more money we make, the more stupid we get. You see we have no manager and no record company, so there's really nothing to stop us.'

One of the best demonstrations of this were the two Saracen tanks that Jimmy bought, which he installed with some serious sub-bass bins. They didn't go down too well with his neighbours, the farmers in south Devon, after their cattle were spooked – 'up to three miles away' – when Jimmy demonstrated his 'noise tank' to some friends.

> **TOP TUNE: 'What Time Is Love?**
> **(Pure Trance 1)', KLF**

9

GOING LEGIT

'Close my eyes and I'm in Jenkins Lane . . . Raindance big tent.'

– 'Glue', Bicep

From 1990 to 1994, I worked for the world's first legal rave promoter, Raindance, handling the press and PR and writing flyer copy, in addition to working on the event – from blowing up the giant balloons and running the guest list to managing the mainstage.

Every account of this era has either ignored or barely mentioned Raindance, probably due to the fact it sprang from Essex rather than London, was basic in terms of production, and featured an unfashionable sound as opposed to Balearic house.

Raindance has a special place in rave history as it was the world's first legal rave in the UK. This is common knowledge. But what is never mentioned is the fact that for a period of around eighteen months, between the introduction of the Graham Bright Bill in March 1990 and organisations such as Fantazia and Universe obtaining all-night music and dance licences from local authorities, Raindance was the only licensed rave taking place anywhere in the UK. Basically, keeping the flame burning for a culture that was under attack from the government, the police and the media.

So how on earth did they get a licence when no one else could? Well, the answer is down to naivety. And mud wrestling.

Like many others watching the media coverage of the orbital raves throughout the previous summer, Loughton cab driver Paul Nelson thought it looked like more fun than driving pissed-up blokes back from the club on a Saturday night. Encouraged in no small part by his music-mad younger brother, Matthew, and his mate, Lou, who owned the lease on a football training ground just off an A13 flyover, he decided he didn't have the balls to run an illegal event, so gingerly approached the council to ask for a licence to do it properly.

'Licensing was different in those days,' Paul remembers. 'No one did events except responsible, sensible people. When I asked what licence we needed to run all night and with more people, the old chap at Newham Council said as we own the land, already had an outdoor licence for the clubhouse and an alcohol licence, we didn't need anything else. I couldn't believe it, and so asked for it in writing.'

By now the team also consisted of a local promoter called Ray Spence who knew his music and the events industry and his mate, Thomas Kibley, who was in his last year at law school. On Saturday, 10 September 1989, Raindance became the first legal all-nighter in the UK. Despite this, the punters were kept in the dark about the licence and had to go to a series of meeting points, even though the venue was secure.

'We were worried that people wouldn't come if they thought it was legit.'

Sure enough, after a few hours the police arrived and after being shown the council letter, allowed the event to proceed.

And proceed it did. Through Saturday night and into Sunday morning, through a car boot sale and two football matches, into Sunday evening and right through the night until Monday morning. The lone police unit parked at the entrance changed shift five times.

Elated at their success, Paul returned to Newham Council, who were a little more inquisitive this time.

'What's the nature of the event, Mr Nelson?'

'Erm, mud wrestling. It's proving very popular at the moment. A bit like boxing except no one gets hurt.'

The councillor pondered for a second and nodded in agreement.

The licence was granted, but only until 2 a.m.

This next rave took place in October and was ended by the police at 2 a.m. precisely.

From this point on, Raindance were open with the council and police, who I suspected saw Raindance as a safe pair of hands and would rather have 5,000 ravers in one place that had a licence than be chasing around Essex trying to extinguish dozens of smaller raves.

This 'bridging' period in the early '90s was crucial to the survival of UK rave culture and Raindance pioneered the way forward, working with the authorities and operating within the law while showcasing local talent. Through

Raindance at Jenkins Lane, new breakbeat-driven sounds emerged from unglamorous Essex towns such as Loughton (SL2), Braintree (the Prodigy), Southend (N-Joi) and Romford (Suburban Base Records).

The events at Jenkins Lane were the only ones in the London area (if not the entire UK) which continued past 3 a.m. They passed off without major incident (as the authorities never found out about the marquee nearly collapsing with 5,000 people inside) and anyway, with the poll tax riots kicking off the night before the first major Raindance party of 1990, the police – who had deployed forces to Trafalgar Square – had other things to worry about. In retrospect, Easter 1990 was a watershed weekend. The Graham Bright Bill had just been passed, effectively extinguishing the possibility of orbital raves, and the Trafalgar Square riot reminded the authorities what real civil disobedience looked like.

The veiled threats from the police to stop the party or block entry amounted to nothing, giving Raindance a chance to show what was possible.

We did the same every few months throughout 1990 and established the concept of a large, licensed dance music event which other promoters adopted. Within a year, Westminster City Council had seen the light and recognised the desire for young people to stay up for ever by offering weekly 6 a.m. licences to West End venues like the Astoria.

While the dance media were bigging up the Balearic house sound of Boy's Own and only had eyes for the 120-BPM West End scene where Danny Rampling, Pete Heller and Terry Farley would ram Leicester Square venues with 400 people, they ignored the less fashionable Jenkins Lane – a recreation ground within exhaust fumes of Essex's

GOING LEGIT

Route 66, the A13 in east London, where a bunch of wide boy DJs and Carl Cox would attract crowds of 4,000 people with a frenzied 140-BPM aural attack of hardcore breaks, cutting-edge techno and the emerging sound of jungle.

Being licensed meant a confirmed start and end time – which in turn meant we could run buses. Raindance pioneered 'park and rave', organising free buses from Trafalgar Square. These were managed by stewards in hi-vis vests, who were in contact at all times with the production Portakabin. The council observers were particularly impressed by this.

A definitive closing time, however, was anathema to many of us, who were used to parties starting at dawn and going on until the generators ran out of fuel or the bar ran dry of water. Or the Old Bill said, 'Enough is enough, you've had yer fun, made yer money. *Songs of Praise* starts in an hour, for Chrissakes, and it's a school night.' Or words to that effect.

This meant that set times were shortened to an hour, and no one liked this, particularly the DJs. But there was only one arena and the flyer needed lots of names . . .

Even in those days, Carl Cox was the number-one attraction, and the big man was always in big demand. I was in the office working on the line-up one afternoon and Ray Spence asked me to book Carl for an upcoming Easter show ('The Egg'). I called him up and told him the date. He said he was available, but the price had gone up from £150 to £200.

This was how we did it in those days, no manager or agent. No contract or technical rider; one phone call and a gentleman's agreement.

Soon after that Carl became the first DJ to get a manager. The mention of the name 'Maxine' will still strike fear into every promoter's heart from that era. Maxine wasn't to be messed with. One named DJ used to maintain she was scarier than any ragga DJ, 'including Jumpin' Jack Frost' (which was saying something). Mind you, compared with some of the managers Carl's had since, Maxine was an angel. She may have been hard work, but she was fair and understood the rave scene because she was part of it.

Moby's first rave

My arrangement with Raindance meant that in addition to handling the press and stage managing, I could book one artist for every show. This is how a quiet guy from Hastings called John Digweed (DJ JD) got to play and why we did an ambient house room at one party that featured Alex Paterson from the Orb and which was empty all night as, frankly, people didn't go to Raindance to chill out. However, I had more success with the next artist I booked.

You won't find any of the additional names on any Raindance flyers; they were always added after ticket sales were deemed strong enough to justify an extra act, or alternatively referred to as 'Special Guest PAs to be announced'. In the summer of '91 there was a tune which you heard everywhere. It had the haunting theme to *Twin Peaks* and a very current R&S Records rhythm track with only one lyric: a chorus of spirits who chanted 'Yeah, yeah, yeah,' prior to an incendiary '. . . *Go!*' It was by an artist called Moby. I had tracked Moby down to NYC and found out he was coming to London on a promotional trip.

That was it! He was booked for £150, but as the flyer was already out, he wasn't advertised.

He was due on at 2.45 a.m. but by 2.15 there was no sign of him. Mobile phones in those days were as rare as rocking horse shit (and about the same size as a rocking horse as well), so there was no way of reaching him to see where he was. We knew from our head steward that there was a mile-long queue of traffic to Jenkins Lane, and ravers were simply abandoning their cars and walking the last few hundred yards to the venue. So we put the call out for security and stewards to keep an eye out for a small American guy who might be carrying a keyboard.

Suddenly, at half-past two, the radio crackled into life: he was here. I pelted out from the Portakabin to the main gate and there was Moby, looking somewhat confused, with a keyboard under his arm and a stand in the other. No tour manager, no hangers-on, no entourage. Just one little guy and his synth.

I welcomed him to Raindance, grabbed the stand and reminded him that he was due on in ten minutes. 'So no time to go to the dressing room, I guess?' he said.

'No, afraid not, but as there isn't one it doesn't make much difference!' I replied.

He followed me past the funfair and into the tent. I climbed up the steps at the back of the stage, set up the stand and gestured for Moby to pass me the keyboard. But he was miles away, stood at the back of the stage, staring wide-eyed at the thousands of ravers vibrating in front of him, blowing whistles and air horns – a multi-coloured ocean of energy.

I'll never forget his words – 'Oh my God, I've never seen anything like this in my life.'

Five minutes later the diminutive New Yorker started playing and when those spine-tingling strings were heard by the crowd, the whole seething mass in that marquee erupted in a wave of euphoria and noise, a fitting reception for the live debut of an all-time classic.

Firestarters in the tent

As glorified Essex cheesy quavers, the Prodigy were regulars at all of our parties. Paul booked them after seeing them play at the Barn in Braintree one night on the same bill as Slipmatt and had been blown away. So they were added to the line-up of the next event. But even if they weren't playing, they'd be at Jenkins Lane raving, Keith down the front, his ponytail whipping through the air back and forth like an eel on the end of a reel. It may surprise you to hear that, at this time, he wasn't the most rock 'n' roll member of the Prodigy crew. He was a pussycat compared with their manager, Mike Champion. I recall one occasion when I was stage managing. It was the end of the night when Prodigy had just played and he was literally rolling around the stage with a bottle of whisky. Until he rolled off the stage. The stage was around 12 foot high and for a second we were worried. We climbed down and found him fast asleep/unconscious on the grass, still cradling his beloved bottle of Jack Daniel's.

'Will you look at him,' said the security fella who helped me recover him. 'What a fucking mess. What hope have they got with him as their manager? They'll get bloody nowhere.'

RIP Mike Champion (1956–2018) and Keith Flint (1969–2019), firestarters.

GOING LEGIT

The Ravers Charter

By late summer '91 it was a crowded market. Local author-ities were granting licences most weekends and the dance music explosion had reinvigorated the clubs, many of whom possessed 6 a.m. licences. Tickets were slow for our Easter event. It was always the first big outdoor rave of the year and, falling in early April, notoriously weather dependent.

Unlike a few years earlier, Raindance was no longer unique and was struggling to be heard among the compet-ition, many of whom overpromised and underdelivered. A rival rave advertised a hugely popular American DJ who we knew wasn't booked as he was scared of flying. Closing times were often left unspecified ('10 p.m. − 'til late'), allowing them to finish early if their late-licence request wasn't granted. As there was no rave regulatory body or quality control, the cowboys were eroding trust and damaging the scene's reputation.

We needed something to show that we cared. Something to guarantee they'd receive everything they saw on the flyer. But how could we do this? This was my job: to ensure Raindance were always one step ahead of the rest.

That night on the news, the blandest prime minister the UK has ever had rode to my rescue.

John Major announced a British Bill of Rights, which addressed consumer confidence with public services and made administrations accountable. It was called the Citizen's Charter and the press loved it. Looking back, it was the only remotely interesting thing he ever did.

More importantly, it gave me an idea . . .

The next morning in the office at Mallow Street, I presented 'The Ravers Charter', which called on promoters

151

to refund their guests if the experience didn't meet their expectations:

> 'IF WE DON'T PROVIDE ANY ATTRACTION OR ACTS MENTIONED ON THE FLYERS, OR PROVIDE A REASONABLE AND SUITABLE REPLACEMENT, WE WILL GIVE YOU A CASH-BACK GUARANTEE.'

We also invited other promoters to sign up to this, in an attempt to show who had honour and who were the cowboys.

I faxed 'The Ravers Charter' out to the press and the smaller dance fanzines like *Blaze* and *Ravescene*. It was completely ignored by the mainstream media, which just reinforced my frustration. I left the office feeling low and wanted to go home. However, I'd promised my mate Marten I'd attend the opening party of his new Cuban bar, Little Havana, just off Leicester Square.

As I mingled, helping myself to rum cocktails and snacks, I found myself talking to a guy in a sharp suit. He was asking about the rave scene, which Marten had told him I worked in, so I explained how we were trying to inject some much-needed confidence into the scene with my charter.

He loved the idea and handed me his business card. It read:

Rav Singh
Showbiz Reporter
Daily Star

Back of the net!

The next day I went down to the *Star* offices and was chuffed to see the artwork they'd created of a medieval parchment scroll headed 'The Ravers Charter', followed

GOING LEGIT

by our statement in full. It ran over half a page and when it came out the following day, it prompted Radio 1 and Kiss 100 to get in touch. Suddenly Raindance was the name on everyone's lips again – and for the right reasons.

Our next party was rammed, everything advertised was delivered and thanks to John Major, we'd exercised self-regulation and stood up for the ravers, without whom there is no party.

New Year's Eve 1991/92

Back in the early '90s, Kiss 100 was huge. The former pirate radio station had finally received a licence and started broadcasting on 1 September 1990. (Their launch party on Highbury Fields had to be cancelled after 10,000 people turned up.)

In many ways, Kiss was the radio equivalent of Raindance – going legit and flying the flag for the sounds of the streets. Their star presenter was Steve Jackson, whose *House That Jack Built* show was so popular he was awarded a daytime slot. His afternoon-show wind-ups with Streetboy are the stuff of legend: pea-shooting hemp seeds into the plants outside 10 Downing Street and getting arrested for cooking 'McStreet' burgers outside McDonald's in Holloway Road on a camping stove. Steve Jackson was the rave scene's answer to Steve Wright and a huge star. The most recognisable voice in London and a damn good DJ as well. So who better to count down to midnight at the Raindance NYE party?

Now, the trouble with booking an in-demand DJ on New Year's Eve is that they will typically have more than one gig. They'll dash from one to another, often with minutes to spare

153

before their set time. It's all part of the excitement. But when your slot is time sensitive (and they don't come more time sensitive than NYE) . . . things can get a little, erm, interesting.

So imagine the situation: it's half past eleven, the atmosphere is building nicely, conducted by MC Hardcore General with Slipmatt in the booth. But this was Raindance, remember – nothing ever went smoothly. We get a message from the police that Steve Jackson is stuck in the usual Raindance roadblock on the A13 and they are bringing him through.

23.45: the stage manager asks for an update. Steve is 'ten minutes away'. Stage manager tells Timmy Hardcore to prepare to hand the mic to Steve as soon as he sees him.

23.50: nervous glances between crew as radio messages are relayed that Steve is 'five minutes away' and will be definitely be doing the countdown.

23.55: the crowd are reaching fever pitch, air-horns blare and whistles pierce the night; a 3,000-strong choir of ravers waiting to see in the New Year.

23.56: 'Where's Steve?'

23.57: 'WHERE THE FUCK IS STEVE?'

23.58: Ray's on the radio. 'Steve's at the main gate, getting searched, he'll be there in five mins – hold the countdown. Repeat, hold the countdown.' WTF???

23.59.30: Slipmatt cuts the music. MC Hardcore General: 'Alright, Raindance. Hold tight, let's hear ya! Everybody in the house: 10 . . . 9 . . . 8 . . . 7 . . . 6 . . . 5 . . . 4 . . . 3 . . . 2 . . . 1 . . . HAPPY NEW YEAR!!!!'

Everyone goes mad; pyrotechnics explode, smoke machines roar, lasers dart and strobes blink. The music kicks in, hugs are shared, kisses given and everyone is smiling. Then, at just gone five past midnight, a flustered

GOING LEGIT

Steve Jackson reaches the stage, 'Where's the mic?' he asks the stage manager. 'We've done it, Steve – it's gone midnight, it's 1992 – Happy New Year!'

Steve's face drops. 'But it's all agreed – I'm doing the countdown,' he repeats. The stage manager talks to the production office, asking the event director to come to the mainstage asap.

Steve is distraught. He's broken his balls to get to the biggest party in town and missed his big moment. He is visibly upset and things are getting quite emotional. This obviously means a big deal to him and he is clearly gutted.

There follows an intense discussion backstage between Steve, the stage manager and the event director as Slipmatt quizzically look on from the DJ booth. Finally, a solution is agreed; at 00.22 Steve Jackson will do the countdown. All over again.

Matt cut the track, Steve took centre-stage and delivered a truly professional countdown, full of energy and excitement . . . in fact, it was so good that the cheer upon reaching 'One!' was every bit as intense as it was at midnight. I suspect that no one really noticed and, if they did, no one cared.

Not one punter mentioned this to any of the Raindance crew. It was only years later when I was having one of those 'once I was so out of it that . . .' conversations with a raver I'd got talking to in Space in Ibiza that it surfaced. 'I went to that "Raindance" one NYE and I was so off my tits that I swear I counted down at midnight twice! Jeez those pills were strong in those days . . .'

I said nothing.

★

Although located in unfashionable E13, Raindance saw its fair share of curious famous faces swap Park Lane for Jenkins Lane. *EastEnders* and Essex gal Danniella Westbrook was a regular. Chris Lowe from Pet Shop Boys would spend all night in a car parked near the fairground 'talking bollocks' to Zero B. And although the guest list read like a who's who of gangland faces, there would never be any trouble.

Socialite Philip Sallon, whose outrageous approach to clothes would inspire Boy George, once turned up wearing nothing but a bin liner coupled with a bin lorry full of West End attitude. He was refusing to queue as it was raining, ('Philip Sallon doesn't queue!') and tried to break through the security cordon which allowed just one person at a time to move forward to the guest list window. But a security guy grabbed his flowing black plastic toga and Philip slipped and fell headfirst into a huge black puddle. His garlanded locks were a mess of dirty water and mud covered his immaculately made-up face.

He was absolutely furious and glared at the security bloke who was gently picking him up from the ground. 'Don't you know who I am?' he demanded, sludge streaming down his face. 'I run the Mud Club.' Cue laughter from all around. You really couldn't make it up.

TOP TUNE: 'DJs Take Control', SL2

10

TURN ON, TUNE IN, DROP ONE

'It's all a rhythm. Everything is pulsating. The universe and everything within it is an oscillating dance.'

– Dr Timothy Leary

If the '60s was a club, Timothy Leary and Allen Ginsberg were Sasha and Digweed in the '90s: conducting the consciousness of everyone within earshot, redefining the norm, blurring accepted boundaries and taking the whole show to another level.

Dr Timothy Leary was the self-styled 'High Priest of LSD' who claimed to have introduced five million minds to acid – including a college dropout searching for enlightenment in India called Steve Jobs, and a charismatic singer-songwriter called Charlie Manson (who was in the cell next door during one of Leary's many incarcerations).

A hugely influential figure, he coined the hippy mantra 'Turn On, Tune In, Drop Out', he inspired the Beatles to write the songs 'Come Together' and 'Tomorrow Never Knows', and was reportedly described as 'the most dangerous man in America' by President Richard Nixon. It was early September 1990 and I was on a plane on my way to Frankfurt, Germany, to interview him for *Mixmag*.

My mates Richard Norris and Dave Ball's band the Grid had just collaborated with Leary on 'Origins of Dance', which featured the good doctor espousing nuggets of cosmic wisdom – 'Think for yourself and question authority' – and explaining the root of dancing lay in elevating consciousness (something I'd been aware of since my 'Sunrise revelation' and was eager to explore and write about) over a lo-fi soundtrack of bleeps and bass.

I'd persuaded *Mixmag* to give me three pages on what I believed was the first 'counter cultural' collaboration betwixt the hippy and acid house eras. I was looking forward to talking to him about the orbital rave phenomenon, his current research into space migration, intelligence increase, life extension, and a belief that computers were the new psychedelic tool. Leary was in Frankfurt to deliver a lecture on emerging technologies and the cyber world. He was regarded by some as a cult hero, a survivor of more than thirty-six different prison cells and five marriages, and was celebrated as an elder statesman of mind-altering substances, much as Howard Marks would be a decade later.

Having been refused an entry visa by the UK Home Office on the grounds that a frail 72-year-old man was 'a threat to public order', his vocals were laid down in Café Largo in LA and recorded as they were played down the phone to Dave Ball (who had 'previous' in this area – having recorded Great Train Robber and part-time Sex Pistol Ronnie Biggs' vocals in a similar way the previous year, for a 12-inch release to promote the *Prisoner of Rio* film).

A few hours later I sat in my bland hotel room preparing my questions. I would be meeting Dr Leary for dinner, an arrangement made by Evolution label boss and mutual friend, Fraser Clark. I was to meet Leary in a small restaurant called Asia. I arrived a little early and waited in the bar area for my guest to arrive. And waited. And waited some more.

Maybe I'd got the time wrong? I decided to wait until 9 p.m. just in case, after which I left my hotel and room number with the maitre d', should Dr Leary turn up. As I foolishly had no contact details for my interviewee, I called Fraser in London from a payphone across the street. He told me he'd been trying to reach me via *Mixmag*, who in turn had been calling my housemate in Bounds Green to pass on a message, should I call from Germany.

Fraser told me the tragic news that Leary's daughter had been found dead that morning, having hung herself in a police cell where she was awaiting trial for shooting her boyfriend. Upon hearing the news, her father had immediately flown back to Los Angeles.

★

I finally managed to catch up with the great man in Amsterdam a month or so later at another of his lectures. In it he explained how he'd revised his 'Turn On, Tune In, Drop Out' mantra in favour of 'Turn On, Boot Up, Jack In' as he believed that the 'PC is the LSD of the 1990s'.

After I'd introduced myself I asked him if he'd like to listen to the recently finished master of 'The Origins of Dance' on my Sony Walkman. He led me by the arm and through the crowd and found a seat in a quiet corner of the room. He sat down and listened intensely, his head between his hands, cupping the cheap fuzzy felt headphones. The tell-tale 'tic-a-tic-a-tic' of the hi-hat spilled out, his left leg now tapping on the floor. A few bars later, his fist banged his thigh in synchronicity with the kick drum. He looked up as a grin broke out across the width of his angular jaw.

I asked him if he was aware of the acid house phenomenon and what he knew about the huge orbital raves of the previous summer.

'I read about them in the papers, all the roadblocks and press hysteria. My friends in London kept me up to speed.'

Was he surprised at the scale of the parties?

'It didn't surprise me that they happened, only that it took so long.'

His blue eyes sparkled with the reward of stumbling across a forgotten memory.

'I love dancing! It was originally a psychedelic way of expressing yourself, a way of getting high. Moving your body can stimulate your inner energies, synchronise your ancient cellular patterns ... and become a wild, ecstatic turn-on!'

He'd previously stated that the sensory elements of a rave were in themselves catalysts of consciousness-raising. 'By simply using lights, combinations of sound and the stroboscope, we can get the marijuana effect, the mescaline effect and the LSD effect.'

I then asked him if he felt any guilt when hearing about acid casualties and deaths resulting from people he'd 'turned on' experimenting with LSD. As an ecstasy evangelist, I was interested in his answer. I had introduced many of my friends to ecstasy, genuinely believing it was a positive process. (It was never driven by profit and although the opportunity presented itself on many occasions in my thirty years in clubbing, I never chose to go down that path.)

'It's accepted that there's inevitably going to be casualties in the exploration of outer space. Likewise with the exploration of inner space. I hope and believe that the greater benefits justify the tragic loss of life. Lemme hear my track again!'

Timothy Leary never did set foot in the UK and died in 1996, surrounded by friends who supplied him with nitrous oxide balloons and his favourite snack, 'Leary Biscuits' – Ritz crackers microwaved with cheese and a bud of pot. His death was subject to a film, *Timothy Leary's Dead*, which shows his head being removed and stored cryogenically in ice. Some of his ashes were sent into space, where they orbited the Earth for ten years. His last words were, 'Why not? . . . Beautiful!' As in life, Timothy Leary was never boring.

Afterglow

As I write this, the *New York Times* reports that a phase 3 clinical trial of MDMA-assisted therapy has shown promising results, potentially marking a crucial step forward on the drug's path to FDA approval.

In spring 2021, the UK's first provider of psychedelic-assisted psychotherapy available to the public opened in

Bristol, and later that year an associate professor of neuroscience at Johns Hopkins University in Baltimore, Maryland, published her discovery from lab experiments that MDMA opens up critical thinking periods and recreates a childlike state of mind to promote mental healing.

Leary's predictions that licences would be issued to grow and use marijuana and a belief that psychedelics possess psychological health benefits were both spot on. As for his claim that computers were the new drug, how's your relationship with your phone?

> **TOP TUNE: 'Origins of Dance',
> Dr Timothy Leary Meets The Grid**

11

THE HILLS ARE ALIVE (WITH THE SOUND OF BASS)

It had to happen. This winter, along with snow, UK club culture will also descend on the Alps. As the hills come alive to the sound of house, après ski no longer means mulled wine around the fire. Mixmag's raving reporter KIRK FIELD straps on his Atomic 195s to bring you the definitive guide to raving on snow . . .

This was the very first account of a phenomena I was involved in and helped shape for the next twenty-five years: clubbing in the snow.

First, some background. I spent successive winters working as a singer and DJ in an Austrian ski resort in 1987 and 1988. Alpine resorts in those days were fantastic places to hide, surrounded by high mountains and sometimes cut off for days from the outside world. In a blissful existence without daily papers, the internet or mobile phones, it was possible to live a simple life which consisted of skiing, drinking and playing music to British, Swedish and Dutch holidaymakers. Those winters are among the happiest times of my life. I had virtually no money and lived day-to-day, dependent on fine weather for mountain-top gigs. But what I did possess was comradeship, access to endless skiing, and a job I loved doing.

It was the start of a long love affair with mountains, snow and having fun with gravity which has lasted more than thirty years. But the next time I returned to the Alps, I wasn't driven by rock 'n' roll but seeking refuge from a war . . .

When the Gulf War broke out in early 1991, there was an anti-war movement that the Evolution collective supported. A fund-raising show took place at the Brixton Fridge venue on Thursday, 17 January headlined by the Shamen, and at extremely short notice I was asked to stage manage it – the guy who was supposed to had dropped acid and was clucking like a chicken around the backstage area, clearly unable to work. This meant changing my plans. I was road-testing a new range of cosmetic products designed for clubbers for *Mixmag*, and hadn't planned on going to the Fridge. Frankly, the whole 'Saddam thing' was getting me down.

1 a.m.

All was going well. Over a thousand were packed in and I went to the box office to check my guests had got in okay. The foyer in the Fridge had a bank of television screens mounted into the wall, and as I walked past I suddenly froze. The multi-screened wall showed missile after missile launching and darting through a night sky, before cutting to explosions across a city captioned 'Baghdad'.

War had broken out and people were being obliterated live on CNN. This was how the air campaign for 'Operation

Desert Storm' began. We stood there dumbfounded. A girl walked past in a MAKE LOVE NOT WAR T-shirt, which was covered in sweat from dancing and clung to her like clingfilm. Above me, a buzzcut US general read a statement about how many missiles had been launched in the last hour and a useful graphic flashed up. Our campaign had failed. They hadn't listened to the people's protests. They never do.

I was deflated but had a job to do. I went to the dressing room to give the band a ten-minute warning before they were due onstage. I knocked and received no answer. This wasn't unusual as they were located right behind the speaker and DJ Harvey from the Tonka crew was at full tilt, with bannisters and windows rattling with each throb of the kick drum. Slowly I opened the door and peered around. 'Ten minutes, fellas.'

The band's founder and frontman Colin Angus was sat before me, head in his hands. 'Colin . . . are you okay? You already know then?'

'Aye, I've just been watching it in the foyer . . .'

He raised his head, and I could see tears streaming down his cheeks.

He looked at me. 'Why are you orange?'

'Orange?'

'Your face is orange.'

'Oh, this! I was sent some fake tan to review for *Mixmag* earlier and am in the process of testing how it handles in a sweaty club.'

After the gig, we sat in the dressing room, despondent and depressed. A former ally of the west, Saddam Hussein was now the big bad wolf. Literally the world's most wanted man with a $25 million reward on his head. I wanted to get as far away from the non-stop TV coverage of him and the Gulf War as possible.

There was a recession at the time and midweek clubs were closing. January is always a quiet time in clubland after the excess of Christmas and New Year's Eve, and back then a lot of London club promoters and DJs would disappear to Thailand. But my budget didn't stretch to that. There was one possible escape route, however . . . my Swiss girlfriend Regina had recently taken a job as a sous chef in the kitchen of a big hotel in Zermatt and had an apartment in the basement to herself.

So, without sleeping, I bought a plane ticket, packed a suitcase and caught the next flight out of Heathrow to Zurich.

I took the train through Switzerland and arrived at Zermatt station to a steady snowfall. I was shocked to discover no cars or buses were allowed in the village, only horse-drawn sleighs and small electric taxis which looked like milk floats. This was revolutionary at the time and gave the place a 'Wild West' frontier town feel, which was only reinforced by a succession of old dark wooden chalets on stilts that I walked past, dragging my heavy suitcase through the snow.

Around me was the smell of woodfires mingled with the spicy aroma of glühwein from a stall on the street. The sleigh bells jingled as they delivered well-heeled, fur-hatted rich Russians to their hotels, their laps covered with blankets and their 'wives' snuggling up to them as they slid by. I arrived at the imposing Zermatterhof Hotel and went inside to wait at the lobby bar for Regina to finish her shift.

A lounge piano tinkled as waiters efficiently moved between the tables of middle-aged, moneyed European hoi polloi. As I sat nursing a three-Swiss-franc coffee, my eyes were drawn to a group of businessmen in black suits standing at the bar in silence. They were the only ones not wearing ski gear, drinking alcohol or laughing and smiling. They were clearly not on holiday. Perhaps it was a business seminar or something, I thought. They all had the same short hairstyles and build, appearing somewhat twitchy. My imagination began to work overtime. Perhaps they were Mormons or from a religious cult? One of the men saw me looking and stared back at me, confrontationally. Instinctively I looked away. Then after a few seconds, returned my glance. His gaze hadn't shifted. He still stared at me, weighing me up. I was considerably younger and more scruffily dressed than everyone else in there, and my appearance was that of someone not rich enough to drink in a luxury 5-star hotel, let alone stay in one. My black leather jacket and green combat trousers were accessorised with a red and white shemagh neck scarf, a Christmas gift from an Israeli girl I knew in London.

It was now dark outside; the gently falling snow was illuminated in the orange glow of the exterior lights, millions of tiny fireflies descending to earth. Dragging the heavy case through the snow had triggered my carpal tunnel syndrome, causing me to cradle my right hand in my left like I was in prayer. I closed my eyes, finally able to relax for the first time in over twenty-four hours. Suddenly I felt my rucksack being snatched from my knee.

'Passport please, sir.' An assured American accent invaded my dusk dreaming. Somewhat startled, I looked up to see I was surrounded by the four men, one of whom had his hand inside his left breast pocket. A bulge indicated he wasn't holding a cigarette lighter. He remained in this position throughout the next ten minutes, looking like Napoleon in a nylon suit.

Naturally, every other customer in the place gawped at this scene, with expressions of intrigue turning to concern as it developed. I instinctively reached into my jacket pocket but was prevented from doing so by one of the men who grabbed my arm, 'It's okay, sir, we'll help you with that.' I could see a wire leading from his shirt pocket to his left ear, which appeared to contain a small flesh-coloured hearing aid.

My rucksack had been taken from me and now my pocket was being picked by a complete stranger in broad daylight, and people looked at me like *I* was the criminal!

The men exuded confidence and oozed power. Upon meeting their gaze, the hotel staff turned their heads, and even the burly doorman in his heavy grey trench coat and peaked cap took a stroll outside through the revolving door.

My rucksack and passport were carefully handed to another man, who walked away with them. This was too much; I tried to stand but was pushed back down again into my chair.

'Just running a few enquiries, sir. All being well, you'll have your belongings back by the time you finish your coffee.'

A waiter nervously plonked down a tray of coffees. One man took a seat while 'Napoleon' moved behind me. I could feel his stare as it burnt the back of my head like a wanton boy's magnifying glass in summer torturing an insect. The man at the table gestured to the coffee and offered me a cigarette from a silver cigarette box in a move straight from the movies.

They were obviously slipping into good cop/bad cop roles.

'No thanks, I don't smoke.'

That's it! They're undercover police. I was relieved that they weren't gangsters or hired contract killers hiding out in the Alps.

'Are you the police?'

'We'll ask the questions.'

Jesus, this is *a movie,* I thought.

'All you need to know is that we are law enforcement officers, and we strongly urge you to cooperate. You carry a British passport. We'll discover shortly if it checks out. In the meantime, please tell us what you're doing here, so far from the warmth of home . . . with no skis?'

The warmth of home? He clearly had never experienced the joy that is north London in January.

'I'm here to visit my girlfriend, she works here as a chef.'

Without hesitation he fired back, 'Her name, please.' This was immediately scrawled with an expensive Parker pen into a small notebook.

He took an interest in my left hand, studying it, before moving his glance up to my face, then down to my right hand, which held the coffee cup. He slowly said the words 'Regina R-E-G-I-N-A Romang R-O-M-A-N-G' into a pin badge on his left label. He paused for a few seconds, before nodding. I could just see he also wore an earpiece in his left ear. He looked at me and smiled benignly, prior to muttering into his lapel, 'Understood.'

After a nod to Napoleon behind me, his manner changed noticeably. 'Sir, your passport and rucksack will be returned and you are free to leave. Enjoy your holiday. Oh, the coffee is on us.'

Moments later the man returned and reunited me with my belongings.

I replaced my passport in my pocket and saw Regina waving to me from the front door, still dressed in her chef's apron and hat.

Over the next few days, I saw more and more Americans in the high street, stood in doorways, sat in cafés and generally hanging round. I avoided the Zermatterhof Hotel bar and went instead to the Papperla Pub, where I got talking to some posh British ski bums who invited me back to their flat for a beer. During the conversation, I casually mentioned how expensive Zermatt was compared with Mayrhofen in Austria.

One rich boy scoffed, 'Switzerland is high end: premium resorts, premium powder. Everyone knows that. Why choose to ski here and then moan about the prices?'

I explained I could stay rent-free in a basement in the Zermatterhof and it was not so much a case of running to but running from the stress of the war – and getting away from people talking about Saddam Bloody Hussein.

On hearing this they glanced at one another and burst out laughing. Their guffaws became hysterical as they exchanged semi-drunk directives.

'Are you going to tell him?'

'No, you tell him.'

'I haven't the heart.'

'Go on . . .'

One of them paused from waxing his skis and composed himself, before collapsing into a high-pitched 'strangled hyena' posh laugh once again.

I'd had enough of their fucking around, so grabbed my leather jacket and made for the door. Much as I had no one to knock around with when Regina was at work, I wasn't desperate enough to be the butt of the jokes for piss-taking posh boys.

'Wait – before you go' – clearing his throat, he assumed a serious tone – 'it's our solemn duty to inform you that your valiant attempt to escape the stress of the war, and in particular, Saddam Hussein, is in vain, dear chap.'

With my hand already on the door handle and my back to them, I asked them what the hell made them so sure.

'Well, because his wife is staying beneath the same roof as you!'

I spun around.

'We have it on good authority that Sajida Hussein and her family fled from Baghdad and are in hiding here. The authorities know of course, there are secret service agents everywhere, protecting them. The place is crawling with trigger-happy CIA agents. They're very nervous that Saddam may try to kill her, before she spills the beans, like he did her brother a few years ago in a helicopter explosion.'

It all made sense. I'd rocked up unshaven, plastered in fake tan and with a tablecloth around my neck, looking like I'd come straight from Baghdad. And rather than avoiding the war, I wound up sleeping under the same roof as Saddam Hussein's missus.

One day at the ice rink, a middle-aged man sat down and began to read *The Times*. My hopes rose. If he's English, we could talk about the football and how bloody expensive everything was here, I thought.

A few minutes later, he was joined by a thin blonde lady who handed him a warm drink. As they spoke, I thought

I recognised a voice which was distinctively thin and quite high for a man. There was undulating background noise from skaters on the ice, but in quieter moments I could hear the odd word: 'Mike . . . the album . . . tour schedule'. He was a musician! Then the penny dropped. Phil Collins! Phil Bloody Collins!

Who'd just bought a house in . . . Zermatt.

I saw him a few times around town with his wife, or alone at the ice rink. Should I say hello? This was my chance to chat about the football, the local beer, the bloody war if I must, with a fellow countryman. It wouldn't hurt to pass the time of day with him, would it? I needn't even let on I know who he is. I was hardly spoilt for choice and in a position to choose my company. 'Any port in a storm' and all that.

But despite having no one to talk to all day long, and desperately in need of company, deep down I knew that I would feel like a fraud after everything I'd said about him over the years. And so, I chose solitude over Phil Collins. He's probably a decent chap, but that would only have made things worse. We may have got on like a house on fire and become great mates and I'd be writing this wearing a Genesis T-shirt. But there's no place for revisionism in revolutions, and isolation is infinitely preferable to insincerity.

The winter Ibiza

I knew that despite the sun being no hotter or the sky bluer in Ibiza than it was in neighbouring Mallorca, when it came to clubbers choosing where to spend their summer holiday, Ibiza would always win hands down (or in the air, to be more accurate). I felt it only a matter of time before skiers and snowboarders would similarly select their winter holiday destination based on the quality of music and venues in a resort.

Having spent two winters as a singer and DJ in the lively Austrian resort of Mayrhofen, I had witnessed first-hand the energy and exuberance of partying surrounded by mountains and how après ski was, for many, as important as 'ski'.

But when the familiar face of my former boss had appeared at the guest list window of Raindance's 'Indian Summer' party the previous autumn before my winter in Zermatt, I was still gobsmacked.

Hotelier Erich Roscher was in town to check on this new youth culture and what he saw that night convinced him to build a venue beneath his car park. It would be the first club in Austria to showcase house music and host the next generation of superstar DJs and acts. As he told me at the time, 'Clubbing is massive and impossible to ignore – and will define the next decade. They rave in England and want to rave on holiday, at the Arena they can do this every night!'

Erich invited me to come and see his vision: a split-level, state-of-the-art 1,500-capacity subterranean superclub in the snow. Roman pillars framed a central staircase which led to the dancefloor. With bars in each corner, a VIP cocktail bar above the stage, and a DJ booth boasting more technology than the bridge of the starship *Enterprise*, the Arena was to alpine raving what the Grand Ole Opry was to country music. My subsequent *Mixmag* piece on this clubbing revolution led to interest from *The Word*, the anarchic youth TV show – hugely popular at the time – going out live every Friday evening on Channel 4.

It's the day of the club's opening and I'm in a cable car with John Digweed, Crescendo's Jon Crosse, Guru Josh and Altern-8's robot. The robot is on stilts and the locals' eyes are on stalks.

Every artist who comes out gets free ski lessons – it was the clincher for Diggers, who is dressed in jeans, a leather jacket and no gloves. Over the years, I count myself lucky enough to have skied with everyone from Eddie the Eagle to John Bishop, from Skrillex to Hot Chocolate, and from Pat Sharp to the Prodigy. But to this day, John Digweed remains the only one who ever wore denim!

Guru Josh had blagged a one-piece ski suit from Erich the night before but insisted on rolling up the sleeves to his elbow in a Don Johnson/*Miami Vice* style. A few hours later Josh was interviewed while milking a goat outside the Scotland Yard Pub, live on Channel 4 to an audience of millions.

The Arena's first season was a huge success, with a different show every week gleamed from my list of contacts in London. Dancers from the Hippodrome, angle-grinding fire breathers from the Camden Palace, and chart-busting stars like Maxine Harvey who sang on some of the KLF hits. I remained in Austria, and worked as artist liaison for the club, picking the acts up from Munich Airport and looking after them for the duration of their visit, which would usually involve taking them skiing.

The climax of the debut season was the closing party with Boy George's band Jesus Loves You headlining. Their fusion of electronic dance music, traditional Eastern music and Western pop was happening. 'Generations of Love' was a massive Balearic anthem. The artist Eve Gallagher was on George's own record label More Protein and was living in Switzerland at the time. As her single 'Love Come Down' was also blowing up, she jumped on the train and joined the fun.

I'd booked George through his close friend, Andria Law, just before he signed with a very powerful player in the dance music world. When George's record label in Vienna heard that their most famous artist was finally bringing his exciting new band to Austria – but playing in a tiny village in the mountains – they went berserk, calling up his manager at the time and asking him why he was allowing George to play in a 'cow shed in the middle of nowhere'.

George's new manager called me up and told me that the show was off, and that if George was to play in Austria, it would be in a club in Vienna, not a barn in the middle of the mountains that no one had ever heard of. He was then somewhat rude to me, telling me that the money we were paying George was an insult and that he didn't get out of bed for less than £12,000.

The flights were already booked, the promotion was out, and all tickets had been sold. We were only five days away from the show. I had to think fast. I asked Andria what was happening. She called up George. George called me and asked if the venue was kosher. I told him it was – and that we couldn't let MTV down.

'MTV? No one told me it was being filmed by MTV. This is great for More Protein! I'll call Andria now.'

Andria then called me and told me the show was on, and that the MTV thing made up for the low fee.

I immediately called up Erich and asked him if he'd cover the cost of an MTV crew coming out to cover his big night. An astute man, who understood the value of the media, he of course agreed – it *was* pan-European promotion for his club and hotel after all. So I had the show, an interesting location and a budget. I just needed to get MTV onboard.

In the event, I knew this would be fairly straightforward as my raving buddy Simone also happened to be an MTV presenter. I'd met James Hyman her producer at Tom Watkins' Atomic Records launch party. I put a fax together outlining the proposal, and by noon the next day MTV were onboard. It really was that easy in those days.

George has gone through many phases in his career. His image has changed every few years, as has his consumption/ abstinence of illegal substances. In April 1993, when he came out to Mayrhofen, he was in his Buddhist phase with a shaved head, face paint on his forehead and a super-strict vegan diet.

Tyrolean food is very basic. It derives from a time when no fresh food was available throughout the snow-covered winter months and is loaded with energy-giving carbs for manual labour. So there's a reliance on high-energy dishes featuring preserved smoked meats, fermented cabbage and dried sausages. This meant George went hungry and was left walking up and down the high street fruitlessly looking for a health food shop, which in the early '90s in the Alps were non-existent.

Whenever an artist visited Mayrhofen, they would usually ask to go skiing or snowboarding, or use the opportunity to learn. George had a different request. He had a fantasy of being taken around the mountain on a skidoo being ridden by a hunky blond ski instructor. So naturally I obliged and lined up a tanned hunk called Andi, whose 400cc snow bike George straddled, before accelerating away across the snow, his arms around the waist of a very nervous-looking Andi.

Half an hour later we were sat in a mountain restaurant with George and Eve. For those non-skiers reading this, Austrian mountain restaurants are owned and run by the farmer and his family, who are more useful with ploughs than paprika, and so the menu is pretty basic and more 'Motorway Services 1970' as opposed to Michelin-starred.

George was aghast to find everything contained meat. 'Even the pea soup has got fuckin' meat in it!' he complained. Which was somewhat true, as you could order the green broth with pieces of frankfurter floating around in it, like menacing shark fins. But despite my reassurances that *ohne fleisch* was a valid vegetarian option, he still insisted on the chef confirming this. So a portly red-faced Austrian fella poked his head out of the kitchen, waved his steel ladle to catch George's attention and shouted the words, '*ohne fleisch*'.

Upon the said dish's arrival, he sifted through the bowl with his spoon like an ever-hopeful gold prospector, prior to finally taking a spoon to his mouth. Everyone around the table finally relaxed and also began tucking into their lunch. Suddenly the air was filled by the sharp crack of steel on porcelain as George dropped his spoon and let out a blood-curdling scream. He stood up, mouth wide open, and pointed to his mouth in utter horror. I leant towards him and could see a piece of cured meat wedged between his two front teeth. Without stopping to think, I plucked the offending offal from his mouth, wrapped it in a serviette and said cheekily, 'Oh, do sit down, George. I'm sure it's not the first bit of gristle to pass your lips.'

The following night, I'd arranged for George to meet the famous climbers Reinhold Messner and Peter Habeler – the first men to climb Everest without oxygen. Both were good-looking, rugged mountain men and

George swooned when Messner walked in. I was looking forward to hearing first-hand what it's like to stand on top of the world, but his tales of derring-do appeared disjointed and he kept losing concentration, which was a little disappointing. The next day I found out why this was. Apparently, George was playing footsie with him under the table throughout dinner!

The show was a great success, and the Arena went on to host more legends of dance music than any other club in Austria. Not bad for a 'cowshed in the middle of nowhere'.

> **TOP TUNE: 'Spiritual High (State of Independence', Moodswings**

12

LOVE OF LOSS

In October 1990, the city of Coventry made dance music history – again.

A decade on from when Jerry Dammers' 2 Tone Records label fuelled the first multi-racial working-class dance music explosion, the 'motor city' was once again at the forefront of youth culture when it hosted the first weekly, legal all-night rave in a city centre club. It was called the Eclipse.

Within a few weeks, this former bingo hall on Lower Ford Street had the crowd excitedly shouting, 'House!' once again at what had rapidly become the epicentre of the UK rave scene.

Stuart Reid and Baz Edwards[7] had followed the M25 orbital party organisers' ploy of selling tickets to 'members' only and avoided the sale of alcohol (which required a

---

[7] Together with Raindance's Ray Spence and Paul Nelson, Stuart and Baz kept the strobe flashing throughout 1990 and deserve to be inducted into The Rave Hall of Fame as torch bearers who carried the flame during a period of darkness.

separate licence). As a result, a seething Coventry City Council were powerless to prevent the parties from happening. It was game on.

In June 1991, I formed my first club promotion, 'Fusion', with Adam P and Richard M. I was responsible for the concept, line-up, press and PR – while Adam handled all aspects of production, leaving Richard to run the financial side of things. It was a strong team with people I knew well and trusted. We weren't to know it at the time, but our first party would hold a special place in rave folklore . . .

> *'OUR TEAM HAVE WORKED ON MOST LARGE-SCALE OUTDOOR RAVES SINCE APRIL 1989. ALL THE TIME WE HAVE BEEN LEARNING. NOW IT'S TIME TO UNLEASH OUR IDEAS . . .'*
>
> – Solstice flyer

I approached the Eclipse and was offered Friday, 21 June, which I was well aware was the summer solstice. This gave me an idea for a theme. Stonehenge was controversially sealed off to the public at midsummer, challenged vociferously by pagans who regard the stones as a sacred site. Druids in particular feel the site is a place of worship and regard it as a temple rather than an ancient antiquity. So what better time to recreate Stonehenge in the middle of Coventry? I decided to invite some of my Druid mates down to perform a ceremony at the precise moment of the sunrise. Nestling under D in my telephone book was Tim Sebastian, leader of the Ancient Order of Druids, who I'd met briefly in Primrose Hill at the autumn equinox ceremony the previous September. As they were denied access to the actual stones by the High Court, my idea of

them celebrating the rising sun at a rave in Coventry was
something which appealed to Tim.

Together with the help of designer Daz Jamieson we
made a dozen long screens which were suspended above
and around the dancefloor (which were perfectly aligned
to the sunrise, replicating the position of the ones on
Salisbury Plain). Onto each screen was beamed an individual image of one of the dolmens, creating the spectacle
of a dancefloor surrounded by a huge stone circle . . . a
rave replica of Great Britain's number-one visitor attraction
except with a smoke machine, a strobe and a laser. Adam
and Daz did a top job and it's no surprise that they both
went on to enjoy successful careers conceiving and delivering top-end events all over the world for some of the
biggest events and brands.

I had a 2K artist budget and spent it thus: Laurent
Garnier, Sasha, Nipper, Dave Seaman, Richie Malone
(Xpansions), the Invasion DJ Team from my home town
of Barrow-in-Furness, with special guest Alex Paterson (the
Orb). It was a strong line-up and represented quite a finan-
cial risk for us, but as nowhere else could get a licence,
there was no competition. It was too good to be true.
Because it wasn't.

Perception announced they'd secured Milton Keynes
Bowl and advertised the 'biggest ever line-up in the UK'
for their 'A Midsummer's Day Dream' event that was
to take place on the same weekend. When I saw their
flyer, I wept. It read like a who's who of the UK dance
music scene.

All acts confirmed: 808 State, the Shamen, the High,
Nomad, N-Joi, Candyland, Gary Clail, Stevie V, Coldcut,
Evolution, Flowered Up, Ruthless Rap Assassins, Paris

Angels, Dream Frequency, PKA, Shades of Rhythm, Sasha, Paul Oakenfold, Mike Pickering, Graeme Park and to (big) top it all off, 'amazing alternative circus acts'. This was to be an era-defining event. One to tell your kids about. Even Radio 1 were covering it with their new dance music presenter, Pete Tong.

Suddenly our pretend Stonehenge and a few disappointed Druids didn't look all that appealing. But we were committed financially and many of those DJs playing were my mates, so I couldn't let them down, or for that matter the ravers who had already bought tickets.

As the weekend approached, the skies remained grey and the rain continued to fall every day in June. Rumours reached us from some staging companies that they were unable to get on site at Milton Keynes as the ground was too soft.

Was the Perception show in doubt?

For the first time in my life, I religiously watched the weather forecast. The outlook predicted it would rain heavily in the Midlands every day until Friday, 21 June. As this was the day before the Perception show, there wasn't adequate time for the ground to dry out. Armed with this knowledge, we upped our promo and incentivised our network of ticket sellers by increasing their commission for any tickets sold after any cancellation by Perception.

The days before the show there was so much confusion and conflicting reports regarding the Milton Keynes event. It was definitely on, it was off, it had been moved, it was postponed. No, it's definitely happening. It was exhausting to the degree that we had to block it out and simply focus on our own show. This was a good lesson. There will always be competition and if your concept is successful, it will provoke inferior imitations. The best way to maintain your position is to keep on doing what you do, don't be distracted by the others and up your game even more. Ensure you remain not just the first, but also the best. Just because you thought of doing something in a certain way before anyone else doesn't give you a right to exclusivity. But it does give you a head start . . . and a database.

Totally stoned

The night built steadily from the doors opening and by midnight we had around a thousand in – our breakeven point. Arrivals tailed off and we thought that was it. But then around half past one I was called to the door. Hundreds of people were arriving, all without tickets. At the eleventh hour what was set to be the World's Biggest Ever Dance Party was cancelled as the site wasn't deemed usable after weeks of rain. While this was unfortunate for the scene as a whole, it meant Solstice was the only all-night party happening in the Midlands. Some even presented Perception tickets, saying they'd been told they were valid!

Alex started to play 'A Huge Ever Growing Pulsating Brain That Rules from the Centre of the Ultraworld' as the Druids in their regalia took to the stage.

Richard and his girlfriend Marianne were hand-fasted (pagan marriage ceremony) and after completing his cere-monial duties, Tim Sebastian, leader of the Secular Order of Druids, stayed until the end and presented us with a sacred oak sapling; symbolic of the acorns that John Lennon and Yoko Ono planted in nearby Coventry Cathedral in 1968 (but which were stolen by Beatles fans).

RAVE NEW WORLD

After the ceremony, I told Alex that Dave Seaman was to play. Although I'd told Alex he was only there to play for the duration of the Druids section of the show, he'd forgotten and was incredulous and perhaps concerned we wouldn't be paying him in full. Although I reassured him we would, he couldn't quite believe it.

'You're going to give me £150 just for playing one record?' he asked, part in disbelief and part disappointment at being taken off.

I put my arm around his shoulder reassuringly and gently led him away . . .

'But, Alex, *what* a record . . .'

That night went down in the annals of rave history. People still talk about it thirty years on, and it's mentioned in any accounts of the Eclipse. More importantly, it gave the Druids an opportunity to mark the most important date in the solar calendar. The longest day and the shortest night.

In the event, Sasha and Laurent Garnier didn't show and were replaced by Dave Ralph, who played the best set of the night. Which is saying something as the music that night was top-quality.

A night on the (rep)tiles

As we didn't lose money and even made a small profit, we decided to do another party at the Eclipse under the 'Fusion' banner. This time it was Adam's turn to choose the theme and he came up with a concept called 'Garden of Eden', after getting his hands on lots of scenery from a mate at a film studio. So once again we set about transforming downtown Coventry into something else: a lush, tropical garden with trees, boulders and projections of waterfalls.

The line-up was imaginative and eclectic (all my DJ mates, basically): the Face, Colin Faver, JD (John Digweed), Richie Malone (Xpansions) and a couple of Raindance DJs. Live PAs included Neutron 9000 and Geoff, another raving buddy also known as Cobalt Stargazer from the heavy metal band, Zodiac Mindwarp and the Love Reaction. For good measure, we brought in Raindance's MC Hardcore General. Extra elements included live percussion from Beathead Percussion featuring the two Terrys – Neale and President – plus belly dancers.[8]

But this was three months down the line and as the summer progressed, more councils were granting all-night licences. Consequently, as the day of the party dawned, ticket sales were alarmingly low. We were disappearing in a sea of parties and looking at a big loss.

'Press and PR is your area, think of something,' said Adam.

'It's your daft bloody theme. What do you want me to do, get Alan Titchmarsh in as a special guest?'

I was annoyed as I'd wanted to continue the celestial theme and call the party 'Equinox'.

'It's the Garden of Eden, not a garden in Evesham. Maybe we can advertise that we're giving out free apples?'

Suddenly I had it. I wrote a quick fax in the Eclipse's office and spent the next thirty minutes following it up on the phone. I spoke to every radio station in the Midlands, both the BBC and regional commercial stations. I figured what I was asking was perfect for those chatty afternoon shows.

I said nothing to my business partners or the venue, in case it didn't come off.

---

[8] The flyer also stated Moby would be appearing, but at the last minute he couldn't get a work permit, as I recall.

Presenter: 'It's coming up to 2.40 on a Friday afternoon. Dear listeners, you are not going to Adam and Eve this next link! As you know, we like nothing more than helping people on this show. So when we received a rather unusual request from a rave party organiser asking for our help, we told him, "Of course."

'Tonight's Garden of Eden party at the Coventry Eclipse on Lower Ford Street has a line-up which includes a wealth of top DJs, a multi-colour laser, and they've turned the venue into a tropical garden with trees, boulders and even a waterfall [okay, I was over-egging the pudding, but the men's toilets on the second floor *always* overflowed, so it was kind of true . . .]. But the guys are missing one essential item. See if you can guess what it is? The winner gets two tickets for tonight's show. Here's Rick Astley with "Never Gonna Give You Up" . . .'

The song ended and Jean from Leamington Spa called in, suggesting it was a fig leaf. 'Very good, Jean, but incorrect.'

Annabel from Radford asked if it was a spare rib, which went right over the presenter's head. Then Dennis from Walsgrave correctly guessed it was a serpent.

'That's right, Dennis! You're on your way to the Garden of Eden. Are you a bit of a raver yourself?'

'Not really,' came the disinterested reply. 'I'm a pastor at the Coventry Bible College. I want people to remember that the serpent represents temptation but that ultimately, the choice to sin is ours. We DO have a choice and . . .'

'Err, thanks for that, Dennis. Now then, if you're a custodian of a cobra or partial to the odd python or two and want to earn a few bob, take your slimy friend along to the Eclipse tonight at 10 p.m. and save the rave. Ooh, that's got a nice ring to it, hasn't it? Save the rave! Here's Duran, Duran with "Union of the Snake" . . .'

Result! This was brilliant promotion. The venue, theme and line-up were all mentioned and what's more, it didn't cost us a penny!

I shared the good news with Richard and Adam, who agreed it was genius. I thought it best not to mention anything to the venue. It was highly unlikely anyone would turn up at 11 p.m. on a Friday night with a snake. Or so I thought . . .

It was 11 p.m. and I was chatting with Dave Seaman, who'd just arrived.

'Kirk to front door. Kirk to front door IMMEDIATELY.' My radio headset, usually hard to hear over the noise of the party, was very audible indeed.

I walked down the crowded staircase, past sweat-soaked, gum-chewing ravers and reached the front door. A huge security man was comatose and being attended to by the in-house first aid team.

'What happened?'

One of the managers of the club, who was kneeling at the guy's side, raised his head and glared. 'Big Ken's got a thing about snakes.'

He pointed to the door. I walked outside and all down one side of the building was an orderly queue . . . of pythons. Some held by bald blokes with large earrings, others cradled by attractive middle-aged women. One was curled around a goth's neck and another flirted with tongues with a huge black mamba that was being supported by a couple with facial tattoos.

The manager dragged me back inside. He was incandescent with rage.

RAVE NEW WORLD

'Are you responsible for this? They're saying the radio asked them to come down tonight 'cos the promoter wanted a snake and was willing to pay £50.'

I swallowed hard and muttered something about it being free promotion for his venue.

'Get rid of 'em all. NOW!'

Methodically, I moved down the line of serpents, thanking them for coming, complimenting their forked-tongue friends and giving them each a tenner for their trouble.

We were never asked back, but that night I learnt one of the first principles of promoting – make sure everyone knows your event is taking place!

Pummelled in Plymouth

Buoyed by our success, but banned from the Eclipse after the snake incident, we sought new party pastures. And in early 1992, found ourselves in Plymouth. We'd heard there was a gap in the market after the biggest local promoters had split up. So we booked the Academy and put together a very London/Raindance orientated bill which read: Guru Josh, SL2, Slipmatt and Lime with Terry Turbo's sound rig (the best in the country at the time), the Raindance laser and free guarana. SL2 had just gone straight into the top ten with 'On a Ragga Tip' and had appeared on *Top of the Pops* the previous night. But perhaps wary of this new promoter coming into Plymouth, the Warehouse venue across town tempted the local promoters to do one more show on the very same night, by offering them the venue for free.

All's fair in love, war and rave promoting, remember! They had the local network, a loyal customer base and a tried 'n' tested product. By comparison, we were flash out-of-towners with no reputation who, in retrospect, must've looked like we were muscling in on their territory.

So once again, advance ticket sales were spectacularly unspectacular. Our flyer teams had switched sides and our ticket sellers, all of whom lived locally, pushed the rival event's tickets (and why wouldn't they?). We were in deep shit . . . and looking at a big loss.

The venue had a glass front, so we deliberately left one section undraped so someone standing on the pavement could see the level of production we had installed. At one point I remember standing outside like an Ibiza PR in the San Antonio West End, trying to persuade people to see for themselves what we'd brought down from 'the big smoke' (a smoke machine, naturally). I even allowed them in to go in and have a look at the smoke-filled, laser-lit, bass-pounded, *empty* dancefloor!

I implored one guy, 'We've got Guru Josh, SL2, who've just gone top ten, Slipmatt and Lime, the Face, a 20k Turbosound rig and the laser from Raindance. What more could you possibly want?'

The guy looked at me and said, 'A crowd. I want to go where everyone else is going' and walked off up the hill to the Warehouse.

We lost £25,000 that night. They were expensive lessons. Eton would've charged less *and* we would've ended up in the Cabinet in Number 10.

Love of Life

Undeterred by our chastening experience in Plymouth, we decided to continue on our home turf (well, not far from it).

Also in early 1992, in return for being granted the east of England's first all-night music and dance licence at the Kelsey Kerridge Sports Hall in Cambridge, we agreed to make a substantial charitable donation to Addenbrooke's Children's Hospital.

Half a dozen phone calls later, we'd put together a line-up featuring a live set from the Prodigy, established names such as Ray Keith and Slipmatt, alongside emerging hopefuls straight from the Raindance dancefloor like Beamish. So we had a venue, a headliner, a line-up and a crowd to market to. We even had a slogan: our strapline was *'Live the life you love'* – which we all agreed was perfectly in tune with the utopian theme of self-expression and hedonism.

However, what we couldn't agree on was what to call the party. As it was to take place on 29 February, I wanted to call it 'Quantum Leap'. But it was Richard's turn to name the show and he felt strongly that it should be 'Love of Life'. But Ray, who was another partner, was adamant that we should call it 'Life of Love'.

All week in an office just off Old Street roundabout in Mallow Street, the debate raged on. And on. Each protagonist energetically trying to persuade other staff members of his choice, rightly suspecting that if they couldn't agree by the print deadline, it was going to come down to a vote.

In these pre-internet times, artwork was delivered to the printers, who would fax through a proof to be signed off before the presses rolled.

The printer had already received the artwork some days earlier with an empty space left where the name of the event could be added – when we had decided! We'd already signed off the proof, and as the style of font was known, it was simply a case of confirming the name over the telephone for the printer to create and add to the artwork.

Thursday came – print deadline day – and all afternoon the debate continued to rage unabated, one side imploring 'It's gotta be "Life of Love" because the message is "live the life you love".' While the other would insist, 'Nah, "Love of Life" sounds better, as the message is love life.'

At 6 p.m. a vote was held. It was a tie. Stalemate. The 6 p.m. deadline came and went, as did the one at 7 p.m. we'd extended it to. More extensions were requested, and reluctantly granted by an increasingly irate printer, who just wanted to get the presses rolling and leave the night-shift workers to fold and box the flyers.

Finally at 9 p.m. precisely, the phone rang. I picked it up knowing it would be the printer, who by now was clearly at the end of his tether and demanding an immediate decision or, 'you can sho . . . yer . . . kin' flyers where the s. . . don't shine'. Although it was a very bad line, and he sounded like Norman Collier, I understood perfectly.

Exchanged glances revealed no one was prepared to back down and so a coin was tossed. Heads for 'Love of Life', tails for 'Life of Love'.

'Heads! It's Love of Life, Love of Life – go to print!'

We left the office, exhausted but relieved to finally have a name to run with and the knowledge that 75,000 flyers would be delivered to the office the next morning for distribution.

Friday morning dawned. It was a bright but cold January day and as I walked up the subway from Old Street Tube station, I had a spring in my step. It was always great when flyers arrived, when you saw the words you'd written in print – words which weren't just read but would be *devoured* by thousands of ravers across the south-east. I always tried to add something to any flyer I wrote to make it stand out, something extra (or a USP, as it's called these days). This flyer was no exception: in addition to 'BIG QUADROPHONIC SOUND RIG' and 'LASERS TO SURPRISE EVERYBODY', it also boasted 'A BALCONY TO VIEW THE MIND-BLOWING VISUALS'.

Anyway, back to the flyers. I emerged onto Old Street and took the first left into Mallow Street. Halfway down, on the other side of the road, a white Ford Transit van was moving off, hazards still flashing from where it had been parked outside the office. THE FLYERS HAD ARRIVED.

I walked in expecting to see the corridor partly blocked with brown cardboard boxes stacked to eye level, awaiting collection. But oddly there were none.

I walked into the office and instead of the usual chatter, everyone was sitting in silence. No one looked up or acknowledged my entrance.

'I see they've arrived. How do they look?'

Without speaking, Ray handed me the flyer he had been staring at . . . the flyer *every* person in the room had each been holding and staring at in silence. The only flyers from the 75,000 which weren't making their way back to the printers in the white Transit van, in fact.

I looked down. The front showed the raver silhouetted and throwing shapes against a concentric pink and blue laser tunnel, beneath the name of the party, proudly emblazoned in green across the front of 25,000 full-colour A4 flyers.

It read . . . 'LOVE OF LOAF'.

Shit.

Afterglow

Looking back, Solstice was all very *Spinal Tap* (which I hadn't seen at the time, otherwise I may not have suggested it), but this party was underpinned by integrity as well as insanity: the ceremony was authentic and as anyone who was there that night will testify, it was a very special party.

At Glastonbury the following year, Tim Sebastian inducted me into their order at the stone circle at dawn. I was honoured and inspired to mark the 'Wheel of the Year' (equinoxes, solstices and midpoints) at raves. Another pagan promoter, the much-missed Paul Shurey, invited me to perform rituals at his Universe's Tribal Gatherings in Oxford and Munich. As 'Pagan Pulse' (myself together with DJs Beamish and Oberon), we visited Croatia, Hanover, Penzance and Dublin, celebrating the sun's passage through the sky, music and dance while promoting an awareness that we are a part of nature rather than separate from her.

The 'Love of Loaf' flyers were pulped and redone, and although we did a number of 'Love of Life' parties in 1993 at the same venue, we never made money on any of them. We'd invariably overspend on licence fees, venue hire, police, medical and production costs (Adam Proto always went over budget, justifying the expense by saying, 'But it'll look the bollocks' – and to his credit, it always did). Our breakeven was therefore too high and the licence conditions too strict to be able to generate sufficient revenue – for example, there was strictly no entry allowed after 11 p.m. But they were always great parties with a top soundtrack and appreciative crowd. So we kept on doing another party, throwing good money after bad, to no avail.

It didn't seem to matter that the events weren't financially successful – they looked and sounded fantastic, and so we kept throwing them regardless. To the degree they were referred to as 'Love of Loss' by some cynical mates.

TOP TUNE: 'Outer Space', Prodigy

13

FROM RUSSIA WITH A DOVE

*Globetrotting Kirk Field jets off to Moscow with Guru Josh in
tow and witnesses the ultimate act of perestroika: Russia's first
ever full-scale rave in the Olympic Stadium . . .*

In early June 1991, Dave Seaman called me with another
overseas assignment. He had received a fax inviting a
Mixmag reporter to attend the Soviet Union's first 'rave',
which was to be held at the Olympic Stadium in Moscow.

Due to the scarcity of flights in those days from London
to Moscow, it would mean staying for five nights. I accepted
of course and eagerly awaited the visa and plane ticket to
drop through my letterbox.

A week later, I was still waiting and starting to get nervous.
Calls to the Russian Embassy yielded nothing other than
being on hold for an eternity while listening to an endless
loop of Sergei Prokofiev's toiling dirge 'Dance of the
Knights'. Eventually I was told to present myself in person
at the Embassy at 9 a.m. the following morning . . . the
day of departure!

So, on a bright summer morning, I emerged from Notting Hill Gate Tube station and sauntered towards the rather imposing Russian Embassy in Kensington Palace Gardens.

I was summonsed officiously through the automatic gate, past a security guard and inside the building. I was then shown to a red carpeted lobby area that was decorated with portraits of Russian leaders in ornate frames. After ten minutes, a diplomatic type in a suit walked past me and opened the oak-panelled door adjacent to my seat. Thirty seconds later, I was told to come in. As I opened the door, the gentleman who just walked past me could be observed hurriedly concealing a hip flask in the top drawer of his desk. The smell of vodka was overpowering. He looked dishevelled, pale, and frankly disinterested.

'What is the purpose of your visit?' he enquired, without even looking at me or even raising his eyes from the visa application form. I told him I was a music journalist, and my intention was to cover the first dance music event in the Soviet Union.

He lethargically looked through the pile of envelopes before him and handed me a large brown envelope into which he'd folded some documents, before indicating the door and formally wishing me a pleasant visit to the Soviet Union.

Upon arrival at Heathrow for the Aeroflot to Moscow, I spotted Annabel, Guru Josh's PA, who told me that Josh was also flying out to play the event, having been booked at the last minute as a replacement for (the much more Soviet-sounding 'keyboard wizard') Adamski.

I knew Josh well, having seen him most weekends over the past few years. His top-five hit, 'Infinity', had brought him international success in the autumn of '89 as the piano-led Italo house sound stormed the charts with tracks like Black Box's 'Ride on Time', Starlight's 'Numero Uno' and the Technotronic smash, 'Pump Up the Jam'.

He was always great fun, and we shared a mischievous and anarchic sense of humour.

When I got to the check-in desk, I handed the Aeroflot rep my brown envelope. Although my visa was in order, there was no plane ticket and my name was not on the passenger manifest. Neither were Josh's (Paul Walden) or the stand-in sax player, Dave. Annabel made a beeline for the Aeroflot office. Frantic phone calls were made to the promoter. We tried everything. Impressing on them that our visit was a charitable one, we had come to save the Soviet soul from rock music and that Boris Yeltsin was expecting us and had requested a meeting. Yet we were always met by the same stony-faced reply, 'Sorry, no name, no ticket.'

In desperation, Josh managed to reach over the counter and grab the passenger list and saw at the bottom, Mr Gary Josh and band. We identified ourselves and were handed hastily handwritten tickets and boarding passes. There was no time for a drink, or even to buy a large Toblerone in duty free. We only just made it. Time for a drink.

The five-hour night flight was a riot. The plane was practically empty except for a few pale blokes in suits who sat at the front, a huge woman who spent the whole flight praying and fiddling with rosary beads, a lank-haired bloke at the very back, and a group of girls who were flying out to Japan for a three-week stint dancing in a Tokyo bar.

Within ten minutes of the seatbelt sign being switched off, Josh had nicked a bottle of vodka from the passing drinks tray and we'd moved to sit with the girls and party. Josh invited the lank-haired bloke at the back over to join us. After a few vodkas he confessed he had dropped a tab of acid. (Never a good idea on a plane. As a certain south London promoter can testify after his flight from Gatwick to Ibiza took NINE HOURS after electrical storms caused diversions to Mallorca and Menorca. I was sat next to him, and the memory of his sweating face and fearful eyes as the plane was tossed around in the storm will never leave me.) Rave code states that when someone's having a bad time, you offer them support, and so I clicked into *Bad Trip Buddy* mode. I told him that no matter how bad he felt, it wasn't reality, and the effect of the drug would pass. Things would get better.

He disagreed, telling me he really was doomed and there was no escape from his fate. He was struggling big time, so I called for the cabin crew and asked for an orange juice for my friend into which I would dissolve some vitamin C – or 'Vitamin Comedown' as it was called back then due to its perceived ability to counter bad trips . . . which is an urban myth by the way.

As she delivered the OJ, the stewardess clocked he was acting oddly as he examined his acne-ridden face in the small plane window like it was a mirror, while preening his eyebrows. This perhaps would not have been so strange had the grey plastic night screen not have been pulled down.

After plonking a Berocca into his weak orange squash (this being Soviet-era Aeroflot, there was no fruit juice, just cordial) and after some encouragement from me and him drinking it, there was no improvement. He insisted he was condemned to confinement by the authorities for drug smuggling.

I laughed. 'A trace of acid in your urine is not what they'd class as a significant bust.'

He reached under his seat, handed me a scruffy canvas rucksack and calmy said, 'No. But this is.'

I looked inside the rucksack and there was a green A4 cardboard folder. I removed it and looked inside. There was an *Argos* catalogue with something sandwiched between the lawnmowers and ladders. It looked like a sheet of stamps. Except instead of the Queen's head, there were lots of purple Om symbols. I flicked through the catalogue and there must've been more than a dozen sheets, literally thousands of tabs of acid.

I tapped Josh on the shoulder, who was sat in the seat in front. As he peered through the gap in between the seats at the magazine, his eyes nearly popped out of his head.

As we approached Moscow the guy became more and more agitated. And Josh was getting more and more nervous.

'Listen, when we get off, stay away from Peter Panic. Don't let him walk with us. We don't want to be associated with him; he's got the demeanour of a dead man walking. That rucksack is a one-way ticket to a Siberian salt mine. I don't want it anywhere near me.'

When we landed, we made sure we were first off the plane, but our new shifty friend was not far behind. We started walking faster, along endless empty corridors, following signs marked таможня/ Customs Control Zone. By now we were doing that half-walking/half-running thing that late mothers do towards primary schools at 3.30 p.m. But as we speeded up, a glance over our shoulders showed us so did Peter Panic.

As we rounded the final corner, we found ourselves in the large customs zone. We skidded to a halt as the eyes of every uniformed official in the cavernous room greeted our entrance. As we were the first arrivals from our plane, we approached the two border cabins and presented our papers. I hoped they'd be swift. But as I was to find out, nothing in Soviet-era Moscow was efficient, and my worst fears came true when the world's most conspicuous drug dealer appeared at the other end of the hall, spotted us and started making a beeline in our direction. If they thought we were his travelling companions and found the illicit contraband, there would be no rave, no report from the rave and no return to the United Kingdom for a very long time. My fingerprints were on the catalogue, and I had told the cabin crew he was my friend.

Then a door opened to the left of us. A girl I recognised as the Aeroflot flight attendant who'd brought the orange 'juice' to me on the plane earlier emerged. Flanked by a gaggle of border guards brandishing handguns. She pointed out our acid friend companion, who was quickly escorted away at gunpoint after being separated from his rucksack. I caught his gaze as he turned to go. It was a mixture of horror framed by an air of resignation. His eyes seemed to say, 'I told you so.' Then the pathetic creature was led away to a side room, where rubber gloves lay waiting . . .

My thoughts were interrupted by the loud double thud of a stamp hitting my passport. I was done. I grabbed it at exactly the same time as Josh was handed his at the adjacent booth. But Dave the sax player was still being held at the custom officials' kiosk. Although possessing the same documentation as us, he had different coloured skin and the USSR was blatantly racist in those days. Dave was being denied entry to the Soviet Union probably because he was black. We waited for two hours before they let him through, hoping Peter Panic wouldn't implicate us in his crime and involve us meanwhile.

I thought about his expression as he was taken away and acknowledged Josh's idea.

'Fuck me, that was close. That was a good move, making sure we didn't let him walk with us. I never realised that flight attendant would be so on it.'

There was a long pause. Josh didn't do pauses. There was something on his mind. As we stood waiting for the conveyor belt to jolt into action, he shifted uneasily from one foot to another before confessing that it was him who'd tipped off the flight attendant when she started asking him questions about 'your strange friend'.

'Look, if I didn't grass him up, they wouldn't have believed we weren't involved. Besides, he would have got caught anyway. He was a shite drug smuggler, right?'

I was dumbfounded. While there was a selfish logic to his reasoning, I couldn't help but think about the hapless hippy who was grassed up by one of the biggest stars in the rave scene. This was the first time Josh showed me his true colours. 'Looking after number one' was always his primary objective. 'If Dave doesn't get in, you'll have to play sax for me. It's a playback show. Just miming. Piece of piss.'

'But I've never even held a sax, let alone know how to play one!' I explained.

'Neither does Dave, he's just a mate I've brought along for company,' he replied.

When Dave finally appeared it turned out the delay was because they questioned the validity of his ticket. 'Because it was handwritten, you mean?' I ventured.

'No, because it's one way,' he replied.

Like a comedy choreographed move, we all simultan-
eously retrieved our flight tickets from our pockets and sure
enough, they were all 'one way'. I was stuck behind the
Iron Curtain with a nutcase popstar in a fake leopardskin
coat and a pretend sax player, with no credit card, very
little cash and no plane ticket home.

Mugged in Moscow

My room was in one of the top tourist hotels in Moscow
at the time, towering over the city with spires topped with
large red stars. One exception was a large modern-looking
edifice called the Intourist Hotel – a tall, box-shaped
building notorious for its black marketeers, and sex
workers who hung around the foyer in short skirts and
high heels.

Our handler for the trip – Viktor – proudly told us that
it was a Soviet expression of cubism and was at the time
the tallest reinforced concrete building in 'whole of
Soviet Union'. In truth it was a gaudy hostel, two decades
out of fashion and tired-looking. The Status Quo of
accommodation.

I was housed on the fourteenth floor, which afforded
views over the whole city. The décor reflected the height
of fashion . . . in 1970 when it was built. Above the desk,
a large wall mirror reflected the kitsch cabin which would
be my home for the next five days. From the window I
could see the red stars lit up on the roof of the Kremlin
in Red Square and other towering tourist hotels; a grand
greyness which reminded me of Fritz Lang's *Metropolis*.

My head suddenly began spinning. I started feeling naus-
eous and was violently sick. I spent the next six hours

vomiting and testing the Soviet toilet's capacity to flush away gift after gift from the West. It felt – and smelt – like food poisoning. Probably from a crusty chicken sandwich I'd eaten on the plane.

By the time 9 a.m. came, I was a pale, weakened shell and couldn't face the prospect of breakfast. Just before 10 a.m. my room phone rang. It was Viktor reminding me there were buses waiting downstairs to transport all artists and media to a press conference for the event, which was going to take place at the venue. I was in a bad way and told him I was sick and couldn't make it.

'But it is in programme, you must attend!'

I told him I'd need some time to get ready but would take a car to the stadium as soon as I could.

I pulled back the curtains. It was a warm, sunny summer's day. Smog hung over the city like a grey ghoul as cars crawled around the roads. I took the lift downstairs and jumped in a cab. With no knowledge of Russian, I simply asked him to take me to the Olympic Stadium.

A few minutes later we entered Pushkin Square and passed a huge crowd of people milling about a doorway. The mass of people stretched around the side of the building. Passing cars slowed as drivers rubber-necked the scene. Militiamen in uniform stood nearby, keeping an eye on them.

The cabbie could see my interest and caught my gaze in his rear-view mirror and muttered one word: 'McDonald's – first in Soviet Union.'

'But the queues, they'll be waiting for ages!'

In the rear-view mirror I watched a wry smile break across his face. 'We're used to standing in line. We stand in line for hours, sometimes days. We are accustomed to this.'

RAVE NEW WORLD

Viktor later told me that after fourteen years of negotiation with the authorities, McDonald's had finally opened in Moscow a few weeks earlier. On its opening day, 38,000 people turned up to sample a burger which cost them the equivalent of half a day's wages.[9] This is how desperate the people were to embrace the West at this time. This was not the only queue I saw from the back seat of that cab. Crowds gathered around lots of shops as there were food shortages in Moscow at the time. Reformer Mikhail Gorbachev took the brunt of the rage.

The cab driver told me a joke: 'People were queuing for bread. They'd been queuing a long time and they were getting very irritated. One man turned in the queue to his neighbour and said, "I'm fed up with this, I blame Gorbachev, I'm going to kill Gorbachev," and off he went. He came back two days later and the people in the queue said, "Did you kill Gorbachev?" "No," he replied. "The queue to kill Gorbachev was just too long."'

The Berlin Wall had fallen, perestroika was four years in, and Ozzy Osbourne had played to 30,000 people the previous summer. But they'd seen nothing yet. The influence of Western decadence was about to go to a different level – the gurning gift of rave music.

The venue was the Central Lenin Stadium (now called the Luzhniki Stadium), a sprawling, decaying concrete monstrosity in the south-west of the city, which had been recently repaired to host the 1980 Olympic Games – and which my driver hadn't the foggiest clue how to get into.

---

[9] As this book was being completed, McDonald's closed all their 'restaurants' in Russia as a consequence of the invasion of Ukraine.

FROM RUSSIA WITH A DOVE

I noticed he kept glancing in his mirror and appeared to grow ever more nervous, accelerating for about a minute before pulling over. Removing his glasses, he stopped the meter and indicated for me to get out, pointing across the wasteland to the stadium.

I was confused but had no choice. I climbed over the metal barrier and began walking towards the concrete complex, some 200 metres away. As I looked back to watch my cab speed away, another one pulled over at the same spot. A dark figure emerged, and similarly climbed over the barrier into the wasteland. Great. I was being followed. I broke into a run and soon reached the first building. Doorways were open and it was clearly unoccupied. I walked down a deserted corridor into a cavernous room with holes in the roof and puddles of water on the floor. Graffiti adorned the walls and my entrance caused a huge black crow to take flight and disappear through a gap in the roof. A sunken area in the centre stretched for exactly 50 metres. I knew this because it said so on the wall of the cavern. It dawned on me that I was alone in the Olympic swimming pool where Duncan Goodhew had won a gold medal a decade earlier. I gazed in silence around the decaying edifice, this was the empire I had grown up being threatened by. But here we were a decade on from the Olympic Games and the place was a derelict shell. Once the pride of the USSR, it now stood forgotten and forlorn, a ghost stadium which reflected the Soviet state's decline and decay.

Behind me, I heard footsteps. I left through an open doorway, past turnstiles, across a courtyard and into another building – a snaking collection of musty, litter-strewn corridors – until I stood before a large grey metal door marked Выход/Exit, which was locked from the outside. I was trapped.

I hid around the corner in a former communal shower area which stank of piss, the air rancid, burning my nostrils. Instinctively I held my breath. The footsteps got louder, then stopped, unveiling the sound of heavy breathing. The bloke was really panting. He was clearly unfit and very possibly no match for a dancefloor-fit 29-year-old raver.

But I was scared. Alone in Moscow, trapped in a shower, hiding from someone unknown to me, who could be armed or dangerous. Or even armed *and* dangerous. There were no witnesses either. What had I got myself into?

Murdered trying to get to a twatting Technotronic press conference. 'Hello, Kirruk. Helloooo! It's Viktor.' The words echoed around the room.

I stepped out, rather sheepishly and smiled weakly at my flush-faced, rotund pursuer. Viktor explained that by chance he was also delayed and saw me leaving the hotel, but just missed me and jumped in the cab behind me. He was surprised to see me get out on the ring road and was worried I was getting lost, so decided to follow me and lead me to the press conference. Hmmmm. I was starting to have my doubts about him.

I was too late for the press conference in any case, but Josh and stand-in sax player Dave had a huge bowl of fruit and smoked salmon sandwiches in their dressing room, which I devoured and began to feel better.

I asked Viktor, who wouldn't leave my side, which DJs were playing. After some discussion with a stern-looking middle-aged bloke with a RTR lapel badge, he moodily showed me a running order. It was clear that the rave I'd travelled 3,000 kilometres to cover wasn't a rave at all, but a fund-raising pop-music television spectacular for the children of Chernobyl, the nuclear reactor that had exploded five years earlier. This was the Europop equivalent of the Moscow Music Peace Festival of 1989, which featured Mötley Crüe, Ozzy Osbourne, Skid Row, Cinderella, the Scorpions and Bon Jovi, as well as local acts.

The dance version was rather more lightweight: artists included FPI Project, Technotronic featuring Dutch singer Daisy Dee, Guru Josh and, rather bizarrely, a Michael Jackson tribute along with a German version of KLF called Recall IV. Looking back, it was a hotch-potch, cobbled-together collection of one-hit wonders. And a Michael Jackson impersonator. It was at this point we all realised the absurdity of the situation and decided to make the most of our time behind the Iron Curtain and have as much fun as possible.

TOP TUNE: 'Infinity', Guru Josh

14

DROP ACID, NOT BOMBS

It was a hot summer's day in Moscow and I decided to change my Levi 501s for a pair of baggy white board shorts. As I threw the jeans on the bed, a few small flecks of paper fell out of the turn-ups. I picked them up and examined them. OH. MY. GOD. They were two pieces of *Berlin wallpaper* – LSD-soaked wallpaper on which sheets of acid tabs were dried after being immersed in liquid lysergic acid.

It was ideal for the overseas trips I was increasingly doing. Having already taken some to Ibiza in my turn-ups when I covered an event at Ku (now Privilege) for *Mixmag*, I'd obviously brought some back as well.

Clearly my jeans weren't washed before my Moscow trip a few days later. If I'd known my Levi's were still 'loaded', I would've jettisoned the stuff without a moment's hesitation. Instead, here I was with the craziest bloke in the rave scene, some industrial-strength LSD and five days ahead of me.

Josh was very welcoming of my contribution but, being Guru Josh, he naturally insisted on washing it down with a bottle of vodka he'd ordered from room service.

DROP ACID, NOT BOMBS

After an hour, fortified by the native grain and frazzled by the Berlin wallpaper, we went outside for a taxi, on the way bumping into Viktor in the foyer, who offered to be our guide and show us Moscow's jewel, St Basil's Cathedral in Red Square. This collection of swirling, multi-coloured domes is the finest example of artistic architecture in Russia, the most unorthodox Orthodox Church in Christendom, which would even give Gaudí's gargantuan gothic vision Sagrada Familia in Barcelona a run for its money in the *Trippy Churches Olympics.* And through 'wallpaper and vodka glasses' it was something else, believe me . . .

Viktor explained the church is shrouded in legends and myths. People say that the cruel Russian Tsar had the architect blinded to prevent him from building a more magnificent building for anyone else. Legend has it that Napoleon wanted to destroy the cathedral when he realised he couldn't relocate it to Paris, as he so wanted. The pigment used to give the amazing colours to the domes are said to be taken from a biblical description, in the Book of Revelation, of the kingdom of heaven.

Our warped Western minds were well and truly blown. We walked on across the cobbles as Mongolian wedding parties posed for group photos and convoys of black cars snaked into the Kremlin. This is where every May Day Parade, Russian leaders view from a balcony their prided arsenal of nuclear missiles rumbling past on trucks in a show of Soviet strength.

In one corner, there was a low red-brick building, around which a huge queue snaked the length of the Kremlin wall. We thought it was an exclusive private members' club. This was a red rag to a couple of blaggers from London, so we pestered Viktor to get us to the front of the queue. Once inside, we followed the crowd into a darkened cavernous room adorned with paintings and statues. We went off in search of the VIP area (as you do) but instead, only found a Very Important Corpse: the waxy embalmed body of Lenin (as you do in a mausoleum). An hour later, Josh was still shaking and staring into the distance.

'It was only a dead body, mate,' I reassured him.

'I could handle that part. It was when he winked at me, I lost it,' he shuddered.

Showtime

After a shower and change of clothes, we headed back to the venue on a bus that was accompanied by an outlaw biker motorcade courtesy of the local security, Night Wolves. I learnt they were the Soviet equivalent of the Hells Angels, who formed after coming together to organise illegal rock concerts in the 1980s. In a shrewd move, Putin has embraced them and politicised their cause by being filmed riding with them. They are considered by some to be a paramilitary and propaganda arm of the Putin regime.

Showtime drew near and the stadium filled up to the sound of silence. There was no warm-up DJ and this was a crowd who seemed to be as cold as a corpse – 40,000 of them glumly sat there like they were in the dentist's waiting room. It then dawned on me – they didn't behave like a crowd at a pop or rock concert, simply because they had never been a crowd at a pop or rock concert before.

The stage stood 50 metres from the nearest seat, a vast void patrolled by dour-looking soldiers acting as security and archaic-looking television cameras on tripods. A large screen flickered to life above the stage. An unseen voice introduced the heroic workers of Chernobyl. This was the cue for a closed-circuit television link with Kiev, where several dozen employees of the Chernobyl power station had assembled to watch the concert in a studio (off camera). They chatted about the accident, but the crowd started talking among themselves because although they could hear the workers, they couldn't see them. At one point, the Moscow audience were asked to stand in silence as the workers in Kiev read a roll of the twenty-three people who had died as a result of the disaster.

Although deserving respect, this is what's known in the game as an atmosphere killer. As dance music is largely non-verbal, visual or messages using music work the best. On the night Michael Jackson died, Paul van Dyk closed with 'Billie Jean'. No announcement was needed, and everyone participated and showed respect to the 'King of Pop' in the best way imaginable – by dancing.

As the show progressed, the crowd politely applauded each act, and then returned to a stony silence. Recall IV were going through their Teutonic tribute to KLF, which was causing mild intrigue, but there was no feeling of unity or elation. There was a lot of work to do if rave was going to get a foothold in the Soviet Union.

Josh took to the stage and played his follow-up hit, 'Whose Law (Is It Anyway)?'. Devoid of a hook, it failed to register with the crowd. People began talking among themselves as Josh's fist pumps and head-banging fell flat. This was embar-rassing. All this way to die onstage in front of the world's largest country at the time, stretching nearly 7,000 miles from east to west.

Then, the welcome fanfare of 'Infinity' appeared like a knight on a white charger to save the day. Ripples of recognition moved through the crowd. Josh grabbed the mic again, 'Moscow, let's 'ave it!' From the front row, the crowd began to stand, then jig . . . and then dance. It was going off! But the most memorable sight was not the flailing arms or pumping fists: it was the sea of smiles. I'd been in the country for twenty-four hours and this was the first time I'd seen a natural smile. 'Crazy man, crazy music,' shouted a stage security man I recognised to be one of the Night Wolves. I gave him the widest grin and a thumbs-up. Okay, so it was only a four-minute pop song, but before my eyes I was witnessing the music which had turned my life upside down hitting the nerve of the coldest crowd. A non-verbal, energy-filled dance anthem was rocking the Russians and hastening the shabby oblivion of the Soviet Union with smileys and the best sax riff since 'Baker Street'.

'I must tell you that you are esteemed guests of the chairman of the Supreme Soviet of Russia, Boris Yeltsin, who will be welcoming you tomorrow to express his gratitude at your service.' Viktor beamed like a proud parent at prizegiving.

'What?'

Josh confirmed it. 'That's right. All artists have been invited to meet bladdy Boris tomorrow morning at the Kremlin.'

Now it's not every day you get to meet a world leader, while having a pocketful of psychedelics. When I told Josh about Timothy Leary's plan to deliver psychedelics to world leaders in order for them to work through their insecurities and trust issues, it gave him an idea. Josh would present Mr Yeltsin with a small bottle of minibar vodka, into which my remaining pieces of Berlin wallpaper were marinated overnight, and we would propose a toast there and then. Yeltsin had a reputation for being partial to a drink, so we figured he'd accept the toast and, in a show of bravura, down it in one, providing the acid house movement's greatest moment . . . and maybe . . . just maybe . . . world peace. I went to bed so excited I couldn't sleep.

Every raver at the time possessed a missionary-like zeal regarding ecstasy. We felt it was a wonder drug and should be prescribed to EVERYONE. Raising consciousness on a global scale was the endgame and here was my chance. One shot. One chance to make a difference. This was our moment.

Whether it would've worked or not will never be known as Boris had to fly to Chechnya early the next morning to quell the uprising, so we met another dignitary instead. Although disappointed, we went along, posed for photos and each accepted a certificate thanking us for our charitable service to the Soviet Union.

Looking back on it, fate decreed that he dodged a bullet – and so did we. What were we thinking? If Boris had taken the bait and Viktor had spilled the beans, the consequences would've been grisly. I think we'd have been bumped off in a road 'accident' on the way to the airport or detained at customs on the way out after drugs were planted on us. I shiver to think what would've happened. Each year on 10 January, Chechnya's Independence Day, I raise a glass to the Grozny rebels whose insurrection may have unknowingly saved a couple of space cadets from the Siberian salt mine!

As I was swiftly finding out through my travels to far-flung dancefloors, rave was an international language and trance-ended borders and cultures.

Afterglow

The tension in Russia boiled over a few weeks later. The hardline political and military leaders wanted an end to Mikhail Gorbachev's Reform Program, angry at the well-publicised loss of control of the eastern European puppet states. Tanks peppered the parliamentary building, but the attempted coup failed. This was thanks largely to demonstrations in Moscow led by future President Boris Yeltsin, who rode onto the streets triumphantly sat on a tank.

Democracy and civil society had won the day, further boosting popular belief that dictatorial control was a thing of the past. Yeltsin transformed Russia's state socialist economy into a capitalist market economy, but economic collapse and inflation ensued. Amid the chaos, a small number of oligarchs obtained a majority of national assets and corruption continued.

> **TOP TUNE: 'If Only I Could'**
> **(Extended Mix), Sydney Youngblood**

15

MARBELLA MADNESS

By 1993 the British rave market was becoming saturated. Seemingly everyone was out to get licences from local councils, who realised that the only way to prevent illegal parties happening was to reluctantly sanction legal ones at sports centres, showgrounds and at many provincial nightclubs with extended 6 a.m. licences.

As innovators, Raindance felt the natural progression was to pull off an all-night dance event overseas. Having discovered Ibiza a few years earlier and watching its influence and popularity grow, I felt it was the obvious place to take Raindance. In May the previous year I'd even scoped out a possible venue, the disused Can Bufi arena on the outskirts of Ibiza Town. I had photos and had even sounded out the local record shops as ticket sellers. This would've been the first British rave in Ibiza and would launch Essex breakbeat on the island, which was stubbornly still preoccupied with the slower Boy's Own London sound.

I was utterly gobsmacked, then, when I found out that the location for the show would not be Ibiza . . . but Marbella.

Marbella? No clubbers went to Marbella! Back in the '90s, it was merely a washed-up, seedy ex-pat Costa del Crime town with a reputation for low-rent nightlife. Apparently, some of the Raindance crew had gone out there on a scouting mission, got talking to a couple of local ex-pat pillheads in a bar, who told them that in addition to being DJs, they could promote the party all along the Costa del Sol. And not only that, but they also had the perfect venue . . . the local bullring in nearby Puerto Banús. Millionaires Row.

That, to my knowledge, was the extent of the feasibility study and location suitability exercise for an event costing somewhere in the region of £150,000.

So, despite my protestations and deep reservations, Marbella it was.

In early August, a party of around twenty of us boarded a plane at Gatwick in an attempt to conquer the Costas, with an advertised line-up including Shades of Rhythm, SL2, Psychotropic, Trevor Fung, Vicki Edwards, Slipmatt, DJ Face and a '6-metre-high laser robot' (which was a misprint, the man on stilts reached a dizzying 10 feet – half the height promised). Guru Josh, who unlike the others had a hit single under his belt in Spain, was also present, but missing from the flyer. Not a great start, but a pretty good indication of the misadventure to come . . .

There was also a handful of Spanish names on the flyer. These were local DJs who were tasked with selling tickets and bringing in the local clubbers. Needless to say, they failed to deliver anything except a long list of mates for the already-heaving guest list.

When we got to the hotel, there weren't enough beds for everyone, so I chose to sleep in the open air on the small balcony for the next ten nights – and got eaten alive by the mosquitoes, who couldn't believe their luck. I was woken at ten sharp each morning by a loud '*Buenos días, señor!*' from an old Spanish man with a hosepipe washing down the pool area, which my al fresco boutique balcony overlooked.

My role was press officer, same as it was back in the UK, except instead of dealing with Kiss FM (or Kiss 100, as it was then), I had to get some coverage on the local English-speaking radio stations like Coastline Radio and OCI (Onda Cero Internacional).

Rather than being a radar of musical trends, these stations were – and probably still are – a community-orientated voice for the large British ex-pat community who shelter from the grey skies and endless rain of their home-land on the sunny southern coast of Spain. Here, they have created a whitewashed ghetto of fry-ups, sports bars and supermarkets which stock Heinz beans to enjoy with all-year-round tans.

Our radio ad campaign featured the usual 'bloke stuck down a deep well' voiceover, urgently running through the line-up like his life-support machine was about to be unplugged. The event's virtues were breathlessly extolled while he still had breath, repeating the name of the event for good measure in every other sentence, as a manic stac-cato breakbeat rattled threateningly throughout the ad.

Compared with the other adverts on the station (swim-ming pool cleaning services, Spanish bookkeeping and satellite TV engineers), our commercial was not so much incongruous as positively disturbing – confirming the preju-dices many felt about the rave scene as an aggressive, urban youth culture, fuelled by tribal rhythms that worked those present into a frothy-mouthed frenzy.

I insisted, therefore, that any stations on which we bought advertising also gave us the chance to talk to the listeners in a studio interview and address any concerns which were starting to be voiced about the forthcoming acid house party on their sun-kissed doorstep.

It was agreed Slipmatt would accompany me on the radio station promo trail, and as we walked into one station to appear on the mid-morning show, we decided to be our charming best and let the listeners know that there was nothing to be scared of, and try to coax some to attend and see some fantastic lasers (as the show was called 'Laserdance Spectacular' rather than Raindance, as Paul Nelson also had reservations about the idea and chose not to be involved).

'Hearts and minds,' I reminded Matt when we arrived at the station in downtown Málaga, aware that we would probably be introduced as 'Evil Acid Barons' intent on getting their twelve-year-old children hooked on drugs.

As we sat down in the studio, the DJ, a smarmy 'Smashy and Nicey' type, welcomed us and asked our names, which he casually scribbled on a whiteboard over the console while he lined up the next tune.

[DJ reading the flyer] 'You may have heard about the party in the Puerto Banús bullring this weekend. The "Laserdance Spectacular" features the cream of the UK dance scene. I've got Kirk and DJ Slipknot in the studio to tell us all about it.'

I then proceed to give a general overview about the event and talk about its amazing production values.

[DJ reading] 'Yes, it says here a 6-metre laser robot! – where DOES he find his trousers?'

Slipmatt puts his head in his hands.

The mad mayor

The day before the show, I was asked to attend the present-ation of a cheque to the mayor in Marbella's town hall. I understood that in order to get the council's blessing, a charity donation of 400,000 pesetas (around £20,000) was requested. I had the idea to knock up one of those huge cardboard cheques like Lottery winners receive for the cameras, which we did.

As we were driven from our hotel in Puerto Banús to our appointment, we entered Marbella beneath a rather grand triumphal arch erected by the mayor. Often found in the Middle East, they are the tell-tale sign of a tyrant with too much concrete and should've acted as a warning to us. The driver of our minibus, Mateo, told us a little about the man we were going to meet. His name was Jesús Gil, the eccentric president of Atlético Madrid football club. He'd recently won a landslide[10] victory in the mayoral elections and the first thing he did was bulldoze his prede-cessor's house, because he claimed it stood in the way of a new road he intended to build.

Mateo explained that he was swept to power on a promise to clean up Marbella and admonish undesirable elements. 'This town needs a sheriff' basically. A year into his tenure and crime rates and signs of poverty were indeed falling (as they do if you deport foreign criminals, bribe homeless

---

[10] It wasn't the first time the word 'landslide' had appeared alongside Señor Gil's name. In 1969 he received a five-year sentence for criminal negligence after a restaurant complex he constructed near Segovia collapsed, killing 58 and injuring over 100 people. It tran-spired that his company had cut corners, built without the assistance of either architect or surveyor, and used substandard cement.

people to live in neighbouring towns and look the other way as your police beat up prostitutes). When the media and women's rights groups insisted, he stepped in, touring the port after midnight, megaphone in hand, shouting obscenities at the street girls to *'vete à la mierda, putas'* (fuck off, whores).

Arriving at the town hall with comedy cheque under arm, we were ushered along a corridor into a room which featured a life-size bronze bust of some bald bloke in an army tunic, who I later discovered to be the Spanish dictator Franco. Various flags and medals were mounted on a wall behind a huge pine desk, at which sat a large man with thinning hair. He slowly rose, surveyed us all and politely introduced himself as Jesús Gil.

Photographers and a TV crew appeared from a side door to capture the moment the cheque was presented by a beaming Ray Spence. Gil then said a few words, welcoming us to Marbella and wishing us well with our fiesta.

Silver trays of bubbly miraculously appeared, and flutes were sipped as the Mad Mayor proudly showed us an artist's impression of his next project: a giant offshore island existing exclusively for gambling and entertainment which would rival Ibiza as the playground for the rich and famous.

The Spanish Donald Trump

Nearly two decades after his death, Jesús Gil is often described as the 'Donald Trump of Spain' – a politically successful, outrageous figure whose infamy lives on. As does the debt he saddled Marbella with after winning three elections for mayor. His 'This town needs a sheriff' schtick carried a pledge to remove 'undesirables' (illegal immigrants, sex workers and the homeless) – effectively to 'Make Marbella Great Again', in a decade of dodginess and daftness between 1991 and 2002, before his house of cards came tumbling down.

During the final two decades of his life, he was president and later owner of Atlético de Madrid, hiring and firing managers on a comedown (during the 1993/94 season he hired and fired five such managers). Edited highlights of his reign include threatening to shoot underperforming players with a machine gun, refusing to sign Jürgen Klinsmann because he (wrongly) suspected he was gay, a sham shirt sponsor deal (the sham sponsor being his municipality, Marbella), closing the youth academy and overseeing the club's only relegation since the war. Nice work, *señor*.

Naturally, he was a headline writer's dream and his larger-than-life persona led to him getting his own prime-time variety show. Titled *Las noches de tal y tal* (*The Nights of Such and Such*), the show featured a shirtless Gil bobbing about in a jacuzzi with bikini-clad models, while he cracked gags and told stories about his own life.

His 'revitalisation' of Marbella involved vast expansion of the city and an 'imaginative' approach to planning and the environment. After his election in 1991, not a single school or health centre was built in the city.

His legacy was to leave the city with huge debts following accountancy irregularities estimated at around €200 million, the fruits of a massive corruption ring centred on urban planning excesses and bribery initiated under Gil's mandate.

When we approached the authorities in Marbella about using the bullring as a venue for our event, the response was super positive. Looking back, it was in Gil's early reign and fitted his plans of putting Marbella on the map as an international entertainment venue. But it didn't quite work out – he may have wanted Julio Iglesias, but instead he got Guru Josh.

A Spaniard in the works

The day of the show and tensions were high, unlike the ticket sales, which were lower than could have been imagined. Less than 200 had been sold and there was no buzz on the streets. Our advertising hadn't yielded anything, and it was now evident that Marbella was the wrong location for a rave, even if dressed up as a laser spectacular.

I remember being woken at 9 a.m. and summoned to Ray's room, which served as a production office. I was met with frowns and furrowed brows. Our laser guys were at the bullring to continue the installation, setting up the mirrors and running some tests, but had been refused admission. The gates were locked and the old Spanish bloke with the keys spoke no English.

'Have you called the mayor's office?'

I was met with a stony silence. Someone explained that the town hall had instructed the venue to remain closed until we paid the rent for that day.

'What? But we paid them £20,000 yesterday!'

'A misunderstanding,' said Ray. 'It's £20,000 a day, apparently. He said pay or take your stuff out and find somewhere else.'

It was classic Jesús Gil. We had nothing in writing and with a show to deliver, we had no choice but to cough up another £20,000, which we transferred within the hour. And this meant we had a cashflow problem.

The production crews – sound, lights and lasers – were all to be paid, as was the hotel we were all staying in. Usually, once the event had been delivered, ticket money could be drawn on to cover these costs. But unless we could turn it round and get a huge 'walk-up', we were up shit creek without a paddle.

Homage to Catatonia

As expected, the show's attendance was poor. Fewer than 500 people, many of whom were on the guest list after 'helping us to promote the show or sell tickets'.

To make matters worse, there was a shortage of E and so the crew who'd come over (around thirty people including production crew, artists and staff) clubbed together and gave a couple of Spanish girls who were dancing on the stage a considerable wad of cash to supply them with the relevant mood modification. We all agreed it didn't look good for the crew or artists to go round asking for pills. The girls agreed to buy in bulk for the entire crew and were given a significant sum of money as they'd all worked hard and had been let down when an individual was intercepted at Heathrow.

So we had an amazing venue, fantastic production, incredible lasers, but no icing on the cake. After ten minutes the girls reappeared and dished out the pills to everyone. 'Careful, the dealer said they are very strong!' they warned. This was met by much bravado of 'we're hardcore', 'don't worry about us' and resulted in some stagehands double dropping to prove a point.

The girls weren't lying. They were strong alright. Strong sleeping pills. An hour later, six people were asleep in the chapel (all bullrings have a chapel), using unsold merchandise as pillows and mattresses. This reduced the crowd even more and led to one act not performing after we were unable to rouse them from their deep slumber. At the end of the show most of the lighting crew were comatose, a couple of soundmen were curled up on a bass bin, a laser operator was found under the stage and the act who slept through their showtime were still snoring loudly in the chapel . . . in their full-size lobster and swordfish costumes.

Those who did stay awake were treated to a mind-blowing production, which climaxed when a dancer from Shades of Rhythm fell through a gap in the stage. He carried on like a pro and the few who were watching probably thought it was part of the show. The other highlight of the event was at dawn when Guru Josh scaled some scaffolding, gained access to the roof and ran across its apex for an entire circuit of the arena, leaping from one arched section to another, to the horror of the Spanish custodians of the site.

The production office was in the chapel, deep below the stands where matadors pray for salvation before walking into the arena of death. At one point I was alone in there, 'guarding' the merchandise that represented more money down the Swanee (who buys long-sleeved T-shirts and hoodies when it's 40 degrees?), its sanctity and stillness corrupted by an echoey kick drum and bass which reverberated around the wooden stands above. It sounded like God was stomping, too. The aroma of incense hung in the air, which only served to increase the surreal sight of seeing our walkie-talkies charging on their cradles, laid out like sacrificial offerings before an altar, above which stood a crucified blood-stained Jesus Christ. Crowned with thorns, wounded by a spear in his ribs, pierced by nails, his eyes were raised skywards to avoid looking at the awful T-shirts that no one would ever buy.

Above Jesus's head was a scroll which contained the sentence, '*Padre perdónalos porque no saben lo que hacen*'. From my days as an altar boy, I knew this was Spanish for 'Forgive them, Father, they know not what they do'.

And, as usual, JC wasn't wrong. We were absolutely fucking clueless.

Vamos!

After the crowd had departed (a process which took all of five minutes), all senior staff were called to a meeting in the chapel – but we couldn't get in as there were so many people fast asleep. So we assembled in the tunnel, down which they drag the lifeless carcass of the bull from the arena after it has been dispatched by the last plunge of the matador's sword. A spent hulk whose chance of glory ended in slaughter, good only for the butcher's knife. It absolutely felt like the most appropriate location for us to gather.

As I walked along the corridor, I heard laughter from inside the room where the cash was kept. I opened the door and found Richard, the guy who financed the show, sat at a desk. He was counting money and laughing manically.

Gingerly, I approached. 'How've we done, Rich? Is it as bad as you feared?'

He calmed a little, looked at me. 'Around £150,000 down, no money to pay the production or hotel and we need to be out of here by midday or we'll be liable for another £20,000-charity donation to the mayor . . . and all the crew are asleep.'

And he started laughing again.

In the meeting we were informed that we would not be returning to the hotel, but that someone was collecting our belongings and we'd be reunited with them at a lockup, where we would spend the remainder of our time in Spain, hiding from the hotel, police and Jesús Gil's heavies.

To avoid suspicion, a few rooms were kept on which were to be paid for, but the vast majority of the rooms were simply abandoned. The hotel were told that we were delayed at the venue, breaking down the production. It was hoped that no one would notice we weren't there by the time we were on the plane back to Blighty the next morning. The hotel knew we all slept late and their suspicions wouldn't be aroused until around midday, when we failed to check out.

That night was spent in a dingy lockup beneath the cliffs in a secluded cove between Marbella and Fuengirola. There was myself, Josh and six other people (with another eight next door). There were no windows or bedding; we slept on fishing nets and woke up stinking of fish. As there were no showers and we had to keep a low profile, we weren't even allowed a quick dip in the nearby ocean. At first light we nervously emerged and piled into the back of a Ford Transit. As we sped along the autopista, the sun turned up the heat. It was sweltering in the back of the van, so we opened the side door to let some air in, and took turns in gasping at the breeze as we headed for Málaga Airport. But the road to the airport was blocked, the driver said that police were checking vehicles and asking for passports. The game was up. We were all looking at a spell behind bars in a Spanish prison and/or being taught a lesson by the Mad Mayor's truncheon-happy police.

As we slowed down, I saw another exit at the roundabout signposted GRANADA. There was an airport there and I suggested we try our luck. We had no tickets, but a one-way standby ticket back then was sometimes around £40 or £50. It had to be better than the alternative.

An hour and a quarter later we arrived at Granada Airport and to our relief, there was a plane departing imminently for Gatwick.

Between us we cobbled together the money (as Richard had given us all a few hundred quid in pesetas for our hard work) and bought the tickets – all while trying not to look suspicious, each of us smelling like a trawlerman's jock strap.

When that plane took off, my heart felt like it was going to explode through stress AND relief. We all breathed out and ordered some drinks from the trolley.

Upon returning, everyone wanted to know what it was like. *Mixmag* called up, asking for a review of the first ever rave in Spain, but I declined to put pen to paper. I couldn't lie to the readers. And to tell the truth, it would've damaged the Raindance reputation, which, in an overcrowded market, they didn't deserve.

'One day I'll tell the story,' I told my editor . . . but not until the scars heal.

Afterglow

To my knowledge, no footage exists of the Raindance Marbella show. It is the great lost rave footage from that era. Although shot professionally on multiple cameras, the video company refused to edit or hand over the footage as they hadn't been paid and had to find their own way back. During the course of writing this book, I tried to track it down.

After many months of disappointment and endless blind alleys, Daz Jamieson, who was involved in visuals back then, got in touch to tell me his father had discovered a dusty VHS cassette in his loft marked MARBELLA. It was sent to me and as it hadn't been played for nearly thirty years, I meticulously cleaned and dried it to remove any dampness or mould. After a slow band of static rose up the screen, a fuzzy image formed: a figure in brightly coloured clothing and floppy hat throwing shapes in what looked like a hotel room. Clearly larking around for the camera, I vaguely recognised him as a dancer from Shades of Rhythm, who appeared on the Marbella bill. This was it, I'd found it!

But my glee turned to a frown when after three minutes of pre-show tomfoolery, another wave of white magnetic interference ascended the screen, to replace the rave-dancing loon with the title sequence of *Easy Rider* starring Peter Fonda and Dennis Hopper. My worst fears had come true. It had been taped over and the visual record of the most expensive mistake in the rave era was probably lost for ever.

TOP TUNE: 'Hablando' (Accordeon Mix), Ramirez

16

OH, WHAT A LOVED-UP WAR!

Q: *Who are your biggest influences?*

Genesis P-Orridge: *Aleister Crowley, Anton LaVey, founder of the Church of Satan, Charles Manson and pornography.*

I was made aware of Genesis P-Orridge by Marc Almond and Dave Ball in the early 1980s, when I worked with Soft Cell on their videos. I understood him to be the High Priest of Thee Temple Ov Psychick Youth (TOPY), a cult of experimental British artists who created subversive art and used ritual magic. This was expressed through audio-visual band Psychic TV, whose aim was to raise global consciousness by recruiting fans to become Psychick Youth – a sort of cross between a fan club and shadowy cult. Members donned paramilitary gear and submitted bodily fluids as part of their initiation on the twenty-third day of every month: blood, semen and saliva. Along with these, they had to write down in detail their sexual fantasies, which would all be placed in a vault.

There were rumours that 'Gen' was a modern-day Aleister Crowley, the English occultist, or, even worse, Charles Manson. Either way, he was said to be a demon-raising occultist who was the biggest threat to the nation's youth since Johnny Rotten and punk rock.

From the industrial ashes of 'shock rock visual arts group' Throbbing Gristle, Gen formed Psychic TV (PTV) and in doing so embraced drum machines, dayglo psychedelia and the use of samples.

In 1988, a collaboration with ex-Soft Cell lurker and keyboard player Dave Ball and Richard Norris resulted in what was the first 'acid house' album, *Jack the Tab*. Although largely ignored by the dance music press, the album became hugely influential – with Andrew Weatherall citing it a major influence for his production on Primal Scream's *Screamadelica*. However, neither *Jack the Tab* or Psychic TV were on the rave radar, something which irked Gen.

This was how I came to be invited to accompany PTV on an overseas engagement in the former Yugoslavia in January 1991 for *Mixmag*. This was shortly followed by Gen winding up at the centre of a satanic panic in the UK, culminating in a raid of his house by Scotland Yard and leading to his self-imposed exile in New York. But that's another story completely. Working in the music business as I did, I was used to being in the company of famous people, but a satanic cult leader was another matter entirely.

Things started to go strange shortly after I met them at Heathrow for the flight out to Zagreb. As Gen filed through the metal screening gate, the buzzer sounded. The airport security officer indicated he would have to remove his boots. He tried again. BUZZZZ. The security official pointed to

OH, WHAT A LOVED-UP WAR!

Gen's belt, which was removed and placed on a tray. Gen walked through again. BUZZZZ. The customs guy raised an eyebrow and asked Gen to turn out his pockets, then to remove his rings and necklace. He did so and attempted the manoeuvre once again. BUZZZZ. Clearly perplexed, the security man explained to Gen he'd have to accompany him to a private room for further examination.

'He's not going to like that,' I said to the band's sound engineer, who I was stood in line with, waiting to go through.

'On the contrary, Kirk, that's exactly what he was hoping for. He's just had twenty-three piercings between his balls and his arse and loves to show 'em off.'

Having cleared security, we waited for Genesis to emerge from the room. The door opened and Gen walked out grinning from ear to ear, while behind him a customs official stood motionless in the door frame, ashen-faced.

Having spent the previous month in Zermatt hiding from the Gulf War, I was unaware that the political situation in Yugoslavia was brittle. The country wasn't a country at all, but a federation comprising Bosnia and Herzegovina, Croatia, Macedonia, Montenegro, Serbia and Slovenia. When someone on the plane mentioned that the show was nearly called off as a civil war was expected to break out at any minute, I was shocked.

After leaving the airport, we rode the bendy bus to the hotel. I saw an impressive large building and wondered what it was. A man standing next to me explained it was the Glavni kolodvor – the train station.

'Thank you, this is my first time in Yugoslavia.'

Everyone stared at me like I'd just sworn. An old woman spat on the floor of the tram. The man leaned towards me and said quietly but firmly, *'Yugoslavia? Ne. Croatia.'*

RAVE NEW WORLD

As I took in a new city from the packed tram, I began to notice armed soldiers stationed on every corner and outside banks. Armoured cars were parked at junctions and people scurried about their business, heads bowed. The tension was palpable.

At the hotel we were met by the show's promoter, Dinko Bazadona, a softly spoken Slavic George Clooney who had a mischievous glint in his eye. He was to become a good friend and a catalyst in the spread of clubbing culture to Croatia, long before it became hyped in the twenty-first-century teen years as 'the new Ibiza'.

Over a few beers in the hotel basement, the band and crew gathered each evening as there was no hotel bar. Gen told me how the first record with acid house in the title 'Tune (Turn On the Acid House)' got banned because he used a picture of Superman on the label, and Warner Brothers sent a really heavy letter along the lines of, 'We own Superman – you've got to destroy all the copies and give us the masters and say sorry – or else . . .' They even sent someone around on a motorbike to get the tapes, then to the warehouse to get all the copies they could find. 'What they didn't realise was that 5,000 had been already shipped to America!' said Gen, grinning.

I asked him about his singing style, having noticed he purposely droned some notes.

'I've done some work with the Tibetan technique of finding your true voice by getting stones to resonate with your voice. I started to incorporate those ideas into the microphone and discovered that it was possible to make the microphone vibrate and resonate the same way stones or metal do. And once that happened, I realised there were no limitations at all . . .'

OH, WHAT A LOVED-UP WAR!

We talked long into the night. Genesis was clearly enjoying controlling the conversation, eliciting sexual confessions from everyone sat around the table and revelling in his role as ringmaster of rude stories.

The day of the show was tense. Banks and shops closed and only supermarkets were open for essential items. I went in search of chewing gum and could only find a tasteless local brand in one flavour. Dinko explained that this was state-produced and despised, but as it was the only choice, everyone bought it. However, it was rapidly losing its flavour. From the Black Sea to the Balkans, people wanted to taste a new flavour – one which they were prepared to smash through walls, topple statues and go to war for.

Psychic TV's concert was like nothing the crowd had seen before. Two and a half hours with a break during which a DJ played, followed by another ninety minutes that gradually morphed into a mass happening. Gen blurred the line between crowd and performer, inviting people to join them onstage, to bang drums, dance (or in my case, MC), as rave culture was to do in the decade ahead.

The songs lasted fifteen minutes or more and felt more like the grooves of Madchester a few years earlier: jangly, loose jamming sessions over which random vocals stuttered and exhorted those present to participate. Gen in a kitsch psychedelic suit with lots of sequins and tiny mirrors: a fractal minstrel or psychedelic Pied Piper, a satanic seducer helplessly hypnotising the children and leading them to goodness knows where with his magical flute.

Although disappointed at my lack of camera, Gen sent me a nice message when he saw the feature in *Mixmag* and invited me down to Brighton for 'afternoon tea or to drink some blood of a newborn baby'. He was joking . . . I think.

Gen liked to play the big bad wolf and loved to shock. I never did get to taste that afternoon tea – or the blood of a newborn for that matter – as his house was raided by Scotland Yard's Obscene Publications Squad after the Channel 4 programme *Dispatches* claimed to have footage of him abusing children in sex-magic rites. They alleged he was the leader of a satanic cult. For a few weeks he was public enemy number one, with the *Daily Mail* calling for him to be exiled or imprisoned and Tory MP Nicholas Winterton describing him as an 'evil wrecker of civilisation'.

The material was later found to be a video performance artwork from the early 1980s (that ironically was funded by Channel 4 itself) and which, importantly, featured no children.

Although no charges were filed, Gen went into self-imposed exile in the US. Badly injured fleeing a fire at a party in Def Jam producer Rick Rubin's house, he won $1.5 million damages, before moving to Manhattan, where he met his partner-to-be in a New York City bondage dungeon. Their union was expressed in a 'pandrogeny' project, which involved the duo undergoing body modifications to resemble one another, thus coming to identify themselves as a single pandrogynous being named 'Breyer P-Orridge'. As a Pet Shop Boy might concur, (s)he was never being boring.

Under City Rave, 1993

After inviting Dinko over to London to witness and experience the dance music revolution at Rage in Heaven, he flew back to Zagreb to become his country's first rave promoter. His first party took place underground in the

OH, WHAT A LOVED-UP WAR!

1,000-foot long Grič tunnel, a subterranean Second World War construction which offered the military and government swift and safe access across the city in the event of an air raid. I attended the party on behalf of MTV *News*, for whom I did a piece for camera, interviewing promoters, ravers and DJs against a backdrop of sandbags at the entrance to the dark, damp passage which was only 10 foot wide (except for the central area, where the stage was sited: a spacious 18 feet).

There was no ventilation and throats rasped as dark grey clouds of generator smoke hung above the heads of the seething, sweating, sultry crowd. The tunnel walls were literally dripping with moisture. Zippos refused to spark, causing confusion among wide-eyed ravers, who had turned up in greater numbers than expected as they were sick and tired of the violence and wanted a release from war and atrocities. The numbers in attendance was assisted by Dinko and Damir's naivety in printing 500 paper tickets which people simply photocopied.

The city's fire department, police and council were aghast and tried to shut it down but were unable to seal off the entrance to the tunnel as that was the only source of fresh air. A tent had to be brought in and set up over the decks to combat the constant dripping of water onto the vinyl, while the floor, formerly dusty, had turned to mud in all the condensation, sweat and spilt beer. The strobe flickered relentlessly, freeze-framing dark-eyed, beautiful girls. The tribal techno cacophony echoed above the crowd which now stretched as far as the eye could see.

I asked Dinko how many tickets he'd sold. 'We printed 500, but there's over 5,000 people here – and more outside,' he replied, ruefully.

The fact the party was happening at all was a miracle. The authorities hadn't wanted to issue a music and dance licence and were delaying the application, telling Dinko, 'We haven't received it . . . it's lost . . . it's incomplete . . . please reapply . . .', so a lawyer was engaged by the promoters.

When that was smoothed out another issue arose. Before Dinko and Damir's Future Shock events, there was no rave scene in Croatia. Similarly, there were no lasers in the country, so Dinko had to hire one from Germany. The day before the show, he went to the airport to collect it and was told it was subject to import tax. The customs chief wouldn't accept that it wasn't a purchase and merely a rental and duly impounded the laser. Dinko was bereft. This was the first-ever laser show in Croatia and was an important part of the marketing. One of the dancers who was rehearsing on the stage overheard the conversation and asked to speak to Dinko privately. She explained she was the customs chief's secret mistress and offered to call him. Within half an hour the laser was delivered, free of charge, to the venue . . .

I performed a PA with vocalist Melanie and the London rave scene's most legendary dancer, Troy Zulu King. In my introduction I bigged up the fact we'd come from 'London, England', which prompted boos. Something suddenly appeared in the lights and narrowly missed me. This was the cue for a barrage of more missiles, empty plastic water bottles. Then the spitting started. Translucent streams of gob caught the lights before landing on my arms, chest and legs. What was the problem? Was it my leather trousers?

Backstage, Dinko approached me looking embarrassed, handing me a towel to wipe the saliva from my cocoon-like torso. 'They believe the British are on Serbia's side and that London is their enemy. They do not know that without you, this party would not have happened. I am sorry.'

At 6 a.m. we filed out covered in mud, sweat, dust and smoke residue. But under the city that night, the earth gave birth to rave in Croatia . . . and I played my part in planting the seed.

Score and peace

In June 1994, I was back in Zagreb (this time performing as MC Vitamin K, and accompanying a robot) with Daz Saund, Trevor Rockcliffe, my good pal Colin Faver, and Richard (aka the Shamen's Mr C) at Future Shock.

After landing at Zagreb, we queued to get our passports stamped and Mr C was shocked to see lots of uniformed soldiers wielding machine guns. Outside on the tarmac, UN vehicles sat next to army helicopters as weary-with-war expressions hung on every pallid face. I could see Mr C was agitated, as the queue we were standing in showed no sign of moving. I took the opportunity to gently point out that we were in a war zone. A dirty civil war which no one knew how, when or even if, it would end. It was a complex situation involving ethnicity, border disputes, genocide and religion, all governed by regional politics more sensitive than a vegan on Facebook. And so I told Richard it was probably best not to get involved or say anything incendiary or controversial to the media. He took all this in. 'Genocide . . . ? Jesus!'

Having completed our entry paperwork, we collected our luggage – a few holdalls and two big silver record boxes – and emerged into the arrivals hall, where a few camera crews were waiting. This was de rigueur. The raves were big news and a welcome distraction from the war which had been rumbling on for three years, showing no signs of ending.

They immediately recognised the bleached-haired Mr C and three microphones were subsequently thrust in his face. A pushy young female reporter edged in front of the other two news presenters. 'Mr C, welcome to Zagreb! Is this your first time in Croatia?'

'Yes – and I'd just like to say, what the fuck is going on with you lot and the Serbs? You all need to smoke a spliff and calm the fuck down . . .'

Well, that went well.

Richard went on to build and open The End nightclub in London, which was always very well-programmed and held in high esteem by those who played or danced there, so respect to him for putting something back. He now lives in LA and can look back on his time as an MC, popstar and club owner with pride. That career in diplomacy on the other hand . . .

Air-raid!

However trying the circumstances, life finds a way to carry on. This was a fact I found to be true on my very next visit to the war zone in 1995, this time for *DJ* magazine. The Serbo-Croat War had entered its fourth year, and as ever in extraordinary times, the strange eventually becomes accepted as the 'new normal'. So despite the constant threat of air raids and missile strikes, life went on as usual: children went to school, postmen delivered parcels, footballers dived and cheated, and huge raves took place in the most unusual of venues.

OH, WHAT A LOVED-UP WAR!

This time it was the 7,000-capacity Dom Sportova gymnastics hall. The artists' area was situated upstairs above the stage and boasted a balcony overlooking those below, affording a fantastic view of the crowd in their dayglo necklaces and whistles.

Suddenly, without warning, the music stops and all the lights go out, with ironic cheers from the crowd thinking DJ WestBam from Germany has removed the wrong record. But he shrugs and gestures to the crowd that he is as confused as they are. Tech guys scurry beneath the decks and check multi-core cables, beams of Maglite torches in mouths. Five minutes go by and another five. Damir appears onstage with a megaphone, but the murmur of the crowd drowns him out. I've never seen Dinko look so worried. Usually, when confronted with a problem, he adopts a fatalistic 'what-will-be-will-be' persona. Tonight, he looks pale and drawn. I walk over to him and ask him what's going on.

'Power cut.'

'Have you told the power company?'

'They are the ones who turned it off.'

'Did they say how long it will last?'

'Until the air raid is over.'

Holy shit. Tonight, of all nights, with 7,000 kids gathered in one place.

DJ WestBam beckons me over to the balcony and below us we see something take place I'll keep with me for the rest of my life.

After half an hour with no power, a beat begins to resonate from the front left of the stage. Closer inspection reveals a group of ravers have raided the cleaner's storeroom, found half a dozen wooden mops and brushes which they'd

snapped into makeshift drumsticks. Around a dozen drum-
mers stand around some upturned flight cases for the bass
bins and mid-range speakers, beating out a primitive tribal
rhythm, while others mark the offbeat with short blasts on
whistles. We watch the pulse spread like a wave through the
crowd with more and more joining in, dancing, clapping
and chanting: 7,000 fluorescent silhouettes illuminated only
by glowsticks and the emergency IZLAZ (Exit) lit signs.

We are witnessing a primal relationship and response to
rhythm. Raving without the lasers, amplified sound or a
DJ. Pure primitive, pagan partying. A shiver runs up my
spine. DJ WestBam appears to wipe a tear from his eye.
Even Mr C was lost for words.

Eventually, after nearly two hours, the power came back
on to huge cheers. At one point I was introducing a DJ in
my role as an MC. Every sentence was greeted with a roar.

'Zagreb, are you ready?'

HUGE CHEER.

'Put your hands together and give it up for our next DJ.'

HUGE CHEER.

'Here she is, all the way from Frankfurt, Germany.'

HUGE CHEER.

'Say hello to Marusha!'

HUGE CHEER.

I walked to the side of the stage where Genesis P-Orridge
was standing. Dinko had invited him over to see what he'd
created. He looked at me and said, somewhat disdainfully,
'They'll cheer anything. Like dogs, they don't understand
what you're saying, simply reading the emotion in your tone.'

I was a little offended and disagreed.

'Give me the mic, I'll show you.' Gen walked out into
the front of the stage in front of 7,000 seething Croatian

ravers, held out an upward turned palm and said, 'Always fit the best. Always fit . . . Everest,' and received the biggest cheer of the night.

He walked nonchalantly back to me, tossed me the mic and shrugged.

I was gutted.

The pain event

'Amy's hands are tied to the rafters. The first of many needles pierces her upper arm. She exudes a long, loud moan of pleasure. Not everyone looks impressed. But everyone is looking.'

— *Ministry* magazine, 1998

In 1997, I witnessed another 'first' when London fetish Torture Garden (TG) brought their stocks to Zagreb. For the innocents reading this, TG are purveyors of all things fetish. BDSM, whipping, handcuffs, nipple clamps, ball-gags . . . you name it, it was probably in their suitcase and made for an interesting day at work for the airport customs officials.

Having attended a few fetish parties in London in the naughty '90s, I was very aware that in addition to the PVC catsuits posing on the dancefloor, there was lots of intimate interaction in darkened corners and 'playrooms', and wondered if the fledging nation's youth were ready or knew what they'd let themselves in for.

Dinko told me that he'd already received anonymous threats, probably from far-right puritans, who were opposed to any Western liberalism 'infecting' their proud Christian, exclusively white society. This was triggered by a feature about AIDS which had appeared in the country's largest newspaper the previous day and which carried an illustration from Torture Garden's recently released coffee table book, depicting a leather-clad nun posing with her hand between stockinged thighs. The state is staunchly Catholic and therefore averse to any sort of physical fun which might have felt a bit too outré. When it emerged that the model was a demure Croatian nanny who was working in London, a tabloid frenzy ensued. Her parents were alerted, embarrassed and shamed. The girl was harangued in London by Croatian media and there were calls to ban the party and talk of a candlelit vigil outside the venue at which the souls of those attending would be prayed for. Undeterred, the devilish Dinko decided to proceed.

'Everyone knows our politicians visit whores, they are hypocrites.'

1.30 a.m.: Downtown Zagreb. There's a crowd outside the Gjuro II club and after giving my name the doorman points to my legs and says, matter-of-factly, 'Please to remove trousers.'

I ask him why and he points to the flyer, where it states: 'Dress Code: Bizarre/Glamour/Fetish'. I tell him I'm a journalist. He reluctantly allows me to keep my trousers on. I walk past the cloakroom queue, which is essentially a line of young men holding their trousers.

Emerging into the main room through the cyberpunks, goths, fetish freaks and body art enthusiasts, I spot and wave to Allen TG, who's playing some Lab 4 in the booth. Lots of rubber catsuits and sub/dom couples are standing around the edge of the dancefloor, which is filled with trouserless blokes gawping at two girls dancing with exposed breasts and pierced nipples.

OH, WHAT A LOVED-UP WAR!

I spot Dinko, who's responsible for putting on this show of show-offs.

'Why is no one wearing any trousers?'

'I told the doorman there is dress code. He asked me what he should do if they looked normal. I told him to tell them to take their trousers off. This is a win-win. If they don't want to do it, this party isn't for them, and we don't want them here. If they do it, it makes the party more interesting – and also my friend doing the cloakroom makes money!'

He winked, before adding in a whisper, 'And maybe next time they will make an effort.'

Despite the absence of fetish-friendly retail outlets in Zagreb, locals had improvised and used what Croatia had on offer after nearly five years at war – stormtrooper helmets, gas masks, leather holsters and jackboots. This though wasn't the full list of military items, as my mate Beamish once discovered while playing a gig in Zadar near the front line. After his set, he was congratulated by the promoter for his bravery and continued to play on despite some pissed-up war veteran firing rounds into the ceiling and threatening to kill his girlfriend after seeing her dance with someone else.

This was hardly surprising. It was estimated that there were half a million illegal firearms circulating in Croatia at the end of the war. Croatia produced its own weapons as it feared it may have to arm the entire population. And when the war ended, many held onto the guns, explosives and ammunition rather than hand them in. Zagreb's football ultras are the 'Bad Blue Boys', who allegedly carried pistols. I recall one after-party taking place in their supporters' club HQ, with bulldog mascots and nationalistic slogans everywhere. Fully armed football hooligans who had the government's blessing . . . nice, eh?

I'm welcomed by one of the TG's promoters, Katsu, who is dressed in a skintight rubber nurse's uniform and has bright orange hair and eyebrows. She's hugging an old lady in a matching bright orange woolly hat who I later observe wandering around selling romanticism in the form of single red roses. There appear to be no takers until a tall girl in a rubber mini-dress purchases one, which she uses to thrash the backs of the legs of the trouserless lads on the dancefloor. Blood is drawn. Realising her roses make a useful instrument of torture, this pleasant lady sees a brisk upturn in trade as others make a beeline to purchase the option to administer pain through petals.

As the centuries crossfaded, Croatia opened its borders and the Adriatic coast resorts played host to large raves and festivals.

With the Croatian War of Independence won, the city's football heroes, Dinamo Croatia, were allowed to call themselves Dinamo Zagreb once more. Inevitably, Croatia became referred to as 'the next Ibiza', due to its balmy summer climate, azure sea, spectacular open-air venues and cheap bar prices (Ibiza superclubs, please take note!). Today it's been the home of 'Love International', 'Defected Croatia', 'Ultra Europe', 'Hideout', 'Sonus' and 'Hospitality on the Beach', and Zagreb hosts 'INmusic', the huge indie/rock gathering.

Even TG has left its legacy: fetishism and experiment-ation in sexuality has become visible and acceptable to the mainstream. In 2015, the Museum of Torture opened and is now, along with the Grič tunnel, listed among Tripadvisor's 'Top twenty things to do in Zagreb'.

It all seems a world away from the 'Under City Rave' in 1993 when the airport customs impounded the DJs' record boxes and demanded import duties – because they didn't believe anyone would bring two heavy boxes of vinyl to merely play and not sell.

TOP TUNE: 'The Age of Love', Age of Love

17

LETTING THE CAT OUT
OF THE BAGLEYS

In early 1996, I was approached about getting involved in a new project: turning a grim warehouse behind King's Cross station into London's biggest weekly club night. Kevin Millins, who ran Heaven for Richard Branson at the time, was collaborating with Debby Lee, a successful club-runner and a mischievous like-minded soul. Along with the shrewd Mark Sansom, whose father held the lease on the site, they headed up a well-connected and talented team. With Colin Aubrey booking the line-ups and myself handling press and themes, Bagleys had a team which would transform it.

Upon arrival at the office, I was told to introduce myself to Terry, the Roy Kinnear-esque owner of the site, who had asked to meet the new press and PR man. I walked along the grubby carpeted corridor and found him behind the bar, decanting a brand of vodka I'd never heard of into a huge Smirnoff bottle. The red funnel was wobbling as he held the bottle, so I instinctively steadied it as he poured the cheap Polish vodka. After exchanging pleasant-ries, he earnestly outlined the house rules.

'Now then, son, I hear you're good at your job – maybe the best in town. Hopefully you'll help us turn this place around.'

'Well, I'll do my best.'

'I'm sure you will, son. Now we don't work with contracts 'cos we don't need 'em. If someone's pulling their weight, they'll get the rewards, and if they're not up to scratch, we'll let them know. And if they don't shape up, we part ways, understood?'

'Er, yes, Terry.'

'Good boy – oh, one other thing. If anyone approaches you from Camden Palace offering you a job, make sure you tell us. You're under our umbrella now and it's always good to have an umbrella, son. Believe me. Now, can you pass me that bottle of Indian whisky.'

I was baffled. Why would I need an umbrella? Maybe it was his way of warning me not to go and work for a rival club – not that I would've done as I was aware that north London nightlife was reportedly divided up between two rival families, and I was firmly in one camp.

Every day in that office was like being back at school with your mates. But in addition to fooling around, we were all good at our jobs – a bunch of disparate misfits whose faces didn't fit into the increasingly corporate clubs of Ministry of Sound and Home. It felt like being in *The Magnificent Seven*; we were mavericks who would build the biggest weekly club night London had ever seen.

After much discussion, it was agreed to turn the perceived negative aspects of the vast two-storey former coal ware-house (it's too big . . . there are too many rooms . . . there's no seating) into positives. A 'flow' was established, similar to that which Heaven possessed. This meant people could wander from room to room while *always* moving forward. I refer to this as the 'nocturnal narrative' – all the best clubs have them. They encourage exploration along a linear framework. This was something Kevin felt very strongly about and it was a major improvement.

We couldn't decide which of the rooms to use. House and garage both attracted different audiences, who each had a tendency to sneer at the other. It was hardly a mods and rockers on Brighton beach conflict though, more a mistrust born out of insecurity. The house crowd felt garage could take over, leaving them nowhere to go, and the garage crowd were all former house heads who still responded to house, but felt they'd moved on. So we decided to make the most of the space at our disposal and host both a house and a garage room. This left a meagre £500 budget for the third room, the Bunker Bar. The room's resident, Ariel, suggested we give it to him in return for playing all night. His epic ten-hour 'Journeys Through Dance' sessions (later to become eight hours) became the stuff of legend, revisiting a Balearic approach, traversing from Latin to house to techno and trance, while embracing 'a decade of dance music'.

There was still one room to fill. The downstairs room with the low ceiling and very few seats. I felt this would be an ideal space for harder sounds that I was aware the Aussie and underground clubs were playing at the time. This we called Fast Forward.

We had the concept, the music styles, the line-ups and a name: Freedom.

The opening night, Saturday 16 November 1996, was busy, which, as anyone who works in clubland knows, means absolutely nothing as launches are 'comped out' to the max with invitations and free drinks for everyone. What was encouraging though was that the following few weeks also had around a thousand people through the doors. But then the press started to dry up and we started disappearing from the 'recommended' listings section in *Time Out* magazine. I called up clubbing editor Dave Swindells, with whom I had a good relationship, and asked him why they had cooled on us. He told me he was down the week after the opening party and felt that as much as the night's ethos was freedom, in reality it was turning into a bit of a sausage fest, attracting a homogeneous crowd of north London ravers, most of whom were straight males who dressed to sweat. While there was nothing wrong with that, it was hardly the polysexual festival of tolerance, expression and diversity we were claiming to possess.

We called up Matthew Glamorre, a flamboyant promoter of nights which included 'Smashing' and HARDERFASTERLOUDER!, who was – and remains – one of British nightlife's most significant innovators. He possessed everything we lacked: outrageous dress sense, a fearlessly extrovert attitude and a crowd of hedonistic peacocks who, in addition to not giving a damn what anyone thought about them, would 'go anywhere there's a free bar'.

Matthew's mantra is 'A nightclub should challenge current ideas and aesthetics, break new boundaries and be a beacon to the dispossessed'. Which I think is spot on.

So instead of spending the £500 in Ariel's room on a live PA, we put it behind the bar and gave Matthew 100 invites and 500 drinks tickets to attract and distribute.

His crowd would descend on Freedom around midnight in all their finery, drink like fishes and transform the vibe into one that reflected our name . . . before moving on at 2 a.m., fully loaded, in search of more fun.

Although they were only present for a few hours, Matthew and his crowd set the course of the night. Within weeks, Freedom was getting star listings and regularly named 'Club of the Week'. It sent out a message of tolerance to the sweaty straight males and encouraged an increase in bi and gay couples. We were now getting 2,500–3,000 people through the doors every Saturday, which also had the effect of rejuvenating the venue in the eyes of other club promoters, who, after seeing it rammed, also wanted to work there.

Occasionally we hosted one-offs and in March 1996, I found myself drafted in to work on 'The Sex Maniacs Ball' alongside Debby.

This was an annual naughty charity bash organised by Tuppy Owens in aid of 'The Outsiders Club' – a group aiming to help disabled people achieve a full sex life. The pervy party had already moved from Brixton Academy after the venue pulled out, and Bagleys had agreed to step in as a last-minute host. But following word from Brixton's police that the venue would be prosecuted under the Obscene Publications Act they also cancelled, leaving an enraged promoter and a salivating press in search of a story.[11]

---

[11] In protest at the police harassment of the Ball, the Sexual Freedom Coalition marched on Downing Street a month later with placards proclaiming, 'Hands Off Our Balls!' before a petition titled: 'Sex Please, We're British' was presented to the prime minister.

LETTING THE CAT OUT OF THE BAGLEYS

Debby and I took call after call and explained over and over again the reasons why Bagleys acted like they did, and by late afternoon we were both exhausted by the repetition, leading to us reducing our sugar-coating of the more graphic details in order to get them off the phone. One conversation is particularly memorable though . . .

Debby: 'Hello, Bagleys.'

Caller: 'I've received a press release from the Sex Maniacs Ball confirming cancellation of their charity event at your venue. Can you explain why you refused to allow this party to take place?'

Debby: 'The Metropolitan Police believe the promotional material is obscene, which may lead to the venue being prosecuted.'

Caller: 'Why's that?'

Debby: 'It graphically depicts an act of anal sex in the presence of more than two people.'

Caller: 'How?'

Debby (wearily): 'There's a cartoon of a penis penetrating a pair of bum cheeks, the gender of which is unclear.'

Caller (long pause): 'Oh, I see, thank you.'

Debby: 'You're welcome. Who's calling again?'

Caller: 'It's Cristina at the *Catholic Herald*.'

Another popular perv party at the time was 'The Rubber Ball' hosted by the aptly named Rubber Ron. I recall one occasion when an incident happened involving another 'outside' promoter. A supposed security bloke (who was employed by the guest promoter) was spotted acting suspiciously by the plain clothes in-house security team. When challenged, he pulled a knife and in the ensuing altercation David Anderson (one of the in-house boys) was killed, and another fella hospitalised.

As a result, at the next 'outside' promotion tensions were understandably high. I was stood on the door totalling up the guest list which had just closed and was just about to head home when the distant plod of the kick drum was superseded by *ACK! ACK! ACK! ACK!* A short staccato series of loud cracks punctuated the party – the sound of gunfire. We all dashed inside as it continued; it sounded like a massacre.

People were ashen-faced. Confusion and fear spread as they saw the grim expressions of the security team rushing through.

A girl in a PVC catsuit holding a whip waved at us and pointed at an exit.

'It's coming from the dungeon room!'

The firing didn't stop, it was sounding like a mass shooting. One of the security pulled out what looked like a pistol, but was more likely a cattle stun gun, as they barged their way across the dancefloor. A girl screamed, instinctively I ran towards the room. Through the small doorway I saw smoke hanging above the crowd. A group were gathered around a prostrate figure writhing on the ground. He was groaning, almost pleasurably. He wasn't wearing any underwear and his bollocks were burnt like a couple of IKEA meatballs. His semi-erect cock appeared to have recently ejaculated and looked to be tied by string. On closer inspection it turned out to be the spent cartridge of a Jumping Jack firework. This was verified by a girl who witnessed him wanking, and lighting them, as he neared his own explosion, climaxing as his knackers popped and sizzled with each 'crack'.

The security looked at each other, shrugged as if to say, 'It takes all sorts . . .' before resuming their positions on the door.

The glass is always half-full

These days the majority of DJs are a brand as much as a person. There's too much money at stake and so their management and agencies usually ensure they remain fit for work. So they're often teetotal and act more like account-ants than artists (an exception is the tragedy of Avicii, which shows what happens when a jockey whips the horse he's riding too hard and for too long . . .).

But back in the day, the DJs were the biggest party animals in the club. Only hedonists, music lovers and stay-awakes would choose to play records after midnight in smoke-filled dens of iniquity. There was no career path or multi-million-pound global DJ circuit, and the DJ was generally regarded as only slightly more important to a club owner as the cloakroom attendant.

So it's pretty accurate to say that almost every big-name DJ who came out of the rave scene or played in London in the '90s was a participant in the pleasure which was being had. With the possible exception of John Digweed who wouldn't even buy himself a beer, let alone anyone else!

A popular female DJ's artist rider at the time stipulated, 'unlimited bottles of Sol, three sliced limes and two empty pint glasses (with handles, if possible)'. During her two-hour set she would chain-drink bottle after bottle of Sol, and as her bladder was smaller than her inhibitions, would take periodic mid-set pees into the pint glasses. All in front of an oblivious crowd who saw her only from the waist up. When the glasses were full, she would place them at the side of the booth so they wouldn't be inadvertently knocked over. There was not a single occasion where those full pint glasses were still there at the end of the night. On one occasion after the lights came up, we all sat down for a chilled-out end-of-night drink as security checked the toilets for anyone missing in action.

Keith the bar manager said, "There was a bloke tonight who kept complaining that the cider was warm – which is odd as we don't sell cider.'

'What did he say to you telling him that?' I asked.

'He couldn't hear as he was off his tits and the bleedin' music was so loud, so I popped in a few ice cubes and he went away happy.'

A food caravan was situated between Bagleys Warehouse and the Cross. For around 5,000 clubbers each Saturday night, it was the only place you could get a warm drink, bite to eat or chocolate bar. It was operated by a gruff bloke also called Terry, who had a wild-eyed Sardinian assistant called Maria, neither of whom gave the impression they had excelled in food hygiene classes at catering college. There was no green food hygiene rating in those days, so my colleague Debby Lee affectionately christened the caravan the 'Roach Coach'.

Naturally, Terry was unaware of this until he read a copy of *TNT Magazine* left on a table by some Aussies who had attended the messy Sunday daytime strippers and booze party, rather blasphemously called 'The Church'. It was the week I'd written a piece on King's Cross being the new hub of London clubland: three venues, walkable from the Tube and train station with cheap food available all night long from the Roach Coach.

The first I knew about this was at 9.30 on Monday morning when the editor of *TNT Magazine* called to inform me that they were being threatened with a claim for damages to reputation, resulting from my insinuation that the outlet was not up to acceptable public health standards. Unless they printed an unreserved apology in the following issue, the lawyers were going all-out for a juicy pay-out. The editor pointed out that each issue of the mag carried a disclaimer, which basically absolved the publisher of any responsibility in the event of legal action taken, which I was faxed for good measure: 'The opinions expressed in our published works are those of the author(s) and do not reflect the opinions of TNT Publishing Limited or its editors.'

Effectively it meant that my ass was on the line and, given that reputational damage is based on turnover, I quickly worked out that as the caravan was serving 10,000 clubbers every week, with no competition and very little by way of overheads or staff costs – it was doing more than alright . . . it was a flaming gold mine! This meant that any loss of revenue would be substantial – as would any costs awarded. What started as something trivial was getting very serious.

I assured the editor I'd write an apology along with a feature on 'every clubber's favourite caravan' in the forthcoming issue and additionally say sorry in person when I was next in the Bagleys office.

Of course, Ms Lee thought the whole thing hilarious and told the great and the good about the episode, probably reaching more people than my initial column. I grovelled, apologised, congratulated Terry on the egg and bacon baps, with the result that he even laminated my follow-up review and displayed it proudly in his window . . . along with the bluebottles that infested the site every summer.

TOP TUNE: 'Free', Ultra Naté

18

CHOONISIA

James Bond had M, I had Jody Sharp – whose company Icon Artists put together live club PAs to promote happening crossover tracks. In May 1996, Jody sent me another mission: the year's biggest dance club hit, 'Ultra Flava' by Farley and Heller Project had been signed by AM:PM and was expected to chart. The track was fronted by a lithe Latin-American force of nature called Baby. As the vocals and lyrics were somewhat repetitive, the record company figured the track's release would benefit from a third-rate white rapper, who could make the promotional club PAs a little more interesting and perhaps lead to more sales. Wonder why Jody thought of me?

After a few sessions working out a routine in the mirror at Pineapple Dance Studios in Covent Garden, the simple instrumental house groove had been restructured into a seven-minute slice of (loosely) choreographed chaos, featuring a pouty, shouty singer, a gobby rave MC and the obligatory two attractive female dancers. As much as this is a great dance track, there's not a lot going on melodically, so lots of room for dodgy eight-bar raps and call-and-response sections – plus a l-o-n-g breakdown, which I randomly filled with Samuel L. Jackson's pre-murder monologue from *Pulp Fiction*. You know, the one that starts with, 'Blessed is he, who in the name of charity and good-will, shepherds the weak through the valley of darkness,' and ends with, '. . . and you will know my name is the Lord, when I lay my vengeance upon thee!'

While this had absolutely no relevance to the track, it was instantly recognisable to the crowd and filled that suspense-laden breakdown that we performed in the clubs.

As it turned out, we only did two shows, debuting the show overseas with Jody vaguely describing it as 'somewhere in Ireland'. I had visions of fishermen's cottages, country pubs or perhaps a night out in vibrant Dublin. Instead, we played at a pub with a flat roof on a housing estate in west Belfast, my trepidation turning to elation because the crowd were amazing. I said we did two shows with 'Ultra Flava'. Strictly speaking we only ever did the one in Belfast: the other was in Tunisia at the National Stadium, as part of a celebration televised concert to mark the country's fortieth anniversary of independence.

This would be the most chaotic trip overseas of them all, which is really saying something!

Tuning up . . .

First, some background. In 1996, the Republic of Tunisia was not only celebrating twenty years since gaining inde-pendence, they were also about to become the first Arab state to enter into a free trade agreement with the EU. This was a big deal. However, there were some in Brussels who raised eyebrows at the level of corruption, human rights abuses and lack of press freedoms in the country.[12] For example, Michael Jackson performed a concert in Tunisia that year during his HIStory World Tour. Jackson donated the proceeds from the concert to 26-26, a government-run 'charity', ostensibly focused on supporting vulnerable groups in Tunisia. President Ben Ali's government allegedly pocketed more than half the money. Dissenting voices were arrested, tortured and imprisoned on trumped-up charges. There were threats made on the long-serving president's life and he, at the time of my visit, had moved from one of his presidential grand palaces to a safe house.

Without knowing it, I was walking straight into a political powder keg and as a performer was unknowingly being used by the regime to demonstrate they were progressive and culturally open, fun-lovin' guys. Rather than the 'electric-shocks-to-the-genitals' type of guys they really were.

I'd arranged to meet Baby outside the Body Shop in Heathrow Terminal 2, but she hadn't shown. So after checking in alone, I walked to the departure gate wondering where the hell she was. Baby was in the Reel 2 Real posse and appeared in the 'I Like to Move It' video, bringing twerking to the world. At the time of this trip, she was involved in a volatile relationship with Keith Flint from the Prodigy. It transpired she'd nearly missed our plane to

---

[12] In May 1996, the European Parliament for the first time adopted a resolution critical of the 'deterioration' of the human rights situation in Tunisia. The long-overdue resolution, which provoked a sharp response from Tunisia's parliament, called on the European Council and Commission to urge the Tunisian authorities to 'alter their policy toward the democratic opposition and honour their international human rights commitments.'

Africa after waking up to find all her belongings on the front lawn; Keith had thrown them out of the upstairs bedroom window.

'Why did he do that?' I asked, concerned, when she finally showed up.

She broke off from applying her make-up and sighed. 'Because I did the same to him last week, I guess.'

The next single the Prodigy released featured lyrics penned by Keith. It was called, 'Baby's Got a Temper'. There was never a dull moment when Baby was around.

As soon as we arrived at the hotel it was explained there would be a rehearsal and sound check mainly for the TV camera's benefit. So after checking in, we were told to assemble in the foyer, where all the artists would be taken to the stadium in buses. An hour later, I was stood on a small platform in the middle of the football pitch with a few lights overhead and a pathetically small PA system.

The artists, a collection of chart acts from France, Germany and the US, were underwhelmed. There were no visuals because there were no big screens and little in the way of sound. The 'stage' was effectively a dozen of those thin plywood loft boards you buy in B&Q, which were laid on the grass in the centre circle of the pitch, around 50 metres from the stands. There was, I noticed, no cover whatsoever and an exceptional amount of exposed electrical equipment, unsecured cables and lighting.

'What if it rains?' I asked the bossy guy in a fez, who was barking instructions in Arabic to someone in the TV gantry.

He smiled. 'This is Tunis, sir. It never rains.'

We ran half-heartedly through our set and when everyone was done, boarded the buses back to the hotel.

After dinner and a few drinks with the other acts (a French boyband, an Armenian crooner and a brash hip-hop crew from the Bronx who repeatedly tried to coax Baby and Vanessa into an orgy in their room), I decided to have an early night.

On returning to my room on the sixth floor, I noticed someone sat on a chair outside the room next to mine. He wore a suit, dark glasses and held a radio, but was very polite, even bidding me a 'goodnight'.

Weary from the day's journey I soon fell asleep but was woken a few hours later by the sound of thunder. I watched entranced as my room momentarily flickered in a brilliant blue-white light before a huge thunderclap made the windows rattle. I walked to the window and could see it was raining heavily, spots of water bounced on my balcony ledge. Down below, people scurried, and car horns made it sound like it was a once-a year occurrence. The rain kept me awake for another hour, occasional deluges which eventually calmed into a constant soothing *shhhhhhhhh*. I turned over and lost consciousness to natural white noise.

The next morning, I had breakfast with Baby and Vanessa. They'd declined the orgy and had what they described as a 'girls' night in'. An announcement was made for all artists to assemble in the foyer at 10 a.m. It had stopped raining, but the damage from the deluge was still being assessed by hotel staff, mopping up vast puddles and fixing the awning outside the main entrance, which had collapsed beneath the sheer weight of water.

We assembled to be told that due to the storm the venue was flooded, the pitch waterlogged and the concert, due to commence late afternoon, would now start at 9 p.m. that night.

We spent the late morning around the hotel pool, and the early afternoon hanging around to be interviewed by Tunisian TV. The guy asked the same four questions to each act.

'Is this your first time in People's Republic of Tunisia?'

'Yes.'

'Are you enjoying your visit?'

'So far, yes, but I haven't left the hotel.'

Which prompted a supplemental question: 'Do you like the Hotel El Mechtel?'

'Yes.'

And tellingly: 'Have you performed in any other Arab states or is this the first?'

The propaganda exercise over, the hip-hop crew said they'd 'scored some shit from the guy in the laundry room' and were predictably trying to get any female performer present back to their room. All politely declined as many, including myself, wanted to see something of the ancient city of Carthage.

Despite ordering cab after cab from reception we remained in the foyer. After forty-five minutes we gave up and decided to hail one ourselves. I ventured outside past an uncomfortable-looking doorman and could make out an army roadblock around 50 metres on each side of the hotel, preventing any cabs from entering. The soldiers were armed and on seeing us, walked down the road and ordered us back inside. We were told that the situation outside was dangerous, and a guided bus tour of the city was being organised. We should go back to our rooms or 'enjoy the pool' and a bus would pick us up at 4 p.m.

But 4 p.m. came and went and there was no bus. By 4.30 I'd had enough and returned to my room. I was surprised to see the camera crew in the corridor outside the room next to mine, outside of which sat the 'sentry' with a radio. Pissed off, frustrated and feeling imprisoned, I decided to tell the presenter that the artists were not happy, and that this was not a nice way to treat guests. I purposely walked past my room and into the one next door. A burly man stood framed in the doorframe in shirtsleeves. He wore a black leather shoulder holster and on seeing me appear, reached for his gun. I froze. Beyond him I could see a man in a suit being interviewed by the white-robed TV presenter.

Gun drawn, he beckoned me to back out of the room. Automatically I raised my hands, as you do when someone is pointing a pistol at you.

'Who are you? Why are you here?'

'I'm MC Vitamin K from the Farley and Heller Project.'

He was unmoved. Clearly not a cowbell house enthusiast.

'Ultra Flava? You know, der-du-der-der, der-du-der-der . . .' I'm now doing minstrel hands in time with the bassline. The gun is still pointing at me.

Still nothing.

'I'm performing at the concert. The president invited me.'

Hearing this, the man being interviewed rose to his feet and intervened, muttering something to the man with the gun, who immediately put the thing away. He beckoned me to enter the room and offered me a cup of mint tea. As he resumed his interview, I saw framed photos were strategically placed either side of his head and could be seen framed in the cameraman's monitor. One was of the Pope and the other Nelson Mandela. Closer inspection revealed both images also featured the man being interviewed.

CHOONISIA

His interview complete, he turned his attention to me and thanked me on behalf of the People's Republic of Tunisia for my contribution to the 'celebration of independence and for sharing my musical culture with his people'. Was this the show's organiser? He appeared to be – and he was clearly *very* well-connected.

I politely asked him why we weren't allowed to leave the hotel. He feigned surprise before fixing me with his piercing eyes and explaining that it was easy to get lost in Tunis, and he'd gone to great lengths to put the concert on, and would appreciate it if we could make a small sacrifice and remain here until after the show.

Changing the subject, he asked me if I had children. I replied that I didn't. He picked up another photo, one of three girls, presumably his daughters, and told me one day I should. Family is 'the greatest gift a man can possess. Nice to meet you.' Following a handshake and fake smile, he nodded to the man with the gun, who stepped forward and gestured for me to leave.

I found Baby and Vanessa at the poolside, the former rubbing sun oil into the latter's back, avidly observed by the NY hip-hop crew, salivating like hungry dogs under a restaurant table.

Suddenly it grew darker. A hammer-head-shaped cloud was exploding in slow motion to the west, expanding at a rate of knots. Rain was coming. Again.

Sure enough, fifteen minutes later another deluge dropped from the dark grey sky.

We knew what this meant and, sure enough, after being told to assemble in the foyer at 6 p.m. we were given the bad news: the show had been moved to the following day. There was uproar. Tomorrow was a Saturday. Every ass-shakin', hip-thrustin', mic-spittin' club PA act had a show booked somewhere in Europe. Contracts were signed and flights had been paid for.

Baby called Jody. Jody said something along the lines of 'Fuck 'em, if they can't cover their stage, it's their own fault' and confirmed the flight tickets were non-transferable. She'd already received 50 per cent of the fee upfront and after checking the contract, rescheduling at such short notice was not a valid reason to withhold the balance. Everyone's agents said the same. No one had any desire to remain under hotel arrest a moment longer. The hotel telephones were used to plot an escape. We would eat dinner and act like we were all going to bed like good boys and girls and then, an hour later, rendezvous in reception at 9 p.m. and find a nightclub.

At the witching hour, we arrived in the foyer and ordered cabs. But once again, no cabs appeared.

The hip-hop crew had had enough. 'Fuck this! I'm gonna give them some Noo Yoirk!'

Marching up to the desk one of the rappers demanded freedom.

The blokes behind reception pleaded that they were ordering the cabs, as requested.

'Then where da fuck are they?'

At this point I walked outside to see a policeman waving any approaching cabs away.

Just then, another one of the hip-hop crew called everyone into a huddle. His mate in the laundry room had a brother who had a cab company which wasn't normally allowed to pick up from the front of the hotel but could pick us up from the service yard in the underground car park. Five minutes later, around a dozen of us were riding to our freedom in illicit cabs, speeding through the now-dry streets of Tunis. Eager to experience our freedom fully, we opened all the windows and were assailed by the aromas of liberty – jasmine flowers vibrant after the rain, unfamiliar spices from roadside market stalls, the BBQ smoke of lamb stew steaming in homes, and the balmy, humid early-summer North African air. I closed my eyes and inhaled deeply, holding the cocktail of scents in my lungs long enough for it to enter my capillaries and flow around my body. After twenty-four hours in the sanitised, air-conditioned, sterile hotel, it felt good. I finally felt I was in North Africa.

'Where are we going?'

'To my cousin's club in Sidi Bou Said.'

'Whoooo!'

Thirty minutes later, we're stood in a quiet suburb of a quaint Mediterranean-style village, as a somewhat dishevelled nightclub-manager unlocks an arched gateway. We follow him into an alfresco split-level venue. A stage and dancefloor are overlooked on three sides by terraced gallery seating areas. There are large bars on both levels, both drenched from the earlier rainstorm.

Other staff arrive, get busy with dispersing the water and the power is turned on. Impressive uplighting shows the building's classic Carthaginian curves, a dome and whitewashed stone walls. I feel like I'm in Ibiza ... but mortar alone does not make for merriment. Where are the people?

The manager explains that they are officially closed tonight but will open for us, an exclusive private party. As there are only a dozen of us there, I urge him to invite his regulars and maybe we could perform for them.

RAVE NEW WORLD

He jumps on the phone and excitedly spreads the word: a free party hosted by the artists who were performing at the fortieth independence celebration. This results in a steady stream of older, designer-dressed types, obviously the Tunis 'in crowd'. Within an hour there are around 150 glamorous party-seekers, whose numbers are swelled by the rest of the artists who've heard what's happening and managed to escape from the hotel. What followed is a great example of what happens when people come together to celebrate life: performers do their thing, the hip-hop boys spit and rap, dancers dance and singers sing over whatever the DJ plays. It feels the 2,800-mile round trip isn't a waste of time after all.

It's 2 a.m and the party is building nicely. More and more people are arriving. I'm sat upstairs drinking Bouka's, a strong traditional fig-based cocktail, as there is no alternative mood modification. Karim, the affluent 22-year-old son of a junior government minister, is asking me about life in London. 'Do you live near George Michael?' he asks.

I'm more interested in life in Tunisia. He tells me about Law 52, which sentences drugs users for a minimum of one year and up to five years' imprisonment – and a fine of up to 3,000 dinar (£1,000) whatever the substance is, even *zatla* (hashish). I hear how the law was brought in by President Ben Ali, to show he was tough on drugs after his younger brother was implicated in an international drug-smuggling operation between Amsterdam, Paris and Tunisia, which was known as the *'couscous connection'*.

But it gets better. Before he could be arrested, he flashed his diplomatic immunity card and fled back to Tunis, where he was currently evading a ten-year prison sentence for being the 'bag man' for the gang.

Karim explains that President Ben Ali is hated by the country's youth, considered corrupt and is deeply unpopular. 'Certain people want to kill him, that's why he moves around his palaces.'

'Which one is he in now?'

'My father says he is staying at your hotel, as he knows it won't be shelled with foreign artists and media staying there.'

A little later, Karim finds me on the dancefloor as Robert Miles' 'Children' hypnotises all present. 'This is best party ever! Everyone is here – including Moncef.'

'Who?'

'The president's brother – the guy in the couscous connection!'

'Maybe *he's* got some gear?'

Karim laughs. Behind him, a waning yellow moon appears in a cloudless starlit sky. Despite everything, we'd still managed to start the party . . . and the night was still young.

The music abruptly stops. When this happens your eyes involuntarily turn to the DJ, who is flanked by stern-looking men in uniform, some wielding what look like canes. The senior man in the booth, who is wearing a lopsided green fez, says something authoritative in Arabic into the microphone. People around me quietly murmur their displeasure, but shuffle obediently from the dancefloor and out of the exits, each manned by a soldier.

He then addresses us.

'Ladies and gentlemen guests, there is transport waiting outside to take you back to the hotel. We wish you a peaceful night's sleep. Tomorrow is the concert, you will need your strength. Goodnight!'

As I depart, I cast my eyes around the gallery. It has been cleared, except for one table in the roped-off VIP area. A middle-aged man remonstrates with soldiers, who appear to have confiscated an ice bucket containing a bottle from his table. This was the only time I witnessed a Tunisian question authority during my visit, and it may well have been the last time he did it.

We were herded back onto the buses for the silent ride back to the hotel. Pausing at an intersection at a red light, it was impossible to ignore a huge placard from which a man smiled. At the next junction he was there again. In fact, his face was plastered all over the city. I recognised that smile and dark arched eyebrows. It was my hotel next-door neighbour, the man whose interview I'd interrupted. The man I thought was the show's promoter was in fact the iron-fisted, murderous dictator President Zine El Abidine Ben Ali, and his safe house from death threats from Islamic militants and goodness knows who else appeared to be the hotel room next door to mine!

I went to bed, bidding a nervous goodnight to the guard on the chair in the corridor, who this time wasn't so polite, instead completely ignoring me. He had a gun and no doubt the master key to all the rooms, so I made sure to put the small brass chain across the door, telling myself rather optimistically that would keep him out. I barely slept.

I awoke to find an envelope had been slid under my door. It contained a personal message from President Ben Ali, urging us to remain and pointing out that refusing to perform would be considered an insult to our hosts, who had shown traditional hospitality, and deserved consideration before making any decision.

Within fifteen minutes it was faxed to the US Embassy by a clearly very nervous receptionist. Given he had four angry fellas from the Bronx and one hell-raising diva leaning over the desk, he probably felt he had no other option.

Diplomacy took to the dancefloor and executed a series of deft moves. It was clarified that while all artists could leave of their own free will, no guarantees would be made over scheduling reliability or any provision for transport made. Additionally, any artists who remained would be given a $500 bonus and receive a certificate and medal from President Ben Ali himself.

Being honest, I considered remaining for another day or two, banking the money and picking up another certificate to add to those received from the Croatian and Soviet governments a few years earlier, but the moment soon passed. I was going home.

Three days later, I read in the *Guardian* that the younger brother of President Ben Ali, 'Moncef', was found dead 'in unexplained circumstances' at his villa in Tunis. An assassination some observers accused Ben Ali of ordering.

' . . . family is the greatest gift a man can possess.'

TOP TUNE: 'For What You Dream Of' (Renaissance Mix), Bedrock feat. KYO

19

POP: MY GREATEST MISSES

Boys in particular love being in bands. They give the same sense of family as a gang or being in the Army. What's more, girls notice you and you can hide behind a new identity. You also make lots of money and get to appear on telly . . . what's not to like?

I had been in and out of bands from my teens to my late twenties, with the urge deserting me when I embraced rave culture in the late '80s, but after a few years it dawned on me that I was well-placed for a second shot at stardom. I had found myself at the epicentre of a new movement, knew all the DJs and promoters and had a seemingly endless stream of weird and wonderful ideas.

So, in spring 1992, I found myself back in the studio, this time with an old raving buddy of mine, Gavin Mills (formerly DJ Face, now known as Copyright), to record a summer house anthem which used the hook from the musical *Hair* – 'Let the Sunshine In'.

The track sounded great and was picking up traction from the handful of DJs we sent it to, it was even played on Kiss 100. But I was skint and could only afford to press up fifty promos, so it sank without trace. Imagine my glee, then, when a few months later Milk & Sugar had a huge international hit with an almost identical track . . .

Not knowing when I was beat, I sold my next idea to Nick Gordon Brown at DMC. They were the owners of *Mixmag* at the time and put me in their studio to record a dance version of 'Zorba's Theme' for a label they had called Reflex Records, along with Johnny Remould and the best damned bouzouki player in Haringey. Alas, 'Zorba's Dance' by Bouzouki Joe didn't trouble the chart compilers, record shop owners, or indeed the general public.

The vinyl countdown

Just outside the Domesday village of Icklesham in East Sussex, there's a windmill on a hill, which has been converted into Paul McCartney's private recording studio.

In February 1994, Macca, George Harrison and Ringo were gathered together in a recording studio for the first time since John Lennon had been murdered. In order to make their first recording session as the Beatles for twenty-five years a little less uneasy, they pretended Lennon's absence was down to the fact he'd 'popped out for lunch'. This was made more poignant as they were listening to a recently discovered cassette recording of an unheard John Lennon song.

At the same time, just off the M4 in Slough, I was pretending to be the lead singer of hair metal one-hit wonders Europe in the DMC Studios with the one and only Kym Mazelle and reclusive Europop lover and producer of sonic cheese Johnny Remould as I recorded my next assault on the charts. Figuring that with the millennium on the horizon, and the century running out, a Europop version of 'The Final Countdown' was just what the world needed. Imagine Joey Tempest had just popped out for lunch.

Despite penning new words for the verses and bridge, Joey Tempest's people insisted on retaining 100 per cent of the publishing after arguing that it was the horn fanfare which was the hook, and no one really cared about the words. They were right, of course, but it was worth a try.

Initially things looked promising. It came out on the DMC label FBI Records and the guy who ran DMC Greece in Athens thought it had huge potential, inviting Full Power! – as we were overconfidently monikered – to Thessaloniki on a promo tour. Johnny Remould didn't have a passport (as getting one required the possession of a birth certificate, driving licence and bank account – none of which he gave the impression of being familiar with). So I called up an angle-grinding, fire-breathing, razorblade-swallowing redhead called Lucifire I'd seen perform at Torture Garden to form a live act for the promo tour. Our unique fusion of edgy circus self-harm and rabble-raising white boy MCing left crowd after crowd of Greek clubbers speechless. Not so much blown away as utterly bewildered.

'Heavy rock, Europop, rapping, eating razor blades, fire-breathing, blowing an air horn, masks and occult imagery . . . the only thing Full Power! don't do is actually make any sense,' was one clearly underwhelmed reviewer's response relayed to us on the radio the next morning.

The Greeks, along with *everyone* else for that matter, never shared my vision and 'The Final Countdown' never led to lift-off.

Three months later, I return home to an excited voicemail from my mate Terry who lived in Halkidiki and who'd driven us around on the promo tour.

'Hey, Kirk, congratulations! Your song "The Final Countdown" is on TV all the time!'

'It is?'

'Yes, we must hear it eight or ten times every day.'

'Wow!' Then I remembered we hadn't done a video for it.

'Who's performing it?'

'No one. It's the music on a double-glazing advert.'

I put the phone down, deflated.

Around a week later, I was mournfully looking through a copy of the music industry weekly, *Music Week*. It told of a major new multimedia project by the Beatles called Anthology. The phone suddenly rang. It was Jody Sharp. I'd done her press when she headed up Tom Watkins' label Atomic a few years earlier and we got on really well, sharing a pre-rave affection for Theatre of Hate. She told me she had set up Icon Artists, an agency I mentioned earlier, which supplied acts for the burgeoning nationwide networks of nightclubs and 'fun pubs' who would feature a 'Live PA' from a current chart dance hit.

Aware that I was utterly shameless with a microphone and harboured a burning desire to get on *TOTP*, she told me there was a huge dance anthem I was certain to know which was about to chart, and they needed a frontman to perform it on a UK club tour. Strangely, its creator, Dutch producer Patrick Prins, didn't fancy driving up the

M6 every Friday and Saturday to perform it for a few hundred quid.

She sent it over by bike courier the next day. I opened up the package and inserted the CD, which simply said the Ethics – 'La Luna'. A driving tribal intro gave way to a very familiar sample: 'To the beat of the drum, bang. To the beat of the drum, bang, bang!' was a relative blank canvas, allowing me some vocal input in the form of some very dubious eight-bar raps.[13] Jody invited me to Pineapple Dance Studios in Covent Garden to rehearse with two young dancers, which she filmed and sent to Patrick for approval.

For the next few weeks, we toured the hell out of it. Appearing at raves and clubs up and down the country, promoting it to thousands of people. The crowds loved it and I was hearing from Jody the pre-orders were considerable and Virgin were expecting 'chart action'.

Could this finally be my chance?

The record was released on Saturday, 11 November 1995, and we all waited nervously for Tuesday when the midweek chart positions are released to the industry.

The phone rang. It was Gina from Virgin. The track's midweek chart position was number eighteen. This was incredible – straight into the top twenty from nowhere!

The next few nights I couldn't sleep, and even took a Tube to Virgin Megastore, where I rearranged their NEW

---

[13] For three years, I spent each weekend being driven up and down the motorways to deliver two-song fifteen-minute shows of tracks that were blowing up at the time. As there was minimal vocal content in the tracks (often just a sample repeated rhythmically ad infinitum), my job was to engage the crowd, raise the energy level and generally inject a performance element into proceedings.

racks so that the Ethics were prominent, and bought a few copies. Didn't everyone do that with their first impending taste of chart glory?

Sunday couldn't come fast enough. I counted the hours down to Radio 1's *Official Chart* show which started at 5 p.m. After the first hour (in the rundown from forty to twenty), the track hadn't been mentioned. Did this mean it had dropped out completely or gone in higher?

By number fifteen, there was still no mention.

'Last week's number seven, this week's number fourteen . . . that was Happy Clappers with "I Believe". Another new entry at number thirteen, here's the Ethics . . .'

At that precise moment, Mark Goodier was my favourite person on earth. He'd just delivered the dream.

Straight in at number thirteen! Surely this confirmed my appearance on this Thursday's *Top of the Pops*?

Around mid-morning on Monday, Gina from Virgin called to confirm just that.

Membership of the Musicians' Union was swiftly organised and extra rehearsal times in Pineapple booked in readiness. I gave my address for them to send a cab to take me to the BBC, before calling my barber, Daniel, at Cuts to slot me in for a 'TV trim'. I'd waited all my life for this moment and wanted to look my best.

I went for a run over Ally Pally and felt I could run for ever. I was actually going to be on *Top of the Pops*, beamed into millions of homes across the country, following in the platform boots, Doc Martens and winklepickers of everyone who'd made an impression on me down the years: David Bowie, the Sweet, Slade, Alvin Stardust, the Stranglers, the Jam, Soft Cell, the Smiths, Orbital and the Prodigy.

I could now die happy. I may not have played for Man Utd, married my childhood sweetheart Hania Placzek or become a *Blue Peter* presenter, but this was a more than adequate prize. All those who criticised my singing, all those who laughed at my aspirations to shun a proper job and chase adventure would see me and choke on their cups of tea.

On Wednesday morning, the day before the show, the phone rang again. It was Gina from Virgin.

'Hi, Kirk, bad news I'm afraid. *Top of the Pops* have just called us with the news that they've been offered the world television exclusive on the first new Beatles single for twenty-five years . . . it's not coming out for another six weeks, but they *must* run it this week. This means they have to drop an act. Your performance has been moved to next week . . . as long as the single doesn't drop, that is.'

Emptiness.

I couldn't bear to watch the show.

I never watched it again.

'To the Beat of the Drum' dropped five places to number eighteen in the following week's chart. The dream was over. Again.

'NEVER BEEN THIS HIGH . . . GONNA TOUCH THE SKY'

I vowed never to make another record, but I continued treading the boards as I enjoyed performing in the clubs. I was doing pretty good too: fronting the re-release of 'High' for Hyper Go Go and earning lots of cash every weekend as myself, Kate Hollingsworth and her iconic pink rubber dress were driven around the empty motorway network. We were sometimes joined onstage by Alex Bell, who together with James Diplock wrote the music, or were chauffeured by a cast of characters who were seldom boring.

We promoted 'High' for the best part of a year, prompting its re-release in October 1996. Although it went in at thirty-two, it fell the next week without Radio 1 support and without a *Top of the Pops* appearance.

Typically, we'd do a few shows each night, one in, say, Milton Keynes at 10 p.m. followed by another in Sheffield at 1 a.m. On occasion, we'd even play an all-nighter on the way back at 3 a.m. Kate would be asleep on the back seat while I would sit up front.

One of our drivers let it be known that he was a dealer with some very high-end clients. Each week when we'd exhausted the football, there'd come a point when I'd ask him whose nose he'd blown since we'd last seen him. His answers ranged from an Oscar-winning movie star with a weakness for entertaining two black girls at a time ('I might be in the middle of something, but come right in, the dough's on the bedside table'), Premier League footballers ('always jumpy and not the smartest people') and the usual aristocrats and wholesome TV presenters ('I can't resist saying, "Here's one I made earlier" when we exchange').

The failure of 'High' to pleasurably penetrate the soft, moist top thirty merely confirmed my intention to avoid all recording studios and assaults on the charts. Nineteen ninety-nine appeared, and like many of my generation I was celebrating a decade in dance music. I'd achieved a lot in that time while having the time of my life. It was a shame about never having a hit record, but I'd been involved in the most successful raves and clubs in London and made my living doing what I loved.

Croatian promoter and good friend Dinko asked me to put together a track to mark the Back to the Future edition of his 'Future Shock 2001' rave, similar to the way 'Love

Parade' and 'Mayday' in Germany used to release an official anthem each year.

I told him I'd retired, but as Croatians don't play cricket, he won me over by pointing out that it was me inviting him to Rage which had kick-started the Croatian rave scene — and this anthem would be a celebration of that culture.

So in scenes reminiscent of *The Blues Brothers*, I embarked on a mission to 'get the band back together' for one last show, calling up Johnny Remould and delicious Dartford diva, Tara McDonald. Whether it was out of pity or just a love of adventure, they came on board, and we put together a Sonique-influenced slice of Euro-friendly pop dance: I wrote some unity-promoting lyrics which Tara sang beautifully; I sent it to Dinko, wished him luck and thought nothing more about it.

A few months later he invited us over to Zagreb to perform it in front of 5,000 people. On arrival at the airport, the TV cameras were waiting as they usually were for a big-name DJ. I looked around the arrivals lounge but there were no likely candidates carrying record boxes.

We emerged from the airport to a hail of flashbulbs. A pretty girl presenter thrust a microphone in my face as a cameraman scuttled up behind her, pointing his camera over her shoulder at me.

'MC Sundance! Future Shock Team featuring Tara![14] Congratulations on your number one! How does it feel, topping the charts in Croatia?'

---

[14] Despite working with me, Tara McDonald went on to become a successful singer-songwriter, working with David Guetta, Axwell, Todd Terry and Armand Van Helden, as well as being a voice coach on *The Voice*.

'Sorry?' I looked at Dinko. He eyes glinted with mischief.

'I will tell you later, please promote the show,' he gruffly whispered.

'Wow! Hey, Tara, come here. We're number one! Thank you, Croatia, we will see you tonight at Future Shock!'

Tara blew kisses to an entire nation, causing teenage crushes from the Adriatic to Zagreb . . . while also wondering who the bloke with the quiff and conjunctivitis stood next to her was.

As we rode to the hotel, Dinko explained there was good news and bad news. His co-promoter in Future Shock!, Damir Cuculić, hosted *Top DJ Mag*, a three-hour show on state TV each Saturday night, which was sponsored by a soft drinks company. During the show, Damir would count down the biggest dance tunes of the week, and guess what was at number one that week? The bad news was that the track wasn't released as a single, but instead was the opening track on a forthcoming compilation CD.

It was a technicality as far as I was concerned. I'd finally had a number-one record.

Thank you, Croatia.

**TOP TUNE: 'Back to the Future',
FS Team feat. Tara**

20

HUNTING THE HAND OF GOD

It's Wednesday, 25 November 2020, and the death of Diego Maradona has just been announced. Facebook is filled with accolades and Gary Lineker tweets, 'May he find comfort in the hands of God.'

In 2006, Lineker became the first English journalist to interview Maradona since that 1986 World Cup quarter-final goal he scored against England. It was some coup. When it aired again the week of his death, it reminded me of how close I came to getting the scoop myself while in Ibiza in July 1998, working on a feature for London listings mag, *Time Out*.

On my travels I'd struck up a rapport with the genial German owner of a café in a corner of Plaza del Parque, just outside Dalt Vila in Ibiza Town. I got the impression that Stefan was involved in the mythical Full Moon clifftop psy-trance gatherings and cave raves which had been happening in the north of the island but were increasingly getting busted by a noticeably purposeful police force. He told me they suspected the Discoteca Association of major clubs felt threatened by the growing success of the free parties and were tipping off the police.

I liked Stefan. He reminded me of the first wave of idealists who shaped Ibiza before the age of the superclubs and superstar DJs. I'd call in every morning for an avocado toast and fruit smoothie, and we'd swap stories about the underground scene back in London and Berlin, while lamenting how corporate Ibiza was becoming but still wide-eyed affirming its spirit and magic. We also agreed the superclubs were too English-dominated at that time and that the island was at its most potent when embracing multiple influences and cultures.

One morning he introduced me to an Argentinian friend of his. Whenever I met Argentinians in those days, I'd break the ice by reassuring them that there were many in the UK who felt the Crown's claim on the Falkland Islands was questionable, and that the war was an opportunistic throw of the dice by a struggling prime minister, rather than a 'do or die' Dunkirk or D-Day moment in our history. The Argie guy appreciated my words and added that the hated military junta who ran Argentina at the time were equally at fault for the tragic loss of young lives on both sides.

As I rose to leave, he told me I was like no Englishman he had ever met, and that this could *'open a door no other Englishman could open'*. I didn't have a clue what he was talking about and set off on my white PX125 Vespa to interview the DJ Jon Sa Trinxa at his beach bar residency on the island's most glam beach, Salinas.

After the interview had ended, I stayed around and listened to Jon play to the beautiful people. Suddenly there were raised voices. Previously reclining bodies stiffened and sat bolt upright. They were pointing towards a stocky figure who was approaching from the left, swaggering with arms 45 degrees from his thickset torso in trunks, with a towel swinging from his left hand. As he drew level with the volleyball court, a player shouted 'Diego!' and threw him the ball. The stocky figure leant back and chested the ball up onto his head, where it bounced around half a dozen times to much whooping and cheering from onlookers. He then dropped his towel and juggled the ball for around a minute, using every available part of his body.

After this he kicked the ball high above his head, giving him time to pick up the beach towel from the sand, beckon to his group that he was ready to leave, before the ball returned to his forehead – where it was perfectly cushioned and remained motionless, drawing gasps of astonishment from all around. He then strolled off down the beach, balancing the volleyball on his forehead and occasionally gently heading it, always in complete control and never breaking stride. The eyes of everyone on the beach followed him in silence, until he was a mere speck, at which point a volleyball player gestured fruitlessly in his direction and said '*nuestra pelota!*' ('it's our ball!'). The other players looked at him and simply shrugged, '*Dios*' (God). And that's how I found out that Diego Maradona was on the island.

I rode back to Ibiza Town through the sultry evening air, parked my Vespa beneath a palm tree in Plaza del Parque and spotted Stefan chatting outside. He waved me over and I told him about what had just happened at the beach. He told me that Diego's friends were in the café a little earlier and had asked him if he would open for a private party for Diego and a few friends after midnight. Stefan agreed and accepted it would be private, but that he had a friend he'd like to invite who was not like a typical Englishman, and would it be okay if he came along as his guest? This was approved, but they added that Diego would only talk with me if he felt I could be trusted. The British tabloids had given him a hard time after his infamous 'Hand of God' goal helped knock England out of the 1986 Mexico World Cup, and as result he hadn't spoken to the British press since. This was an amazing scoop, which any British journalist would regard as a career-defining moment.

I was due to go to Pacha that night but decided to blow it out and go to Stefan's café instead. I rode back to San An, just managing to catch the sunset at Café del Mar, before grabbing a pizza from Capricci. This I took back to my room in the Manumission Trips Hostel (Es Calo Playa), which Andy had put me in as a sweetener to writing about his burgeoning holiday company. I crashed out, after first setting my alarm for 1 a.m.

I awoke feeling really groggy, as you generally do with less than four hours' sleep, and got on my Vespa. Although I had always hired scooters to get around the island, my Ibicenco friends always told me to avoid riding the main road between San An and Ibiza Town at night. That's when everyone is over the limit on drink and drugs and driving way too fast. But the budget I was on didn't stetch to a return taxi and as I had no plans to drink, I wouldn't have to worry about police roadblocks.

I got to Stefan's as he was opening the shutters. We went inside and he turned a light on, before pulling back down the wooden shutter so it looked as if the place was closed.

And there we waited. And waited. And waited. It got to 3.30 a.m. and the phone rang. After a brief conversation Stefan looked at me ruefully and said, 'Diego's gone to

Pacha tonight, but wants to come here tomorrow for a private party instead.' Although I was on the guest list at Pacha, it would've been long closed by now.

I rode back, shivering and scything through the chilly night air, which grew ever colder as I passed Privilege and rode over the San Rafael ridge, past Quid Pro Quo. The air grew colder, and I was pleased to reach the summit and see the twinkling lights of San Antonio in the distance below me, the familiar shapes of the bungee tower, Es Paradis pyramid and dome of Eden.

A call to Stefan the next day confirmed that I missed nothing and that the party was still on for later that night. Or maybe the next night. So for the next few days I followed the same ritual of sunset, pizza, a few hours' sleep, before a lonely ride through to Ibiza Town, hoping for an audience with Diego Maradona, which always ended the same way. Diego had decided to stay at his villa, Diego was in Pacha again, Diego was everybloodywhere except the place he was supposed to be!

To make matters worse, people I was interviewing were full of Diego stories. Pippi told me how he'd joined in with the percussionist in Pacha, before walking off with two €400 bongos under his arms. Another contact told me how he'd stood on a chair in a restaurant and sang the Argentinian national anthem, prompting applause from all present. A few weeks earlier he'd been given a suspended jail sentence of two years and ten months for shooting at journalists with an air rifle. But he was clearly living large in Ibiza, while the 1998 World Cup reached a climax (the first tournament for sixteen years not to feature Maradona's name in the Argentina squad, incidentally). The myth surrounding the man had reached mystical proportions after he had correctly prophesied both the finalists and winner of the World Cup on live TV some weeks earlier.

But my time on the island was drawing to a close. I'd waited for the diminutive Diego for three nights running and had nothing to show for it. I reluctantly bid goodbye to Stefan, who beseeched me to stay another night as he was 100 per cent sure it would be the night it happened.

I was torn; I couldn't afford to cancel my flight and go through the hassle of trying to find a new hotel (it was high season and San An was like Bethlehem on Christmas Eve), and what would happen if there was another no-show? I couldn't stay indefinitely, waiting for someone who was notoriously unreliable and didn't owe me anything. But I asked Stefan to let me know if Diego's party ever happened.

So I left on the midnight Gatwick flight, and got home to my flat in Arsenal, north London, just as the sun rose on a glorious summer day. As I crept in, not wanting to wake my girlfriend, I poured myself a glass of red wine to help me sleep and as I was doing so, noticed the red answerphone light blinking.

I hit the button and the dawn peace was broken by a robotic voice: '*You were called today at 3.17 a.m. To listen to the message press 1.*' I pressed 1. There followed the sound of what sounded like a party on the other end of the phone, before a genial German spoke, '*Hey, Kirk, the party is happening, where are you?*' I could hear raucous voices, laughter and shouting and singing until the robotic voice interrupted, '*To return this call press 1, to delete press 2, to save press 3.*' I pressed 1, but no one picked up.

I replaced the receiver and went into the toilet for a pee. Just as I was in mid-flow the phone started ringing. Stefan must be calling me back! He'll be with Diego, maybe I could do the interview over the phone! In my rush to answer it, I emerged from the loo, raced to the phone and tripped over my small suitcase in the hallway. I fell headlong into the shelving unit on which the phone and fax machine sat, sending them crashing onto the floor, as a full glass of wine was sent flying into the wall, where it broke.

The phone stopped ringing.

I was being watched. The racket had woken my girlfriend, who stood above me with a look of horror. 'IT'S FIVE O'CLOCK IN THE MORNING, WHO CAN THAT BE?'

I looked up at her and meekly explained, 'I was having a wee and the phone rang, I thought it might be Diego Maradona . . .'

She shook her head in silent disbelief and went back to bed, leaving me to clear up. My copy was filed without the merest mention of Diego Maradona. But I still like to imagine that on the other end of that call one of the greatest footballers of his generation was ruing his missed opportunity at giving a scoop to the man from *Time Out*.

TOP TUNE: 'Belo Horizonti', Heartists

21

JACK OF CLUBS

In the 1990s, I had found myself at the epicentre of the clubbing explosion. Not only was I in the right city, but I was active in all the 'Ps' – *Promotion, performing, press . . . and partying.* Giving me what was seen as an influential profile.

The *London Evening Standard* newspaper chose me as the '90s party-thrower (Peter Stringfellow represented the '80s, with society hostess Sheila Metcalfe representing the '70s) for a feature on what makes a good party after Helen Fielding had reviewed my club, Flirt!

After failing to make any impression in London during the previous decade with my band, it's thanks to the rave culture I'd stumbled upon that I was now 'someone'.

This was the decade where I would turn up at clubs and give my name to the bloke on the guest list and frequently be met with raised eyes and the words, 'Another Kirk Field from *Mixmag.* You're our third one tonight.'

People knew that my name would be on the door of every decent club night in central London and beyond. In those innocent days, no ID was requested and it was quite easy to use someone's name. I was amused to see the ploy used in the *Human Traffic* movie when they were a ticket short, Jip rocking up to the front door before declaring, 'I'm from *Mixmag*.'

After programming ambient rooms at a club in Mayfair and Raindance, I hosted Fridays at Subterania in Ladbroke Grove for around a year or so, in addition to doing the press for London's only legal rave promoters Raindance and World Dance, plus Aquarium Club in Shoreditch.

I lived, breathed and bled club culture. This led to me being seen as a bit of a 'fixer', making connections between DJs or promoters, acting as a consultant. It led to some memorable and motley experiences around club land, not all of them successful . . .

The search for Gerry Maguire

The phone rang in my flat just off Blackstock Road, Arsenal. It was Tall Terry, the guy I'd met in Mayrhofen in Austria a few winters previously. Terry was half Greek and half Dutch and had married a gorgeous Serbian girl called Sandra. Although fluent in three languages, his English was a little patchy at times and delivered with a strong Dutch/Greek accent. They had recently moved to Belgrade and Terry explained that Sandra's family were 'connected' and wanted to start putting on big events there using world-famous DJs and bands, with money no object. The Balkan War had not long finished, and I understood that they wanted to show the world that Serbia was open for business.

As I knew the scene well and was also connected (although in a different way to Sandra's uncles, I suspect), he asked if I could help secure the artists. If I could, there would be a generous introduction commission for me.

As I personally knew (or at least knew *someone* who worked with) all the big DJs at that time, I was confident I could help him and asked for a shopping list of artists. The following evening, he called me and mentioned Fatboy Slim and Carl Cox, both of whom I'd worked with, but excitedly told me the first show had to feature live music rather than a DJ and talked about a guy who was huge over in Serbia at the time: his name was Gerry Maguire.

Even though his name didn't ring any bells, I wasn't deterred in the least. Occasionally unknown British acts make it big overseas. The next few days I put some feelers out to any mates who worked in the major music agencies but drew a blank. I called Terry with the disappointing news and told him I needed more information. Within an hour he'd called me back with some.

'Apparently, the guy's a fantastic dancer.'

'I thought you said he was a singer?'

'Well, he sings AND dances.'

This gave me an idea. Éire had won the *Eurovision Song Contest* for God knows how many years running, Celtic music was very popular in Europe and *Riverdance* had just opened in the West End. Gerry Maguire had to be Irish! So I spent the next day requesting faxes of artist rosters from every traditional Irish talent agent and management company in the UK and Ireland.

By the end of the day, I'd highlighted no less than six performers with the name 'Gerry' or 'Jerry' Maguire. I called up each one's representation to ask if they also danced. By the end of the next day, I'd narrowed it down to two. Exhausted, I went out to the pub for a few pints and returned to an answerphone message from Terry.

'That guy we're trying to book, sometimes he wears a hat onstage. Whatever he costs, my people will pay it, he's HUGE over here right now.'

So the next day I requested photos of both persons of interest. Although grainy, the faxed images clearly showed neither wearing a hat!

I was beaten. I picked up the phone to tell Terry I couldn't help, and would have to give up the 10 per cent introduction fee. But before I could tender my resignation, a breathless Terry interrupted me, 'Ah, Kirk, I was just about to call you to tell you that I made a little mistake with the name of the act . . . it's not Gerry Maguire. It's Jamiroquai.'

★

Around the same time, I booked the live acts for Village Youth, a gay night in the Limelight which ran weekly on a Monday. Memorable nights include Felix, who performed his hit 'Don't You Want Me?' in a tiger costume, D:Ream with a keyboard player called Brian, whose career literally went cosmic, and a new boyband from Manchester called Take That.

Gary and the boys cost £600. They played in late May of 1992 during a London heatwave. It was like a sauna in there that night, and I made the mistake of coming into work wearing a pair of jogging bottoms and no underwear. My role involved welcoming the band, taking them upstairs to the VIP room, getting them drinks and sorting out their technical needs (which in this case was 'five mics, three live and two dummies'). They sat at the top of the stairs, draped around each other like boybands did, and as I walked up the stairs with a tray of drinks for them, one noticed I wasn't wearing any underwear. As both my hands were full, I couldn't do anything as I stood in front of them delivering their drinks. Each time I did this, the same thing would happen: one of them would make a lunge to pull my pants down.

Their show was super-slick, with immaculate choreography, strong singing and flirtatious eye contact with the crowd. They went down an absolute storm and Gordon Lewis who owned Village Youth asked me to rebook them. I called up Tony Denton who looked after them but found their price had gone up to £2,000.

'£2,000? Fuck me, Tony, they're not the Beatles!'

'Not yet, but they're going top ten on Sunday and this time next year they'll be as big as them . . .'

Flirt!

As the decade developed, the vast explosion of dance music revitalised London's club scene. DJs became the main attraction and grew in both status and financial power. After years packing the Astoria with the Trip and Sin, Nicky Holloway became the first of the new generation of DJs to own his own venue. The Milk Bar was a minimalist 300-capacity venue on the narrow one-way street which connected Soho Square with Charing Cross Road at the side of the Astoria.

Dan Prince, who wrote 'Club Country', the nationwide monthly listings for *Mixmag*, called me up and told me Nicky had offered him Thursday nights. He asked me if I wanted to work with him putting on a weekly party. He'd got all the DJs sorted but needed a concept.

I was aware that fetish parties were becoming more and more mainstream as people were wanting to move on from the non-sexual nature of raves. But fetish nights back in those days played dreadful music – industrial dirge or indie/goth. If we could take the best elements of a fetish party – the dressing up, the lure of sexual adventure, the tolerance – and mix it with a decent soundtrack from the hottest DJs, it would be something fresh and interesting.

So it was that 'Flirt!' came into being. We called it 'crossbreed clubbing' – fusing the flirtatious and libertarian atmosphere of a fetish club, a glamorous house crowd and a soundtrack from the world's biggest DJs.

Paul Oakenfold and Graeme Park were our fortnightly residents with guests who included Frankie Knuckles and Dan's mate Sasha (who I'd witnessed when Dave Seaman took me to Shelley's in Stoke for my thirtieth birthday). He was like a god in that club; one bloke approached him as he played.

'Sasha, can you touch me bird.'

Sasha raised his eyes skyward and gestured as if to say, 'Really?'

'Please, she's 'avin a bad trip but you can sort it.'

Sasha looked around, somewhat embarrassed, with the lad passionately imploring him to lay his hands on his trembling, terrified companion, who grasped a glowstick like her life depended on it.

Reluctantly he put his hands on her shoulder. The instant he made contact, her head jerked back and her entire body went into spasm. Sasha removed his hands. Her eyes opened and a smile spread across her face. She exhaled and nodded to her boyfriend, affirming everything was fine. He then made a 'we are not worthy' gesture with his hands, while backing away in reverence. Sasha looked at me and shrugged. No words were needed.

Back down at 'Flirt!' we added masseurs, brain machines, sex hosts, space punch and bizarre cabaret acts – what's not to like, we agreed!

Each week I'd arrive to find a cracking warm-up DJ practising before the doors opened. 'Hi, I'm Brandon,' he said with a grin. I'd heard about Brandon Block from Dan, who told me he was shit hot as a DJ, but to make sure he didn't cane the bar.

Another week I turned up and a gorgeous blonde girl was in the booth, wearing hot pants and heels. 'Hello luv, I'm Lisa. Dan's asked me to do the warm-up.' God bless Lisa Loud, the most glam warm-up I've had the pleasure of working with.

Initially 'Flirt!' struggled with numbers. We'd have a decent week followed by a quiet week. Unfortunately, the quiet week coincided with Graeme Park's slot and so we agreed we'd have to let him go. I respected Graeme hugely. He was one of the very first DJs in the UK to play house music long before it was acceptable, and his role in the Hacienda was as important as anyone's. But we were losing money and Graeme always insisted we pay him his £250 even when he could see it had been quiet.

I called him and explained the situation, but he wouldn't have it. He steadfastly refused to accept he didn't pull in London and started making silly threats along the lines of 'Who do you think you are? You'll never work in clubs again after this.'

Although the decision wasn't pleasant, 'Flirt!' after Graeme left went from strength to strength. *The Face* ran a two-page interview with Sasha, and the bottom line read: 'Sasha plays Flirt!@ the Milk Bar, Sutton Row on Thursday 14 September.' It was his London debut. A major coup.

Thursday came and as I made my way from Oxford Circus Tube towards the Milk Bar, I reached Soho Square, which was lined with people queuing. Surely not? I asked someone at the back what they were standing in line for.

'Sasha at the Milk Bar.' The words filled me with glee! I couldn't afford to lose any more money and was about to tell Dan I had to quit as I was skint and had no savings. I walked along that queue counting the people. There were 273. We'd sold out . . . and it wasn't even 9 p.m.

For the first month or so we had a live PA, usually a singer who was riding high in the charts at the time, like Rozalla or Sabrina Johnson, but as the weeks went on, we started running out of names. Up until now, Dan had booked the PAs and done a good job. But I felt they were overexposed, every club featured them and they didn't really bring any extra numbers in.

'What's the budget?' I asked Dan.

'£150–200.'

'Leave it to me.'

News of the screws

The early '90s was the heyday of the *News of the World*. Every Sunday morning millions of pairs of eyes would read about the latest scandal. All Conservative governments are mired in sleaze, but John Major's was particularly hypocritical and provided a never-ending series of scandals in

1993. If it wasn't David Mellor shagging his mistress in a Chelsea football shirt, rumours of Steven Norris having three mistresses on the go at one time, MPs asking questions for cash or being found dead after indulging in auto-asphyxiation games, it was the PM himself secretly knobbing his health minister (after famously declaring the country should go 'back to basics'; returning 'to core values of neighbourliness, decency and courtesy'). They were the gift that kept on giving . . . and they were perfect to give us our next PA.

As we were leaving at the end of another packed night, Dan asked me who the PA would be the following Thursday.

'I'll know on Sunday morning.'

Sunday arrived and I struck gold. It emerged that Chancellor Norman Lamont was renting a flat to a domin-atrix who charged businessmen, bishops and other respectable types a tidy sum for tying them up, spanking and whipping them. By the time my eggs had boiled, I'd traced and booked Lindi St Clair (aka Miss Whiplash) to appear at 'Flirt!' on Thursday. I then alerted a few contacts at the tabloids, who ran it in the following day's issues.

Miss Whiplash turned up dressed in a leather corset with a bullwhip and after insisting on being paid in cash up front, took up a position at the bar, where she posed for photos, signed autographs and pretended to whip some City boys who were ordering Champagne.

The following week the *NOTW* carried a feature about the 'Sex Maniacs Ball', which had to be cancelled after every venue they approached was warned off by a moralistic, zealous Metropolitan Police. So I did what I did with the Druids in Coventry and offered the ball's organiser, Tuppy Owens, the opportunity to come down to the club and express herself. The media lapped it all up, and soon 'Flirt!' was the club night on everyone's lips. *Sky Magazine* (which rivalled *The Face* at the time in terms of circulation) sent down a girl who interviewed me on the stage.

Her review was glowing. She said that prior to arriving, she was filled with trepidation and expecting to meet a depraved Svengali-type, but was relieved to find that I was in fact a 'pleasant young man'. We chatted for ten minutes after the interview. I told her about my days as a raving reporter and she told me she was hoping to give journalism up as she had high hopes for her book about a normal girl's love life 'which hopefully people find funny'. I wished her all the best with it.[15]

Helen Fielding's feature along with the tabloid coverage of the club led to celebrities frequently turning up. Mark Wahlberg appeared at the foot of the stairs one night with his entourage. They asked to be escorted to the VIP area and for any complimentary drinks to include Krug Champagne. So I led them into the main room, explaining, 'Everyone's a VIP here, Marky.'

I offered them a bottle of Sol each on the house and they spent the next half an hour looking miserable, posing in silence on the staging in the middle of the room, as everyone else got on with having a great time. After they'd downed their drinks they rose and filed out. I was glad to see them leave, to be honest. They were like a grey cloud in an otherwise azure sky, and no one was in the least interested in Marky or his pecs.

---

[15] *Bridget Jones's Diary* went on to sell over 2 million copies and inspired an award-winning movie (the screenplay of which she also co-wrote) and grossed nearly $300 million.

Bone shaker!

In the late '90s a major London venue was carrying out some excavation work in order to create a VIP room. I was promoting a couple of big nights at the venue at the time. A megastar was being flown in at great expense to reopen the venue, and with an enormous international press list invited and a stellar cast of guest DJs, it was essential that the construction work didn't overrun.

I recall there being a lot of tension on site to finish on schedule. One hot afternoon in August, I was sat in a meeting with the venue management when a bloke in a hi-vis vest and hard hat appeared at the door, looking like he'd just seen a ghost.

'Can I show you something?' he said.

'Can it wait? I'm just in a meeting,' came the reply.

The site manager (as it said on his badge) replied, 'I think you'll want to see this now.'

The venue manager excused himself and paused the meeting prematurely.

He returned some minutes later, clearly flustered.

'You look like you've seen a ghost.'

'How did you guess? Do you mind waiting outside for a moment while I make a call?'

I walked outside and waited in the corridor, where I overheard a conversation with someone senior at the head office of the parent company who owned the club.

It transpired that the building works and excavation of the former bank vault had unearthed bones. As the site was in the heart of London, there'd been human settlement there for thousands of years, through Anglo-Saxon, Roman and medieval times. If the remains were human, any discovery would have to be reported, resulting in work being halted immediately until the archaeologists had excavated and examined the site fully. There are instances of office blocks being delayed years after the groundworks unearthed evidence of former habitation or burial.

My understanding from what I heard was that this was perceived as a threat to the megastar-led relaunch, so someone at head office ordered work to continue. I suspect the site manager and the shift were given a generous bonus and told to forget all about it.

To this day, people dance, drink and chat unaware that possibly a few feet away, skeletons of plague victims lie encased in plaster, their bones vibrating with every beat of the kick drum . . .

Der mile-high club

On the opening day of Sundissential, a club I was promoting with Dan Prince at Heaven, a friend from Austria brought her new German boyfriend along. I offered them some Space punch and found them a few hours later, loved-up on the dancefloor, having the time of their lives. However, soon afterwards, at around midnight, they came up to say goodnight.

'You can't leave now!' I shouted.

'We have to, Dieter has a flight to Munich at 11 a.m.'

'11 a.m.? That's not early – have another glass of punch and stay until 2 at least.'

'That's not such a good idea . . .'

'Of course, it is, you can still get five hours' sleep. You said your hotel is right next to Heathrow, right?'

'Yeah, but . . .'

'But what? Sonique's about to play. You'll love her. Stay!'

They looked at one another and swapped 'I will if you will' glances.

'Okay, then, but no Space Punch for me,' Dieter said.

Of course, as the host who wanted everyone to enjoy themselves at my parties, I brought them two cups, knowing they'd both be knocked back.

This happened again at 2 a.m.

Finally, at closing time, they found me to say thanks for a great night.

I wished him a safe flight.

'Who's flying you back?'

'I am.'

I looked at his girlfriend.

She leaned forward and after checking no one was listening, whispered guiltily, 'Dieter's a pilot for Lufthansa.'

'WOAH! Why the hell didn't you tell me?'

'We did try, Kirk! But as an employee of Lufthansa I was influenced by our company slogan.'

'Which is?'

'Say *yes* to the world.'

The most-feared man in Britain

One night in 1999, I was in the Oxygen Bar just off Leicester Square, reviewing the pure O2 cannisters they were selling for my weekly column in *TNT Magazine*. My mate Lou, who owned the Aquarium, called me on my new Ericsson mobile, asking if I was in town as he had someone he wanted me to meet. Ten minutes later I'm sat across the table from 'Bermondsey Dave'. Dave had organised the security at Ronnie Kray's funeral a few years earlier and was known as 'the Yellow Pages of the Underworld'.

A pair of twinkling blue crystal eyes looked at me intensely either side of a 'you should see the other guy' nose. Through the thick cigar smoke, Dave told me what he wanted to happen and asked me if I could help him. I told him I couldn't, but knew a man who could called Neil O'Brien. An hour later, the former gangster-turned-author had an agent, his first spoken-word show and we were drinking Champagne to celebrate.

In the build-up to the show at the Talk of London theatre on Tottenham Court Road, we monitored his preparation. It was to be the first time *An Audience with Dave Courtney* hit the stage. It's one thing holding court in a pub, but another to hold the attention of hundreds of people for a few hours who've paid for the privilege. It soon became evident that Dave had bags of charisma and the confidence to carry it off.

The big night came, and I arrived at the stage door down a quiet side street. A figure in black stepped out from a parked car and handed me a large brown box, which had a white envelope addressed to 'Mr Courtney'. Although two feet long, I was surprised at how light the package was. The fragrance gave the contents away.

A doorman opened the door and let me in. Making my way to the dressing room, I handed Dave the package.

'Looks like an admirer sent some flowers!'

I then left for the sound desk to drop some music off, which would be played before the show.

After placing a few bottles of water on the stage, I returned to the dressing room to find Dave unusually subdued. Asking him if he was okay, he pointed to the flowers. In the open brown cardboard box lay twelve black roses. He handed me the card I'd delivered. The message on the front didn't read, 'Good Luck!' or 'Congratulations!' but, 'In Deepest Sympathy'.

He told me it was either from a bent copper he was having some issues with at the time, or a very well-known underworld figure who was rumoured to be coming down mob-handed to disrupt things if anything was said 'out of turn' during the show.

'Shall I warn the security?'

He took a toke on his huge cigar and pondered. 'If it kicks off, they'll be no use anyway. I'll handle it.'

The doors soon opened and sure enough, the gentleman in question arrived with his 'boys' and there was a palpable tension when Dave walked out to make his London stage debut. The room was packed and looked like a who's who of rogues. The follow spot reflected off his silver suit and bald head, illuminating a plume of powder-blue cigar smoke which rose from a gnarled, clenched left fist.

After a few minutes he told the crowd he'd just returned from Maidstone after visiting Reggie Kray, who had given the show his blessing. From that moment on the tension turned into mirth as Dave relaxed, spinning tale after tale before answering questions from the crowd, who loved it.

Afterwards in the dressing room he signed a copy of his book, *Stop the Ride, I Want to Get Off*: 'To my pal Kirk, you no I fucking luv ya for making it happen 4 me. Dave Courtney OBE'.

TOP TUNE: 'Hideaway' (Deep Dish Mix), De'Lacy

22

END OF THE CENTURY

'Fuck it!' spat the Voice of an Angel.

Charlotte Church's immaculate white dress was now stained with a streak of blood-red ketchup. The 13-year-old threw the culprit – a hot dog from Artist and Crew catering – into a black dustbin and stormed off to look for a wet wipe.

The DJ was playing Prince. He'd waited all his life for this moment and couldn't resist. They never can. If the radio is blaring out the Cure's 'Friday I'm in Love', you can bet your back teeth it'll be Saturday tomorrow. Similarly, January first is the only time you'll hear provincial BBC Radio giving Bono the airwaves to disprove his claim 'All is quiet on New Year's Day'.

'. . . so tonight, we're gonna party like it's 1999!'

I was backstage in a celebrity caravan site in Greenwich. On each Winnebago a sign confirmed the occupants: Eurythmics, Simply Red, Martine McCutcheon, Bryan Ferry. I was there as a guest of my wife Catherine, who was playing violin for the ex-Roxy Music crooner. The concert was being broadcast live on BBC One and would act as a warm-up for the big countdown at the Millennium Dome, a mile down the river.

In an effort to avoid Martine McCutcheon's performance, I strolled the short distance to the river for a moment of solitary reflection. Weeks earlier when rooting around in the cellar, I'd come across some musty rave relics in a damp cardboard box: the green accordion I'd bought in Moscow in 1991 for $10, a Rave! boardgame which mentions 'kurk' in the credits, a certificate from the Croatian government and among the flyers, a small postage stamp-sized piece of what looked like . . . .wallpaper.

Was it? Could it? Would it still 'work'? Fuck it, tonight I would find out.

I found a bench on a quiet stretch of the riverside path which wasn't filled with burger vans, candy floss stalls or flag sellers and sat down. Martine's muffled notes were peppered by exploding fireworks via excitable pre-midnight ejaculations from back gardens and balconies on the Isle of Dogs across the water. The river shimmered with the reflection of the halogen lighting installed along the river-banks. Brightly coloured silk flags fluttered in the cold breeze as searchlights flashed through the sky. It was London's biggest-ever party and had cost £4 million to put on; 40,000 fireworks were primed and ready. It was like a rave without the kick drum – Tony Blair had even fired a laser across the Thames to officially open the London Eye and the Archbishop of Canterbury was rubbing Vicks into Stephen Fry's bare chest. I made that last bit up.

The sound of the generators, which enabled the excessive illumination, grew louder in my head until it drowned out everything else.

BRWHIRRRRRRRRR.

I became lost in its monotone rumble and lapsed into a daydream reinforced by the myriad dancing lights on the water in front of me.

BRWHIRRRRRRRRR.

That sound had been a constant companion throughout the decade. From the orbital raves to warehouse parties and annual festivals.

BRWHIRRRRRRRRR.

I was transported back to the cobbled courtyard of Dungeons under Lea Bridge Road in Hackney, dancing in the drizzle on my first E. Holding my hands out to feel the lasers hit them, as millions of blue sparks sparkled around my head, welcoming me into the future.

The whole decade had been a night out. I must've danced to over a thousand DJs in fifteen different countries, heard and fallen in love with countless tunes, experienced more magical moments than I ever thought possible, and written countless words about it. It dawned on me I'd connected with a generation of clubbers through my print journalism, promoting, performing and partying.

I ruminated on a trip I had taken to a 400-year-old ruined church in Old Goa in 1993. As my girlfriend and I walked around the site, an old blind man approached and stopped me. Putting his hand in front of his face and resting it on my shoulder, he solemnly declared, 'Your words will be read by many thousands of people, but your face will not be seen.'

I thanked him, shook his hand and walked on. Neither of us said anything, walking on in silence. It was quite spooky. But in the last hours of the dying century, his prophecy made sense. Over the years I had written flyer copy for some of the biggest raves and clubs in London, never receiving a name-check. I'd also written adverts for Kiss 100, my Ravers Charter was published in the *Daily Star* and I'd narrated features on Radio 1 and MTV . . . yet my face remained hidden.

Turned out the old blind man was right, I thought. Then I realised I'd managed to make my living for ten years from the culture of dancing. I'd experienced unbelievable things and met some amazing people in incredible places. But maybe it was time to accept that the ride was over. To snap out of my nostalgic stupor and accept the grainy reality of adult life, should I launch a clubbing travel company and continue my adventure? Or should I apply for a secure but boring position writing about the construction of stadiums and hotels for a trade magazine?

I was torn. On the one hand, I was established in the London club scene and loved it. On the other, I'd just got married and was aware Catherine wanted to buy a house and have kids. What should I do?

Just then my daydream was broken by a boat crossing my vision. It flew a huge Royal ensign at the front. I stared more intently and could make out footmen in bright red livery standing at the bow. Another, at midship on the starboard side and facing me, carried something shiny . . . a horn, perhaps? I scrunched my eyes and fixed them on the front of the boat, on which had been placed a throne. On the throne was someone in an orange coat. Bugger me! It was the Queen being ferried to open the Millennium Dome, where she would see in the new century with Tony Blair, the Archbishop of Canterbury and Jools Holland.

She was a stone's throw away from me.

Without thinking I put my hands to my mouth and bellowed, 'HAPPY NEW YEAR, MA'AM!'

She turned her head and waved at me; the briefest of acknowledgements. The Queen was waving at me! I mean, of course, I *think* that's what happened – it's possible the Berlin Wallpaper made me a *very* unreliable witness – but real or not, I saw this as my sign: *an affirmation to choose the extraordinary over the ordinary.* I would follow my chosen path. A travel company that would cater exclusively for clubbers. The universe decreed it! I bounded back into the show just as the Pet Shop Boys took to the stage.

Afterwards, I was in Bryan's Winnebago with Catherine and the other girls from his string section, swapping NYE stories. Everyone had to describe their favourite one. A knock on the door.

'Happy New Century!'

The ginger head of Mick Hucknall momentarily appeared in the doorframe, bottle of Champagne in one hand and a tall blonde woman on the other, who blew a kiss to Bryan before disappearing off towards Dave Stewart's Winnebago, which was going off.

One of the string section girls turned to me. 'Wasn't that Brigitte Nielsen?'

I smiled. 'You're asking the wrong person . . .'

TOP TUNE: 'Promised Land', Joe Smooth

23

NO CAPER WITHOUT COLLATERAL

'What goes up, must come down.'

– Sir Isaac Newton

After reading all these tales of excess, you might be forgiven for initially thinking this account glorifies the recreational use of drugs and trivialises their impact on the individual and society. They say everyone has a book in them. This is mine. I decided to be honest. There are incidents I'm proud of and incidents I'm ashamed of. That's what life's all about.

The rave era was (and probably still is) excessive in terms of mood modification and altered states. I may have overindulged at times, but never to the stage of ripping people off or getting involved in dealing. With the exception of a certain speed dealer in north-west London who keeps his loyal client list tight, and an award-winning artisan kitchen who also provide dessert, every ongoing drug-dealing operation I've been aware of has inevitably ended in tears.

Anyone can go to a party; leaving it is the challenge

I always looked after myself in between raves. I would eat properly, watch my alcohol intake and catch up on my sleep 'cos that's when you heal and grow. I'd dance non-stop for eight hours with my jaw aching from incessantly chewing gum. Connecting with the music was central to my experience. The stimulants I took helped me in this process. And when the rave was over and the 'back to mine' at someone's house had reached the stage of looking for crumbs of coke on the carpet, I knew it was time to leave.

When something's unsustainable, it needs to be handled with care. I was an evangelist for ecstasy and genuinely believe it preferable to alcohol and tobacco – and certainly cocaine. The handful of times I indulged in LSD Lite (aka Berlin Wallpaper) mostly appear here. It wasn't habitual, but a safer alternative to taking MDMA across international borders. But it was 'Acid Lite'. I've always thought that tabs of acid are like bullets in the Wild West: somewhere there's one with your name on it, and the sooner you get out of Dodge, the safer you'll be.

I count myself very fortunate in that (up until now at least), I've been able to walk away from situations and substances and not develop addictions. Others weren't so lucky. For most of us, E wasn't a gateway drug, but for some it was. Many of them aren't around to explain why.

Should the majority be denied something which will enhance their life because a minority don't know when to stop?

Even though I found myself in some scrapes, I was never incapacitated. Even when I lost it, I still knew where it was and delivered my copy on time (even if it did contain reviews of bands that hadn't played). 'Work hard and play hard', basically.

Everything in moderation, except moderation

Like it or not, drugs are a part of life and what's more, they always have been.[16] There are many reasons they have been outlawed, controlled, and their use prohibited. Safety is one. However, ironically, this could be tackled better if they were regulated, and their responsible use accepted rather than vilified.

Being a parent, I worry about their availability and of addictive 'legal highs' like Spice, and a seemingly endless range of cheap designer drugs. The ongoing popularity of ketamine I've always been uneasy about, having found numerous 'k-hole' casualties comatose down the years. Ketamine has caused my guests in Ibiza more problems than all the rest of the drugs put together. Then there's the worrying incidences of cathinones being sold as MDMA.

---

[16] Data suggests opium and hallucinogenic plants (psychoactive alkaloids) were used in the Neolithic era (12000–2000BC). More recently, traces of nicotine, cocaine and hashish have been found in exhumed Egyptian mummies.

Drugs ruin lives

Yes, they can, but it's not compulsory to let them do so. I've usually found that the people's lives who are ruined by drugs are also addictive personalities and also suffer from dependencies on chocolate, frozen pizza, booze, sex, cigarettes, trainers – buying a lot of something they don't need to give them a momentary high.

I appreciate these are different times. Back in the day it used to be so simple: an E for going out and an Oxo cube of hash for when you got home. How things have changed. What it boils down to is choice and taking responsibility for your own actions. If you choose to use substances that society wants to control, be aware of the risks and try to minimise them. Advice to take just a quarter of a pill to test its toxicity and strength and drink plenty of water helps, but in the absence of any regulation, kids are effectively guinea pigs on which new batches are tested each weekend. Why isn't the presence of a drug-testing stall a condition of being granted a festival licence?

I'd like to see psychedelics and MDMA explored as psychotherapy tools. The war against drugs is a blunt instrument. Criminalising young recreational drug users with a zero-tolerance policy won't result in them not taking drugs, just different ones which don't show up in tests.

When Ann Widdecombe introduced random mandatory drug testing in prisons in 1996, it resulted in the demand for heroin soaring. Cannabis leaves a trace in the blood for up to fourteen days, but opiates can't be detected in tests after twelve hours. And it's not just opiates that provide an alternative to those wanting to avoid a positive test: synthetic drugs like Spice are harder to detect, resulting in addiction of epidemic proportions in UK prisons. Yet we still persist in pursuing the 'war on drugs', rather than suing for peace. Have we learned nothing?

More people die from opioid abuse in the UK than anywhere else in Europe. In the north-west alone, drug-related deaths have risen by 77 per cent in the past decade and this number has been rising for a decade. At the same time, drug services have had their budgets cut by around a third.

Declaring war on drugs is like declaring war on the night. No matter what you do, it's still gonna get dark. The genie is out of the bottle and can't be put back inside. The tide will come in regardless of whether a Tory home secretary sits on a throne telling it to turn back. We live in a society that worships the sensual and encourages exploration and experimentation: 'Live Boldly' . . . 'Go Further' . . . 'Just Do It' . . . 'Taste the Rainbow' – but only if means buying something that can be taxed.

The first step, then, is licensing cannabis. This would not only create revenue to fund education and rehabilitation programmes, but also provide some much-needed consistency and offer an alternative to super-strong skunk, which causes psychosis in young minds. We are the world's leading producer of medicinal cannabis, yet deny our own citizens the benefits in favour of selling it overseas.

Young people today are under unimaginable pressure (only exacerbated by heartless and unnecessary lockdowns stealing away some of their most precious years). Understandably, they feel they've got some catching up to do; it's bound to get messy.

RAVE NEW WORLD

Fucking up is a part of growing up. Our misdemeanours and mistakes were soon forgotten (until you write a book!), and we hopefully moved on a lot wiser. These days, moments of madness are shared within minutes and immortalised for eternity on a thousand screens and feeds.

Even when young people do finally switch off from all the (self-) surveillance and lose themselves in the lasers, their moment of release when their favourite tune drops is captured by their mate next to them with a camera phone, ridiculing their off-guard expression for the sake of entertainment. Can you imagine the hell?

We were so lucky growing up, coming up and messing up when we did. A new sound by new artists on new radio stations, a new consciousness-raiser and way of partying. But the naughty '90s were also a decade of innocence; a time before 9/11, pandemics and endless internet anxiety. We didn't know how carefree it was.

One moment in time; like a beautiful girl frozen in the single frame of a strobe, her eyes closed in bliss, framed by wild static hair, the sweat on her forehead momentarily glistening. Then, before you know it, she's gone. The moment has passed, leaving only an imprint.

Novelist Cecelia Ahern nailed it when she said, 'Moments are precious; sometimes they linger and other times they're fleeting, and yet so much could be done in them; you could change a mind, you could save a life and you could even fall in love.'

What a time to be alive.

'When the angels from above fall down and spread their wings like doves

NO CAPER WITHOUT COLLATERAL

As we walk hand in hand, sisters, brothers, we'll make it to the promised land.'

— 'Promised Land', Joe Smooth

Event testing and drug alerts: wearetheloop.org
Facts, support and advice: talktofrank.com

EPILOGUE

This book wasn't written with any idea of it being published. But feedback from the friends, former ravers and writers I sent chapters to was so positive that I decided to send it to a literary agent. Thankfully, he 'got' it (thanks, James), and felt it had mainstream appeal. A few months on, I visited him in his office, and he ruefully handed me the feedback from the major publishing houses. While they had all enjoyed reading it and said some nice things, every single one passed on it as my 'profile' was not deemed sufficiently high enough.

Then Pete Selby at Nine Eight Books sent an email saying he was really enjoying it, but similarly feared my profile would be a barrier to reaching my audience – but asked if there was anything he had missed.

I explained why my social media profile was deliberately low: for the previous eighteen months I'd been in the selection process to become a magistrate. The magistracy advise winding down social media activity as it could lead to blackmail or personal security issues. I was interested in becoming a magistrate as I felt my experience with young people and their problems might be useful and bring a raver's sense of realism to the bench. Also, as it was an unpaid role, it would fit my aim of 'putting something back' into society, which, upon turning fifty-five years of age, is something I've consciously tried to do.

In pursuing the book and becoming a Justice of the Peace, I was effectively riding two horses and, at some point, I had to choose one. Then I received confirmation of my acceptance and an invite to attend an induction day and swearing-in ceremony. One question stood out: 'Is there anything now or in your past which may bring the judiciary into disrepute, or cause embarrassment?'

I had to decide. I didn't sleep all night, and at 7 a.m. I withdrew my application in a brief email.

At 9 a.m., my phone rang. They were naturally curious, as my enthusiasm and belief in what I could bring to the bench were clear at the interviews I'd done. Now, after finally being accepted, I was declining the opportunity.

'Are you in trouble with the police?' the lady from the advisory committee asked.

'No. I've written an honest book about my years in the rave scene – the parties, the busts, the gangsters, the drugs – and I feel there are things in there that may cause embarrassment to you.'

There was a long silence.

'This is such a shame; we need people like you as magistrates.'

She asked me for a couple of examples of the things mentioned in the book and after a few minutes concluded I was doing the right thing and thanked me for being honest. She then added, 'I can't wait to read your book as I used to go to Cream every weekend – best nights of my life!'

Her words were proof that a generation of ravers – *many of whom broke the law* – are now responsible adults, raising children, holding down jobs and contributing to society.

As Seal says, 'We're never gonna survive, unless we get a little crazy.'

ACKNOWLEDGEMENTS

Gracious thanks to my soundboard, Dan Prince, and MuMu mate, Niall Rudd, for your belief and encouragement. James Wills @ Watson-Little for keeping the faith and Liam Mullone for the intro; Pete Selby and Melissa Bond @ Nine Eight Books for taking a chance on an unpublished writer with a Twitter following smaller than the members of Wham!; unsung heroes of '89 Tarquin de Meza, Paul Marston, Jay Pender and Paul Nelson for allowing me to finally tell their stories; acid house archivist Scott Brady (tracklistings.co.uk) for the scans of my features; and the following friends for reading excerpts and feeding back: Richard Norris, Matthew 'Slipmatt' Nelson, Nick Gordon Brown, Debby Lee, Damian Gelle, JP Montgomery, Jody Sharp, Nick Halkes, Norman Cook, Judge Jules, Gavin Mills DJ Face/Copyright, Nick Nicely for the Raindance Bullring vid, Penny Griffiths for the long-lost footage of Guru Josh milking a goat, Adam Proto, Richard Michalski, Jason 'JFK' Finch, Nick 'The Kid' Coles, Mark 'K90' Doggett, JP, Lisa 'Pin-Up' Barretta, Lee Crisp, Sean Cummiskey, Pez, Neil O'Brien, Terry Neale, Erich Roscher, Leam Wilcox, Richard 'Raindance'

Siggins, Mike Parry, Matthew Ward, Vicky Devine, *Proof*essor Sorrel Dryden, Bill 'Zero B' Borez, Julia Antoni, Tim & Jim (Soul Purpose radio), Darren Robinson, Simone 'Angel' Hunt, Kevin Ridley, MC Keo, Georgie Brendon, Toni Tambourine, Nick Stevenson @ *Mixmag* – and Dave Seaman for giving an unknown dole kid the opportunity to write for the clubbers' bible.

This book is dedicated to everyone I ever raved with and is inspired by Robin and Joey Field – who now know what their dad got up to before they got onto the guest list at this amazing club we call life.

'Dance while the record spins.'